GEORGIA CITIZENS AND SOLDIERS
OF THE AMERICAN REVOLUTION

by

Robert S. Davis, Jr.

Design for Title Page and Front Cover:
A Georgia Revolutionary Soldier from a 1777 Currency Note

SOUTHERN HISTORICAL PRESS
%The Rev.S. Emmett Lucas,Jr.
P.O. Box 738
Easley, South Carolina 29640

ISBN   0-89308-169-8
Library of Congress Card Catalog Number: 79 - 67497

ENGAGEMENT BETWEEN THE WHIGS & TORIES.
NEAR KETTLE CREEK, 1779.

An 1840 illustration of the Battle of Kettle Creek. Courtesy of the Georgia Department of Archives and History.

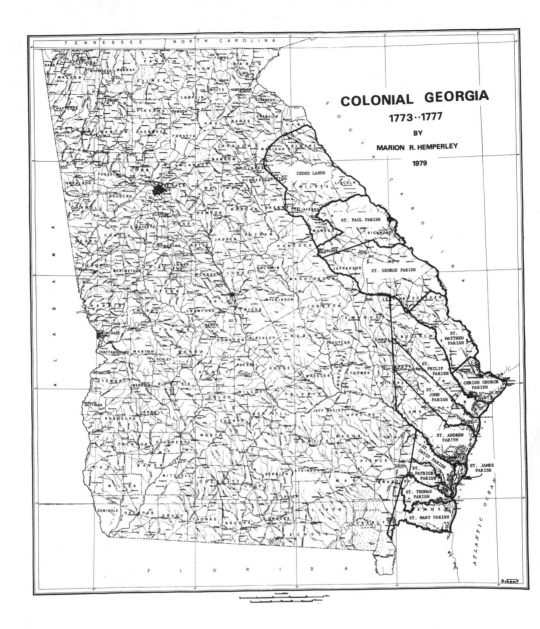

COLONIAL GEORGIA

1773-1777

BY

MARION R. HEMPERLEY

1979

TABLE OF CONTENTS

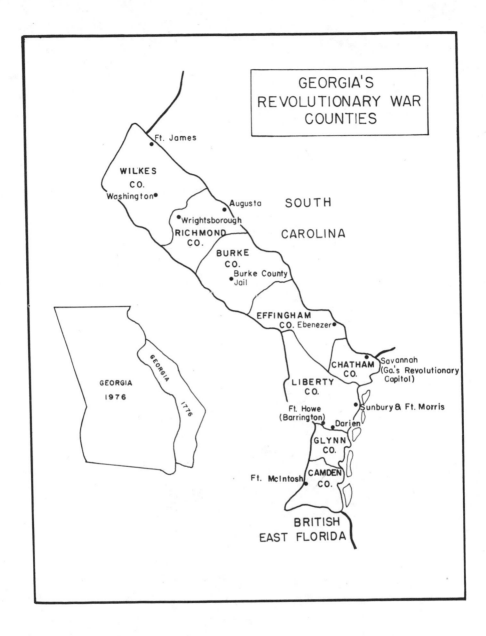

GEORGIA'S
REVOLUTIONARY WAR
COUNTIES

Ft. James

WILKES
CO.
Washington

Augusta

SOUTH

CAROLINA

Wrightsborough

RICHMOND
CO.

BURKE
CO.
Burke County
Jail

EFFINGHAM
CO. Ebenezer

GEORGIA 1776

GEORGIA
1976

CHATHAM
CO.

Savannah
(Ga.'s Revolutionary
Capitol)

LIBERTY
CO.

Ft. Howe
(Barrington)

Sunbury & Ft. Morris

Darien

GLYNN
CO.

Ft. McIntosh

CAMDEN
CO.

BRITISH
EAST FLORIDA

INTRODUCTION

The following is an attempt to describe the American Revolution in Georgia through genealogically significant documents. Among these are manuscripts that explain the reluctance of Georgians to join the Revolution, how politically divided they were, the sacrifices and risks that Georgians made during the war (voluntarily or otherwise), and the penalties both sides dealt the other when they came to power. Included are military rolls that illustrate not only the complexity of the military establishments in Georgia, but also that the American Revolution in Georgia was, above all else, a very real war.

Georgia was the last and probably the most reluctant of the thirteen colonies to join the American Revolution. Although with the smallest and most sparsely settled population on every border Georgia had to face almost overwhelming numbers of potential or real enemies. Savage fighting by American, British, and French armies added to the destruction caused by bandits and Indians, and left the state in ruins and the population badly scattered. Georgia was the only state completely conquered by the British and restored to the status of a colony, complete with royal governor and colonial militia. That Georgia was eventually retaken from the British was seen as a remarkable feat by many at the time. The tremendous losses that Georgia suffered in this country's first war, as an independent country, can only be gussed at, but one researcher estimated that in what is present-day Burke and surrounding counties, one of the most heavily populated areas of Revolutionary Georgia, only some forty percent of the families living there before the war remained after the fighting was over. Hugh McCall, Georgia's first historian, probably best summed it up in the "Notice to the Public" in Vol. I of The History of Georgia (Savannah, 1811):

> No state in the union suffered more than Georgia--none made greater struggles--none had such difficulties to encounter, and none has been so little noticed in the general history of the war.

The documents included herein illustrate that struggle while providing genealogical information on people who lived or served in Georgia during the Revolution. Some researchers may find information in the military rolls or accounts that will help them to meet membership requirements in patriotic organizations, but for many who find an ancestor's name included in these papers, there will be only an idea of what an ancestor felt or thought or believed in 200 years ago.

In keeping with this idea, only non-essential information such as actual amounts paid to each man, the number of days that he served, etc., has been omitted and then with a note that the information in parentheses appears in the original document. All information in brackets is provided by the editor. When the names on the document are original signatures, this is explained in the introduction to the document or signified by "/s/." In many instances, particularly with signatures, the eighteenth-century handwriting has been difficult to read and subject to error. Phonetic spellings of names by different clerks on some of these documents results in different spellings of the same name. In each instance, the spelling used in the original document was kept, no matter how obviously incorrect or how different from a signature or another spelling on other documents.

I would like to express my appreciation to several people who helped to make this project possible. Mr. Kenneth H. Thomas, Jr., of the Georgia Genealogical Society first provided me with the opportunity and then offered continuous encouragement and suggestions as the project grew well beyond what I thought possible. Mrs. Lee Sherry, general editor of the Georgia Genealogical Society Quarterly; Mrs. June Clark Hartel of Crofton, Maryland; Mr. Gordon B. Smith of Savannah; Mr. Heard Robertson and Dr. Ed Cashin of Augusta; Dr. Kenneth Coleman of the University of Georgia, and Mrs. Audry Kenny of the Georgia Department of Archives and History were all very helpful in putting together the documents included here. I also owe a considerable debt to staff members of the various libraries and archives who gave their time and/or permission to use this material.

To no organization do I owe more than to Special Collections, University of Georgia Libraries. Their staff has been, without exception, helpful, courteous, patient and forgiving.

Robert S. Davis, Jr.
Jasper, Georgia
March 20, 1978

PART I: GEORGIA CITIZENS

"RESOLVED, That we were born free, have all the feelings of men and are entitled to all the natural rights of mankind."

Georgia Provincial Congress
10 July 1775

Dedicated to Robert Willingham, Jr., Larry Galley, and Judy Muse of Special Collections, University of Georgia Libraries.

A. IDEAS ON GENEALOGICAL RESEARCH ON GEORGIANS, 1773-1783

1. Pension records.

Individual Revolutionary War pension files are a gold mine of genealogical information on families before, during, and long after the American Revolution. A typical pension claim, even when only filed by a veteran's widow or children, might provide information on a family's movements from 1760 to the date the pension claim was filed, usually in 1832, as well as details and dates of births, deaths, marriages, and military services of not only the Revolutionary War soldier on whose service the pension is claimed but also of some of his family members, officers, and comrades. Of the federal pensions, only the applications filed after 1814 have survived. These records are kept by the National Archives, in alphabetical order by the names of the soldiers, with the abreviations of the state or states in which each soldier served as part of his file designation. A list of the Revolutionary War pension applicants who served in Georgia is included elsewhere in this volume as an appendix. Published lists of all pension applicants, for every state, are available at most large research libraries.

A complete set of the microfilm edition of these pension papers is available at the National Archives, the South Carolina Department of Archives and History, and the East Tennessee State University Library, and is being acquired by the Georgia Department of Archives and History. None of these institutions, however, allow their microfilm copies of these records to be borrowed through interlibrary loan. Photostatic copies of specific pension claims can be ordered directly from Military Service Records (NNCC), National Archives (GSA), Washington DC 20408. Researchers should be aware, however, that when they order such a copy of a pension claim, they will only receive reproductions of a few selected pages of a pension file that may contain forty or more manuscript pages. Some individuals have gotten around this problem by purchasing a copy of the entire microfilm reel that a specific pension appears on from the National Archives.

No index to the contents of the pension claims of the men who served in Georgia during the war is currently available. Such an index would be invaluable as a means of locating references to the thousands of battles, locations, officers, fellow soldiers, family members, charavter witnesses, ministers, and civil officials mentioned within these pension records. Many Revolutionary War veterans who did not file their own pension claim but did appear as witnesses to their friends' claims could be located with such an index.

The surviving records of the Georgia state (pre-1790) and the pre-1815 dederal Revolutionary War pensions are incomplete and scattered. Some information on the Georgia state pensions has been found in the published legislative acts, minutes of the executive council, and other records at the Georgia Department of Archives and History; the county files and other records in the Telamon Cuyler Collection, Special Collections, University of Georgia Libraries; and the original executive council minutes, Georgia Miscellaneous Collection, William R. Perkins Library, Duke University.

Various published lists of pre-1815 federal pensions have survived and may have been reprinted. Some of thes records also contain brief personal data on the pensioners. Among those at the Georgia Department of Archives and History are:

* A Transcript of the Pension List of the United States For 1813. Reprinted ed. Baltimore: Southern Book Company, 1953. Call number G 973.3 UN 1813.

* Ainsworth, Mary Govier, comp., "Recently Discovered Records Relating to Revolutionary War Veterans Who Applied for Pensions Under the Act of 1792." Reprinted from the National Genealogical Society Quarterly. Call number G 973.3 N28r.

* Saffell, W. T. R. Records of the Revolutionary War: Containing the Military and Financial Correspondence of Distinguished Officers. . . New York: Pudney and Russell, 1858. Call number G.973.3. Page 551 is a list of the death dates of Georgia officers who received Revolutionary War pensions, 1799-1831. On pages 410-39 is a list of officers and widows of officers who qualified for half pay.

* Letter From the Secretary of War a Report of the Names, Rank, and Line of Every Person Placed on the Pension List in Pursuance of the Act of the 18th March 1818. Reprinted ed. Baltimore: Southern Book Co., 1955. Call number G 973.3 UN 1818.

* Report From the Secretary of War in Obedience to Resolutions of the Senate of the 5th and 30th June 1834 and the 3d of March 1835 in Relation to the Pension Establishment of the United States. Washington: Duff Green, 1835. Call number G 973.3 UN.

* Rejected or Suspended Applications for Revolutionary War Pensions. Baltimore: Genealogical Publishing Co., 1969. Call number G 973.3.

In the library of the South Carolina Department of Archives and History is a bound copy of the pages of Report of the Secretary of War, 1835, Pension Rolls, call number F 273 S6, relating to South Carolina. Scattered throughout the booklet are the names and former military units of men who served in Georgia during the Revolution but lived in South Carolina after their service and drew their pensions from that state. The South Carolina Department of Archives and History also has thousands of files of accounts, pensions, and other records of claims filed with South Carolina by Revolutionary War soldiers or their heirs, known as the Accounts Audited of Claims growing out of the Revolution in South Carolina. Many Georgians and men who served in Georgia are bound in these files. An index of the names found in these papers is available at the South Carolina Archives.

2. Land records.

Georgia issued certificates for land bounties to her Patriot Revolutionary War soldiers, sailors, citizens, and refugees. Over the years, many of these loose records have been destroyed or stolen. The majority of those that have survived are filed alphabetically, by the names of the claimants, in the Georgia Surveyor General Department, an agency housed in the same building as the Georgia Department of Archives and History. The Surveyor General Department is currently working to prepare a list of these loose records for publication. Many of the certificates that were stolen from the State of Georgia have since shown up in manuscript collections in various libraries, such as those in the Telamon Cuyler Collection, Special Collections, University of Georgia libraries that are abstracted elsewhere in this volume.

Lucian Lamar Knight abstracted many Revolutionary War bounty certificates for his Georgia's Roster of the Revolution. . .(1920; reprinted Baltimore: Genealogical Publishing Company, 1967). Knight, however, overlooked many of the certificates in the Surveyor General Department, made errors in the abstracting of others, and some that he copied can no longer be found.

No means of locating these certificates beyond what is described above is available. Some contemporary lists of the recipients of the bounties have survived, however, see, for instance, Ruth Blair, comp., Revolutionary Soldiers Receipts for Georgia Bounty Grants (Atlanta: Foote and Davis Co., 1928). For background information on the bounty certificates see Alex M. Hitz, "Georgia's Bounty Land Grant," Georgia Historical Quarterly 38 (1954): 337 ff.

Georgia's other land records that provide proof of Revolutionary War service are the later state land lotteries. These records have been published:

* Lucas, Silas E. The Third and Fourth or 1820 and 1821 Land Lotteries of Georgia. Easley: Southern Historical Press, 1973. The Revolutionary War soldiers identified in this lottery were invalids or indigents.

* Houston, Martha Lou. Reprint of the Official Register of the Land Lottery of Georgia 1827 Originally published in 1828, reprinted Easley: Southern Historical Press, 1976. Also indentifies widows of Revolutionary War soldiers.

* Lucas, Silas E. The 1832 Gold Lottery of Georgia Containing a List of Fortunate Drawers Easley: Southern Historical Press, 1976.

* Smith, James E. The 1832 Cherokee Land Lottery of Georgia. Originally published in 1838, reprinted Vidalia: Southern Historical Press, 1968.

* Hitz, Alex M. Authentic List of All Land Lottery Grants Made to Veterans of the Revolutionary War by the State of Georgia. 2nd ed. Atlanta: Secretary of State, 1966.

3. Military accounts.

The account papers for the Georgia continental troops are not always easy to research in. At the American Jewish Historical Society in Waltham, Massachusetts are the Mordecai Sheftall Papers, containing thousands of loose accounts for the four battalions of Georgia continental foot soldiers. Within these papers are the names of roughly 1,000 of these continentals. The Sheftall Papers are not microfilmed, published, indexed, or organized in such a way as to make using them possible except by a personal trip to the Society.

At the National Archives, other loose accounts and some account books for the Georgia continental troops can be found in the Miscellaneous Records in the War Department Collection of Revolutionary War Records, Record Group 93. The National Archives has an index to this collection and a microfilm copy of these records although neither is available on interlibrary loan. June Clark Hartel abstracted the loose Georgia accounts from this collection in Georgia Genealogical Magazine no. 70 (Fall, 1978): 283 ff. The DAR's Pierce's Register of the Certificates Issued by John Pierce, Esquire. . .to Officers and Soldiers of the Continental Army Under the Act of July 4, 1783 (1915; reprinted Baltimore: Genealogical Publishing Co., 1973) is a list of continental officers based upon records from military accounts.

The ration book of Colonel John White's 4th Georgia Continental Battalion and the account book of Colonel Samuel Elbert, commander of the 2nd Georgia Continental Battalion, are at the William R. Perkins Library, Duke University.

Francis B. Heitman's *Historical Register of the Officers of the Continental Army During the War of the Revolution, April, 1775 to December, 1783* rev. ed. (Washington: Rare Book Shop Publishing Co., 1914) contains a great deal of undocumented information on continental officers. When his sources have been located, however, they have generally been found to be reliable.

Almost all of the known accounts paid by the State of Georgia for Revolutionary War service or supplies are in the Telamon Cuyler Collection, Special Collections, University of Georgia. As this collection has no general index, using these thousand of loose papers can be time consuming. The lengthier accounts and those of special interest to genealogists are reproduced elsewhere in this work.

Caroline Price Wilson published a state account book of monies paid for services and supplies used during the Revolution in volume one of *Annals of Georgia* (1928: reprinted Vidalia: Georgia Genealogical Reprints, 1968). Such records are also found scattered through the typescript executive and legislative minutes and the published senate and house journals at the Georgia Department of Archives and History.

State account records of the Revolution and other similar material is included among the colonial deeds and other records known collectively as the Georgia colonial conveyances. William C. Dumont abstracted part of these records in *Colonial Georgia Genealogical Data 1748-1783* (Washington: National Genealogical Society, 1971) and others have been published in the 1961-1973 issues of *Georgia Genealogical Magazine*. The Taylor Foundation has come out with two of the earliest of these books. A cumulative index of all of the colonial conveyance books is currently being considered by the Taylor Foundation.

A few state Revolutionary War accounts are found among the colonial and Revolutionary War business records in the Telfair Family Papers in the William R. Perkins Library, Duke University, and the Georgia Historical Society Library in Savannah. Although these business records carry some information on many famous and not so famous Georgians of the Revolutionary War period, most of these particular documents are of little more than autograph value. More useful loose papers of the Revolution can be found in the Georgia Miscellaneous Collection of the Perkins Library.

4. Loyalist records.

The main source for information on the more important of the Georgia Loyalists are the claims they filed with the British government for compensation for their losses in the Revolution. The originals of these papers are in the Audit Office Papers of the British Public Record Office. A few representative pages from each of these claims are available on microfilm at the Georgia Department of Archives and History. To see all of the papers of a particular Loyalist claim, a researcher would do better to borrow from the complete copies on microfilm at the Public Archives of Canada, through interlibrary loan. The Public Archives of Canada also has microfilm copies of the rosters of many of the Loyalist provincial units that served with the British army in Georgia.

Among the books on Loyalists that abstract the above records or similar documents are William Henry Siebert, *Loyalists in East Florida* 2 vols. (Boston: Gregg Press, 1972), II; Hugh Edward Egerton, ed., *The Royal Commission on the Losses and Services of American Loyalist 1783* to 1785 (Oxford: The Roxburghe Club, 1915); and Alexander Fraser, ed.) Second Report of the Bureau of Archives For the Province of Ontario (Toronto: L. C. Cameron, 1905).

A Spanish census of Loyalists in Florida in 1783 was published in the 1971 issues of the Georgia Genealogical Magazine. The census gives the name, family composition, occupation, and former residence of each Loyalist.

5. Published sources--general background.

Among the best published documents for finding family information or military services for Georgians during the Revolution is Allen D. Candler, comp., The Revolutionary Records of the State of Georgia 3 vols. (Atlanta: Franklin-Turner Co., 1908). Also good are the Collections of the Georgia Historical Society and the Georgia Historical Quarterly. The latter is currently being indexed by the Georgia Historical Society. Their index will be published.

Several valuable guides and catalogues to 18th century manuscript collections of Georgia material have come out during the Bicentennial. Among these are Lilla Mills Hawes and Karen Elizabeth Osvald, comps., "Checklist of Eighteenth Century Manuscripts in the Georgia Historical Society," Collections of the Georgia Historical Society (Savannah: The Society, 1976), XIX; Marilyn Adams, comp., A Preliminary Guide to Records Held by the Georgia Department of Archives and History (Atlanta: State Printing Office, 1976); and Janice Gayle Blake, comp., Pre-Nineteenth Century Maps in the Collection of the Georgia Surveyor General Department (Atlanta: State Printing Office, 1975). The Georgia Department of Archives and History has microfilmed their pre-1800 executive department papers in alphabetical order. A guide to this microfilm is available in the Archives' microfilm library.

The Georgia Surveyor General Department has completed their series of parish by parish abstracts of colonial Georgia land grants and plats, which are valuable for studying Georgia's early families before the Revolution began. Of similar importance are Allen D. Candler and Lucian Lamar Knight, comps., The Colonial Records of the State of Georgia 26 vols. (Atlanta: various state printers, 1904-1916). The Georgia Department of Archives and History has thirteen additional volumes of this series in typescript.

A few indices and catalogues that cover much broader subjects than just Georgia are extremely useful in Georgia genealogical research on the Revolution. These include the new index to the Papers of the Continental Congress being published by the National Archives; Lester J. Cappon and Stella F. Duff, comps., The Virginia Gazette Index, 1736-1780 2 vols. (Williamsburg, 1950); and the American Genealogical-Biographical Index to Genealogical, Biographical, and Local History Materials (Middleton, Conn., 1952-). The latter is a valuable series of books that are not as well known to researchers as they should be. No complete set of these works to date exist in Georgia although all of the volumes published so far are available at the William R. Perkins Library, Duke University, and the Thomas Cooper Library, University of South Carolina. The largest number of volumes of this series in Georgia are at the Atlanta Public Library.

Not all books published on Georgians during the Revolution are as good as others. Among other reasons, many of the older works were written with inadequate or no documentation. These works include George R. Gilmore, Sketches of Some of the First Settlers of Upper Georgia (New York, 1855); Sophie Lee Foster, ed., Revolutionary Reader Reminiscences and Indian Legends (Atlanta, 1913); Louise F. Hays, Hero of Hornets Nest: A Biography of Elijah Clark, 1733 to 1799 (New York, 1946); Mrs. Howard McCall, comp., Roster of Revolutionary Soldiers in

<u>Georgia</u> 3 vols. (Baltimore, 1968); Lucian Lamar Knight, comp., <u>Georgia's Roster</u> of the <u>Revolution</u>. . .(Atlanta, 1920; reprinted Batimore, 1967); and the various undocumented lists of soldiers who fought at the Battle of Kettle Creek.

6. Source materials for local and county research.

For Revolutionary War research on present-day Wilkes and sur- rounding counties see Robert Willingham, Jr., <u>We Have This Heritage</u>. . . (Washington, Ga.: Washington-Wilkes Publishing Co., 1969) for general history and for records see Grace G. Davidson, comp., <u>Early Records of Georgia Wilkes County</u> 2 vols. (1932; reprinted Vidalia: SouthernHis- torical Press, 1968) and Robert S. Davis, Jr., <u>The Wilkes County Papers</u>, <u>1773-1833</u> (Easley: Southern Historical Press, 1979). The latter two works contain information on Georgia Loyalists as well as Patriots. For information on the Battle of Kettle Creek, fought in Wilkes County on 14 February 1779, and the men who fought there, Robert S. Davis, Jr. and Kenneth H. Thomas, Jr., <u>Kettle Creek The Battle of the Cane Brakes</u> (Atlanta: State Printing Office, 1974) and Davis, <u>Kettle Creek Battle and Battlefield</u>. . .(Washington, Ga.: Washington-Wilkes Publishing Co., 1978),

Information on Burke and surrounding counties during the Revolution can be found in Neil Baldwin and A. H. Hillhouse, <u>An Intelligent Student's Guide to Burke County History</u> (Waynesboro: the authors, 1956) and Robert S. Davis, Jr., "Bicentennial Supplement," <u>Waynesboro True Citizen</u>, 30 June 1976. Some Revolutionary War material on Richmond County was compiled by Grace G. Davidson, in volume two of <u>Historical Collections of the Georgia Chapters of the Daughters of the American Revolution</u> (1929; Vidalia: Southern Historical Press, 1968). John M. Sheftall's <u>Sunbury on the Medway</u>. . .(Atlanta: State Printing Office, 1975) covers an important Revolutionary War town in Liberty County.

The Georgia Surveyor General Department has the Dr. John H. Goff Collection on Georgia forts, ferries, and roads. Much of the informa- tion in this collection covers Georgia's Revolutionary War years. George White, comp., <u>Historical Collections of Georgia</u>. . .(New York: Pudney and Russell, 1855) reproduces many original documents of genealogical value in a county histories format.

7. Special Sources
in the Main Search Room, Georgia Department of Archives.

Over the years, the Georgia Department of Archives and History has acquired several unpublished indices, typescripts, and other material of Revolutionary War interest. Among these are typescript indices to Candler, comp., <u>The Revolutionary Records of the State of Georgia</u>; the Georgia Historical Quarterly (up to 1932); Revolutionary War soldiers in White, <u>Historical Collections of Georgia</u>; and early Savannah news- papers.

The typescript books at the Georgia Archives include Louise Frederick Hays comp., "A Census of Penioners for Revolutionary or Mili- tary Service Under the Act for Taking the Sixth Census 1840" and Wanda Hoffer, comp., "Marked Graves of Revolutionary Soldiers and Patriots Buried in Georgia." Original manuscripts from the state records were used to compile the "Georgia Military Affairs," "Indian Affairs," and other typescripts in the 1930's. Not all of these manuscripts can now be found in the Archives. What is left of these records are cata- logued, with many other records, in the Vertical File in the Main Search Room. Typescripts of DAR compilations of family, church, cemetery, and court records are also available at the Archives but the value of these works is chiefly for later periods.

Even some of the pbulished volumes at the Georgia Archives have unique research value. Their copy of Charles Francis Jenkins, Button Gwinnett, Signer of the Declaration of Independence (Garden City, 1926), for instance, has newspaper clippings pasted on its blank pages relating to new finds on Gwinnett since 1926. Their copy of The Revolutionary Records of the State of Georgia has penciled notes as to where complete copies of acts abstracted in those volumes can be found. The copy of W. T. R. Saffell, Records of the Revolutionary War. . .(New York, 1858) at the Archives has attached a special typed index of Georgia officers who served to the end of the Revolution or until their deaths, found in the book. No catalogue to these "amended" editions of these published books has been compiled.

Finally, the Main Search Room of the Georgia Department of Archives and History has some special biographies made up from bits and pieces of published works. Among these are works on Sergeant William Jasper and Elijah Clark. Other such biographical material is kept in file folders, catalogued in the Vertical File.

8.   South Carolina books on Georgians.

Georgia researchers sometimes take the Savannah River took seriously as a boundary. South Carolinian troops often crossed that border to fight in Georgia during the Revolution and vice versa. Consquently, many books on South Carolina in the American Revolution contain a great deal of information on Georgia and Georgians. Those of genealogical interest include:

* Gibbes, Robert Wilson, comp. History of the American Revolution . . .3 vols. New York: Appleton and Company, 1853-1857.

* Johnson, Joseph. Traditions and Reminencences Chiefly of the American Revolution. Charleston: Walker and James, 1851.

* McCrady, Edward. The History of South Carolina in the Revolution, 1780-1783. New York: MacMillan Cp., 1902.

* Drayton, John. Memoirs of the American Revolution. 2 vols. Charleston: A. E. Miller, 1821.

* Draper, Lyman C. King's Mountain and Its Heroes. . .Cincinnati, 1881.

* Bailey, J. D. Some Heroes of the American Revolution. Originally published 1924, reprinted Easley: Southern Historical Press, 1976.

Researchers seeking information on early Georgians would also be wise to check the published indices to the South Carolina Historical Magazine.

9.   Background information.

Only a few good general works on the American Revolution in Georgia have been written. They are Edward J. Cashin and Heard Robertson, Augusta and the American Revolution Events in the Georgia Back Country 1773-1783 (Darien: Ashantilly Press, 1975); Alexander A. Lawrence, Storm Over Savannah The Story of the Count D'Estaing and the Siege of the Town in 1779 (1951; rev. ed. Athens: University of Georgia Press, 1968); and Kenneth Coleman, The American Revolution in Georgia, 1763-1789 (Athens: University of Georgia Press, 1958). Carroll Proctor Scruggs' Georgia During the Revolution (Norcross: Bay Tree Grove

Publishers, 1975) is an entertaining way to read about the events and
see the sites associated with Georgia during that period. For people
interested in specific areas of the Revolution or do not have the time
to study the longer works above, the series of booklets on various
topics of the Revolution in Georgia put out by the Georgia Bicentennial
Commission and the Georgia Department of Education will prove valuable.

Hugh McCall's The History of Georgia. . .(1811-1816; reprinted
Atlanta: Cherokee Publishing Company, 1969) is still valuable for
research on this period of the state's history. Unfortunately, this
work has shortcomings in that like the Revolutionary War pension
statements, it relies too heavily on the memories of old veterans for
names and dates.

The materials for writing a good historical work on Georgia in the
American Revolution are more plentiful than ever. Among the manuscript
collections available on microfilm through interlibrary loan are the
Henry Laurens Papers of the South Carolina Historical Society, the
Benjamin Lincoln Papers of the Massachusetts Historical Society, the
Horatio Gates Papers of the New York Historical Society, and the
British Headquarters Papers of the British Public Record Office.
Reference books that would prove useful include John R. Sellars, et al,
comps., Manuscript Sources in the Library of Congress for Research on
the American Revolution (Washington: Library of Congress, 1975);
Patrick D. McLaughlin, comp., Pre-Federal Maps in the National Archives:
An Annotated List (Washington: National Archives, 1971); K. G. Davies'
abstracts of the Revolutionary War manuscripts in the Colonial Office
Papers, of the British Public Record Office, Documents of the American
Revolution 1770-1783 16 vols. to date (Dublin: University of Ireland
Press, 1973-); Helen Cripe and Diane Campbell, comps., American
Manuscripts 1763-1815: An Index to Documents Described in Auction
Records and Dealers' Catalogues (Wilmington: Scholarly Resources,
1977); and Dwight L. Smith, ed., Era of the American Revolution a
Bicentennial Biography (Santa Barbara: Clio Press, 1975) as well as
the sources cited elsewhere in this section and the various standard
bibliographies of Georgia books and articles.

10. Genealogical magazines.

Georgia's numerous genealogical magazines were publishing material
on the American Revolution long before the Bicentennial. Copies of
these magazines are available at the Georgia Department of Archives and
History, as well as copies of what indices are available to these
periodicals. No bibliography of the contents of these magazines has
been compiled nor do any of the general bibliographies to Georgia
materials contain any references to the genealogical periodicals put
out about Georgia. The following is a list of the current Georgia
genealogical magazines, complied by Kenneth H. Thomas, Jr., of the
Georgia Genealogical Society:

   * Family Puzzlers (weekly)   Ed., Mary Warren.
     Started June 7, 1964.   Heritage Papers
                                    Danielsville, Ga.   30633

   * Georgia Genealogical   Rev. Silas E. Lucas
     Magazine (quarterly)   Southern Historical Press
     Started July, 1961.   P. O. Box 738
                                      Easley, S. C. 29640

   * Georgia Genealogical   Leoda Sherry
     Society Quarterly   Georgia Genealogical Society
     Started April, 1964.   P. O. Box 38066
                                    Atlanta, Ga.   30334

* Georgia Genealogist
  (quarterly; no queries)
  Started 1970.

Mary Warren
Heritage Papers
Danielsville, Ga. 30633

* Georgia Pioneers
  (quarterly)
  Started February, 1964

Mary Carter
P. O. Box 1028
Albany, Ga. 31702

* North West Georgia
  Historical and
  Genealogical Society
  Quarterly
  Started 1968.

Jewel J. Dyer
North West Georgia
Historical and Genealogical
Society
P. O. Box 2484
Rome, Ga. 30161

* They Were Here
  (quarterly)
  Started 1965.

Francis Wynd
2009 Gail Ave.
Albany, Ga. 31707

* Huxford Genealogical
  Society
  (quarterly)
  Started 1974.

Lois A. McAlpin
Huxford Genealogical Society
P. O. Box 246
Homerville, Ga. 31634

B. PETITIONS, 1774

Patriot sentiment in Georgia during the early years of the American Revolution was strongest in the colony's two ports, Savannah and Sunbury. These first Patriots held a meeting in Savannah on July 27, 1774, to consider action in response to what Americans called the "Intolerable Acts," passed by the British Parliament to punish Boston for the Boston Tea Party of the previous December. It was decided that representatives of Georgia's frontier areas should be present before measures could be properly considered. A summons was issued for each area to send "duly authorized" delegates to the next meeting, to be held in Savannah on August 10, 1774.

In St. Paul Parish (present-day Richmond, Wilkes, and surrounding counties), more than forty citizens signed a petition, dated August 5, protesting the coming meeting. Their petition expressed their feelings that the people of Georgia did not "have real grievances to complain of," were "not involved in the same guilt as Boston," that the coming meeting was illegal, and that "the persons who are most active on this occasion are chiefly those whose property lies in or near Savannah and therefore, are not exposed to the bad effects of an Indian war." These Georgians in St. Paul Parish feared their frontier area would be in serious danger with "such powerful aid and assistance as none but Great Britain can give." Leading citizens of St. Paul Parish signed the petition, among them many men who would later join the Patriot cause, including John Dooly, William Candler, Barnard Heard, and Zachariah Lamar.

Representatives of St. Paul Parish and St. George Parish attempted to be present at the meeting of August 10th to present their petitions, but they were refused admittance. Following the August 10th meeting, seven petitions from the Savannah area and the three parishes that made up Georgia's northern frontier (including St. Paul Parish) were signed by more than 500 Georgians in protest to the Patriot activities. The new petitions from St. Paul Parish mentioned the heavy-handed treatment that their representatives and their first petition had received.

The initial petition of St. Paul Parish and the seven petitions written after the August 10th meeting were published in the September and October, 1774, issues of the Georgia Gazette. The Rev. George White published seven of these eight petitions in his <u>Historical Collections</u> <u>of Georgia</u>. . .(New York, 1854). He may have had the original petitions to copy from rather than the edited versions that appeared in the 1774 <u>Georgia Gazette</u>, contrary to what some scholars have suggested. The following is a composite version of those eight petitions, made by combining the names and wording of both previous versions. Names that appear in brackets on the following are bound on the White version of the petitions only or differ from the names on the similar versions in the <u>Georgia Gazette</u>.

[White, pp. 48-49; Georgia Gazette, 7 September 1774, p. 2, c. 1, 2]:

    Agreeable to the directions of the self appointed Committee, Mr. Glen, the Chairman, issued a summons to every parish and district, of which the following is a copy:

    <u>Gentlemen</u>,
                                                July 27, 1774

    At a very respectable Meeting of the Inhabitants of the Province this Day at Savannah, for the purpose of concerting such measures as may be proper to be pursued respecting certain late Acts of the British Parliament, it was (after some Business being entered upon) objected, that many of the Out Parishes might not have had a sufficient Notification of the intended Meeting; and therefore "resolved that all further Business be postponed till the tenth of August next; and that in the mean time, Notice thereof be given to the Inhabitants of the several Parishes, in order to afford them an Opportunity of sending down Deputies to deliver their Sense upon this very important Occasion." In Pursuance of this Resolve I take the Liberty, as Chairman of the Committee, to request you will send Gentlemen duly authorized to attend on Behalf of your Parish, at the next Meeting. The Number expected to join this Committee is agreeable to the Number of Representatives each Parish sends to the General Assembly. The Committee appointed to meet you at Savannah are: John Glen, John Smith, Joseph Clay, John Houstoun, Noble Wimberly Jones, Lyman Hall, William Young, Edward Telfair, Samuel Farley, George Walton, Joseph Habersham, Jonathan Bryan, Jonathan Cochran, John McIntosh, Suchon [?] Baukes, William Gibbons, Benjamin Andrew, [illegible], John Stirk, Archibald Bulloch, James Screven, David Zubly, Henry Lewis Bourquin, Elisha Butler, William Baker, Parmenas Way, John Baker, John Mann, John Benefield, John Stacey, and John Morel. I am you most humble Servant,

                             Signed, JOHN GLEN.

To, &c.

    On the 10th instant a Meeting was accordingly held, to which several districts and parishes, particularly St. Paul's, one of the most populous in the province, sent no Deputies; and although one Lord and another person attended as Deputies for the parish of St. George, yet upwards of 80 respectable Inhabitants of that parish sent down their dissent; Nor was the parish of Christ-Church represented at this Meeting, unless the self-appointed Committee can be considered as their Representatives. This measure left an opening for any to appear at the Meeting in the character of Deputies, who brought down an appointment as such, without any enquiry whether they were constituted by the majority of the parish or not. Several artful falsehoods were thrown out to induce the parishes and districts to send Deputies: In the parish of St. George it was said that the Stamp Act was to be enforced, and in the parish of St. Matthew the people were told that nothing was intended but a dutiful Petition to the King as the Father of his People; and to such lengths were matters carried, that, when some of the Inhabitants of St. Matthew's parish, having discovered the deception, desired that they might scratch out their names from the instrument appointing Deputies, it was refused them.

    The adjournment from the 27th of July to the 19th of August was general, and therefore it was natural to suppose that the last Meeting would be held at the Vendus House, the same place as the first; for, whenever it is intended that a future Meeting of any kind shall be held in a different place than what is usual, notice is always given of the alteration of the place of meeting, otherwise those who may be desirous of attending would not know where to go. In the present case, none knew that the second Meeting would be held at a different place than the first, except those few who were in [on] the secret; but the important Meeting of the 10th of August, in defence of the constitutional rights and liberties of the American Subjects, was held in a tavern, with the door shut for a considerable time, and it is said 26 persons answered for the whole province, and undertook to bind them by Resolutions; and when several Gentlemen attempted to go in, the Tavernkeeper, who stood at the door with a list in his hand, refused them admittance, because their names were not mentioned in that list. Such was the conduct of those pretended advocates for the liberties of America!

Several of the Inhabitants of the parishes of St. Paul and St. George, two of the most populous in the province, had transmitted their written dissents to any Resolutions; and there were gentlemen ready to present these dissents, had not the door been shut for a considerable time, and admittance refused. And it is conceived that the shutting the door; and refusing admittance to any but Resolutioners, was calculated to prevent the rest of the Inhabitants from giving dissent to measures that were intended to operate as the unanimous sense of the Province.

Upon the whole, the world will judge whether the Meeting of the 19th inst, held by a few persons in a tavern, with the door shut, can, with any appearance of truth or decency, be called a General Meeting of the Inhabitants of Georgia.

Having now given our reasons at large, we enter this our Public dissent to the said Resolutions of the 19th instant, and all the proceedings had or to be had thereon, and do earnestly desire that such Resolutions may not be taken as the sense of the Inhabitants of Georgia.

James Habersham, Lachlan McGillivray, Josiah Tattnall, James Hume, John Jamieson, Thomas Johnston, John Simpson, James Robertson, Alexander Thomson, Lewis Johnson, John Irvine, Anthony Stokes, Edward Langworthy, Joseph Butler, William Skinner, James Mossman, Henry Younge, Philip Younge, Thomas Moodie, Philip Moore, Joseph Ottolenghe, George Fraser, John Inglin [Inglish?], David Montaigut, James Read, William Moss, Henry Younge jun., Joseph Farley, John Foulis, James Nichols, Thomas Ross, James Thompson, Richard Wright, John Patton, John Hume, James Edward Powell, Leonard Cecil, Moses Nunez, Andrew Robertson, Henry Preston, Robert Bolton, Noble Jones, James Habersham jun., Andrew Hewar, James A. Stewart, Peter La Vren dissents because he conceives that as an inhabitant of Christ Church parish he was not represented, John Mulliyne, John B. Gerardiau, Abraham Gray, Robert Watts, Alexander Wylly, David Turbere, David Gray, William Moore, Quinton Pooler, Francis Knowles, George Finch, William Ross, John Parkinson, Edward Jones, John Graham, Thomas Ried, John Storr, [illegible] Furse, William Brown jun., James Herriot, John Lovery [Lowery?], Nicholas Wade, Matthew Stewart, Charles Younge, James Muter, Robert Gray, James Dixen, Peter Slighterman, Samuel Shepherd, William Strothers, William Thompson, William Sime, Stephen Britton, Isaac Baillou, George Henley, John Spencer, James Low, George Stewart, Daniel McInnes, Jonathan Holden, Henry Forest, John Mills.

The Following Persons in other Districts of this Parish have subscribed hereunto viz.
Upon the Island of Skidaway: George Barry, Charles William Mackinon, Robert Reid.
In Vernonburgh: David Johnston, George Dron, Nathaniel Adams, Walter Denny, Peter Theiss, Jacob Theiss, Joseph Spencer, Henry Nungesur, John Campbell, George Nungesur, James Noble, John Ranstatler.

[White, pp. 437-38; Georgia Gazette, 21 September 1774, p. 4, c. 1]:

We who have put our names to this paper, Inhabitants of the Parish of St. Matthew and Town of Ebenezer, think it necessary in this publick manner to declare, That, about the 4th day of this instant August, we were told by certain persons that we must send a petition home to our King in regard to the Bostonians, to beg for relief, as a child begs a father when he expects correction, and that all those who would join must sign their names,* that they might know how many would be in this parish; and that, should we decline what was recommended, we must expect the Stamp Act imposed on us. By these and other like flattering words we were persuaded to sign, but we find that we were deceived, for that the people wh met at Savannah on the 10th instant did not petition our King, but made up a paper, which we think is very wrong, and may incur the displeasure of his Majesty so as to prevent us from having soldiers to help us in case of an Indian war. We therefore disagree entirely to the said paper, and do hereby protest against any resolutions that are or hereafter may be entered into on this occasion.

Urban Buntz, George Gnann, John [Jaher] Hangletter, John Paulus, George Gruber, Matthew Beidenback, George Ballinger, John Oexlin, Rentz, George Buntz, John Pfliager, Henry-Ludwig Buntz, Jacob Metzger, John Metzger, John-Adam Fryermuth, John Fierl, George Zitterauder, John Heckel, Solomon Zandt, Jacob Gnann, Jacob Kieffer, Christian Steiner, John Remshart, Sigmund Olt, Israel Leimberger, Leonhart Kraus, George Bechtley, Baltas Reifer [Keifer], Michael Mack jun., Peter Fryermuth, Solomon Prothero, Jacob Tusant, John Grasintine, Christopher Rottenberger, Andrew Gnann.

We the subscribers do hereby certify that we are against Resolutions, this 2d September, 1774. Phillip Dell, Paul Pinck, Matthew Meyer, Jacob Meyer, John Maurer, George Maurer, Daniel Weitman, Martin Rylander, Benjamin Gainer, [illegible], Michael Riefer, John Wertsch.

[White, pp. 283-84; Georgia Gazette, 28 September 1774, p. 3, c. 1]:

We the subscribers, Inhabitants of the Parish of St. George, in the Province of Georgia, do hereby publickly declare, that we entirely disagree to the Paper containing certain Resolutions which were drawn up in Savannah by some persons met there the 10th August, 1774, because although many of us gave our votes that Mr. Jones and Mr. Lord should go to the said Meeting, yet it was because we were told that, unless we did send some persons there, we would have the Stamp Act put in force. By these and such like arguments, we were prevailed upon to do what we did; but as we find we were deceived, and that the said Meeting was intended to draw up a Paper that we think reflects very improperly upon our King and the Parliament, and may be of bad consequence to this Province, and can serve no good purpose, we therefore declare, that we do not approve of the said Paper, and we give our Dissent in this publick manner.

George Wells, James Rae, Peter Shand, Joseph Gresham, James Dayle, William Dayle, Shadrach Barrow, Joseph Tilley, Daniel Thomas, Job Thomas, Gideon Thomas, Drury Roberts, John Thomas, Joel Walker, Robert Henderson, James Red, Francis Lewis Fryer, William McNorell [M. Norell?], John Red, John Kennedy, Philip Morrey, James Worrin, Francis Stringer, James Williams, Paul McCormick, Samuel Red, Humphrey Williams, Alexander Berryhill, John Greenway, Edmund Hill, Robert Blaishard, Charles Williams, Hugh Irwin, Thomas Penninton, Thomas Carter, John Rogers, James Brantley, John Anderson, William Wethers, John Catlett, William

---

*[This is from the version published in the Georgia Gazette. In White's version, this line reads, "...that all those who would not join must sign their name...."]

14

Moor, William Gadbe [Godbe?], John Pettycrew, Richard Curton, William
Catlett, William Curton, David Green, John Rattan, Philip Helveston,
John Frier, Elias Daniel, James Davis, Ephraim Odom, William Milner,
Benjamin Brantley, Elijah Dier [Dix?], Thomas Grey, Samuel Berryhill,
Jeremiah Brantley, Thomas Red, John Green, John Bledfoe [Bledsoe?],
John Burnsides, Starling Jordan, John Forth, Patrick Dickey, Nathan
Williams, Zechariah Wimberly, Edward Wathers [Watters?], Henry Hamon,
Stephen Lamb, John Stephens, Benjamin Warren, Frederick Francis,
Solomon Davis, Moses Davis, John Gray, Arthur Walker, Francis Hancock,
Amos Davis, Pleasent Goodall, Jacob Lamb, Wade Kitts, Allen Brown,
Daniel Logan, Josiah Allday, Myrick Davies, James Douglis, John Roberts,
Landman Asbury [Ashbury?], Robert Douglis jun., Robert Dougliss Sen.,
Charles Golightly, Jesse Scrugs, John Howel, Henry Mills, Bud Cade,
John Dunavon, William Hobbs, Solomon Andrew, James Darcy, Joseph Moore,
James Moore, Amos Whitehead, John Whitehead, John Robinson, John
Sharp, Ezekiel Brumfield, Thomas Odom, Jacob Sharp, William Hobbs,
Clement Yarborough, John Thomas sen., Joshua Shap, James Hunt, William
Young, Barnaby Lamb, John Tillman, Seth Slokumb, Caleb Whitehead, Lewis
Hobbs, Robert Cade, William Cade.

[Georgia Gazette, 28 September 1774, p. 3, c. 1]:

We the subscribers, Inhabitants of Queensborough, and other
Inhabitants of the Western District of the Parish of St. George, in the
Province of Georgia, do hereby publickly declare our Disagreement to
Mr. Jones and Mr. Lord's going to Savannah as Deputies to represent
this Parish at the Meeting held there the tenth day of August last. As
we were not anyways consulted upon the said occasion, nor even had any
notice of their appointment to the said business, we therefore do hereby declare our Dissent and Disagreement to whatever they the said Jones
and Lord may have done or agreed to at Said Meeting.

Queensborough, Sept. 4, 1774.

Roger Lawson, Blassengame Harvey, John Lawson, Daniel McNeil,
William okelly [?], Francis Mountain, Andrew Lyle, Richard Fleeting,
George Cleland, David Cooper, John Cooper, Joseph Beatty, John Harvey,
Samuel Beatty, Robert Cooper, John Allen, Henry Hurd, George Ingram,
John Beggs, Matthew Moor, William Boys, Joseph Johnston, John Twitty,
David Irwin, Jeremiah Payton, James Campbell, Patrick McGee, John
Gilmore, William Hill, Joseph Saunders, Alexander Boys, Thomas Betty,
Thomas Mountain, Andrew Johnson, William Hesseran, Joseph Marshall sen.,
Matthew Marshall, John Marshall, Joseph Marshall jun., James Roberson,
Hugh Alexander, John Brander, Robert Breson [?], William Alexander,
Robert Alexander, David Alexander sen., Thomas Alexander, Matthew
Marshall, John Morason, David Alexander jun., Alexander Chesnut, Francis
Lewis, David Woods.

[White, pp. 603-04; Georgia Gazette, 12 October 1774, p. 1, c. 2]:

[Wednesday, October 12th, 1774.]

A PROTEST or DECLARATION of DISSENT of the Inhabitants of St. Paul's
Parish, against any Resolutions expressive of Disloyalty to our Most
Gracious King, and the Lords and Commons of Great-Britain.

We, the subscribers, inhabitants of the Parish of St. Paul, having
understood that certain persons have attempted, and are now attempting
to prevail on the good-meaning and well-disposed people of this Province, to enter into resolutions similar to those made in the Province
of South Carolina, in order to counteract and render ineffectual some
late acts of the British Parliament, intended to reduce the people of
Boston to a sense of their duty: --

We do hereby, for ourselves and others, protest against any, and
declare our dissent to any such resolutions, or proceedings in any

15

wise tending to express disloyalty to our most gracious Sovereign, and the Lords and Commons of Great Britain, for the following reasons, viz.

First, Because we apprehend this mode of assembling and entering into resolutions that arraign the conduct of the King and Parliament, is illegal, and tends only to alienate the affection, and forfeit the favour and protection of a most gracious Sovereign, and to draw upon this colony the displeasure of the Lords and Commons of Great Britain.

Secondly, Because, if we have real grievances to complain of, the only legal and constitutional method of seeking redress is, we apprehend, to instruct our representatives in Assembly to move for and promote a decent and proper application to his Majesty and the Parliament for relief.

Thirdly, That as the inhabitants of this Province have had no hand in destroying any teas, the property of the East Idnia Company, and, therefore, are not involved in the same guilt as those of Boston, they can have no business to make themselves partakers of the ill consequences resulting from such a conduct.

Thirdly,* Because we understand that the Council and Assembly of this Province have lately applied to his Majesty for assistance in case of an Indian War; and should we enter into any such resolutions, we could not in justice expect any such assistance, but would be counteracting what they have done, and exposing the Province to imminent danger.

Fourthly, Because the persons who are most active on this occasion, are chiefly those whose property lies in or near Savannah, and, therefore, are not immediately exposed to the bad effects of an Indian war; whereas, the back settlements of this Province, and our parish in particular, would most certainly be laid waste and depopulated, unless we receive such powerful aid and assistance as none but Great Britain can give. For these and many other reasons, we declare our dissent to all resolutions by which his Majesty's favour and protection might be forfeited.

James Grierson, William Goodgion, Robert Bonner, John Anderson, Edward Barnard, Andrew McLean, John D. Hammerer, John Dooly, James Hill, Barnard Heard, Amos Stapler, Charles Walker, John McDuffie, Giles Tillet, James Seymour, Thomas Pace, Richard Bailey, Samuel Tillet, William Redman, Joel Cloud, William Miller, Zechariah Lamar, Sen., Jacob Dennis, Littleberry Bosticke, Basil Lamar, James Few, John Baster, Benjamin Webster, Robert Honey, Job Smith, William Barnard, William Mungum, John Chapman, Patrick Jarvis, Joseph Maddock, Jonathan Sell, Robert Mackay, William Candler, Deverix Jarrat, Sherwood Bugg, Isaac Low, Peter Paris, John Henderson, Thomas Grierson, John McDonald, Francis Hancock. August 5, 1774.

[White, pp. 604-05; Georgia Gazette, 12 October 1774, p. 1, c. 2; p. 2, c. 1]:

To Thomas Shruder, Thomas Netherclift, and John Hume, Esqrs.
Members of Assembly for the Parish of St. Paul
G E O R G I A, Parish of St. Paul.

---

*[This is an error in numbering copies from White. In the version of this protest that appear in the Georgia Gazette, 12 October 1774, this and the previous paragraph are completely omitted. What is labeled as "Fourthly" in the above is identified as "3." in the Georgia Gazette.]

WE, Inhabitants of the Town and District of Augusta,* think it incumbant upon us in this publick manner to declare our dissent from, and disapprobation of, certain Resolutions published in this Gazeete of the 17th inst. entered into on Wednesday the 10th day of August, as it is there said, at a General Meeting of the Inhabitants of this Province, though we are credibly informed that the said meeting, so far from being general, was not even numerous, and that one of our Representatives, whom we had provided with a protest, and our reasons at large why we could not agree to any resolutions expressive of disaffection or disrespect to our most gracious King, or the Lords and Commons of Great-Britain, thought it improper to deliver said protest to a few people met privately in a tavern, having also been told by some Gentlemen coming from the place of meeting that they had been refused admittance.

We entirely dissent from the aforesaid resolutions. First, because we apprehend that this mode of assembling, and entering into resolutions that arraign the conduct of the King and Parliament, is illegal, and tends only to alienate the affection, and forfeit the favour and protection of a most gracious Sovereign, and to drawn upon this colony the displeasure of the Lords and Commons of Great Britain. Secondly, because, if we have real grievances to complain of, the only legal and constitutional method of seeking redress is, we apprehend, to instruct our Representatives in Assembly to move for and promote a decent and proper application to his Majesty and the Parliament for relief. Thirdly, Because if we should be silent on this occasion, our silence would be construed into consent; and a partial act of, and resolutions entered into by, some individuals, might be considered as the general sense of the Province.*

We, therefore, in duty to our King and country, and ourselves, do hereby solemnly protest against any of the proceedings of the aforesaid meeting, and declare our entire dissent from the resolutions entered into at the same, as witness our hands at Augusta, this 30th day of August, 1774.

Robert Mackay, Andrew Johnston, Edward Barnard, William Goodgion, James Gordon, James Grierson, John Daniel Hammerer, Francis Begbie, Thomas Graham, Francis Pringle, Donald Cameron, John Frances, Daniel Waiscoat, George Barnard, Charles Walker, John Pratt, William Matthews, Robert Bonner, Benjamin Webster, Martin Weatherford, Abraham Spear, John Lamar, John Francis Williams, Peter Paris, John Bacon, Sherwood Bugg, William Bugg, Daniel Wolecon, William Johnson, Charles Clark, Moody Butt, Samuel Clerk, John Howell, John Dooly, Thomas Grierson, Robert Grierson, Spencer Kelly, Joseph Leslie.

[White, pp. 412-13; Georgia Gazette, 12 October 1774, p. 2, c. 1]:

G E O R G I A, Parish of St. Paul.

We the Inhabitants of the Town and Township of Wrightsborough, and places adjacent, understanding that fourteen persons have drawn up several resolutions respecting the disputes between Great Britain and the Town of Boston, concerning the destroying of a quantity of tea, the property of the East-India Company, and have published them as the act of the province, and which we look upon as a great imposition, having no knowledge of them till after they were passed; therefore, we do in

---

*[On the copy of this petition that White used this word is shown as "Augustine."]

*[The first three sentences of this paragraph are omitted and the last is worded differently in the White version of this petition. These are the same three sentences that are in the White version of the St. Paul Parish petition of 5 August 1774, but are not included in version of the same petition that appeared in the Georgia Gazette. See the preceding petition.]

this public manner deny having any concern in them, and disapprove of them altogether, such proceedings as a few acting for the whole without their knowledge we apprehend being contrary to the rights and privileges of every British subject.

John Oliver, J.P. John Stubbs, Isaac Vernon, Josias Fewgate [Pewgate?], John Jones, Thomas Watson sen., David Baldwin, Henry Ashfield, Samuel Hart, Alexander Ottery, Jesse Morgan, Ellis Haines, Aaron McCarter, Stephen Bishop, Abram Louders, James Oliver, John Greason, William Daniel, Silas Pace, Gersham Wooddell, Absalom Beddell, Phinehas Mendenhall, William Foster, John Clower, Abraham Poter [Parker?], James Jinkins, Oliver Matthews, John Highton, Edward Green, Joseph Jackson, Joel Phillips, Matthew Hobbs, Joseph Maddock, J.P. Thomas Ansly, John Lindsay, Abram Dennis, John Jones, junr., Richard Webb, Benjamin Ansly, John Watson, Robert Day, Drury Rogers, James Anglin, Jacob Watson, Robert Cowin, Lewis Powell, Joseph [Jacob?] Collins, William Childre, Robert Harper, Jacob Dennis, Nicholas White, John Moor, Joshua Sanders, Robert Jenkins, Robert Neisus [Nelson?], Hilleny Guy (Hillery Grey?], James Bishop, John Fairchild, John James, Zechariah Phillips, Richard Holimon, Absolam Holimon, Edward Hill, John Hill, Joshua Hill, John Davis, Isaac Green, Samuel Sinquefield, William Sinquefield, Reuben Sherrill, Morris Callingham, Joel Cloud, John Stewart jun., John Lang, James Rayn, Henry Walker, Peter Purkins, Thomas Gilliland, Uriah Odom, Richard Hokitt, Edward Hagen, Joseph Hallensworth, Abram Hilton, William Michell, John Evans, John Evans jun., Peter Williams, John Stewart, Jonathan Sell, William Bromfield, William Weldon, John Thompson, Joseph Millen, William Penton, Alexander Oliver, Ambrose Holiday, Abraham Johnson, Nathaniel Jackson, George Wagganer, Robert Walton, Walter Drummond, Charles Dunn, Ezekiel Miller, John West, John Hodgin, Peter Cox, Joseph Brown, Henry Jones, John Dennis, Francis Jones, Peter Weathers, Richard Thomson, Timothy Jourdan, Watkins Richards, Abraham Davis, Gabriel Davis, John Davis, Isaac Davis, Edward Peater, John Pirks, Jacob Davis, Jonathan Sell, J. P. Thomas Pace.

[White, pp. 605-06; Georgia Gazette, 12 October 1774, p. 2, c. 1]:

G E O R G I A. Parish of St. Paul.

We the Inhabitants of the Kyoka and Broad River Settlements do in this publick manner think proper to declare our dissent and disapprobation to a certain paper or hand-bill, published and dispersed through the province, entitled and called, "Resolutions entered into at Savannah, on Wednesday the tenth Day of August, 1774, at a General Meeting (as therein set forth) of the Inhabitants of the Province, assembled to consider of the State of the Colonies in America," for the following reasons, viz.

Because we look upon the said paper as a very improper treatment of the inhabitants of the province, and of this parish in particular, for that we have been well informed that the said meeting was not a publick one, as before advertised, it being held at the house of Mr. Tondee in Savannah, and that many respectable persons were refused admittance. Secondly, That the meeting was by no means a numerous one, for where a question of the most serious concern was put there were only twenty-six persons that gave their voices. Thirdly, Because we from the beginning entirely disapproved of the said meeting, and, in consequence of our disapprobation, we sent to Savannah a protest and reasons at large, which would have been produced at said meeting on Wednesday the 10 inst. had not a number of Gentlemen been refused admittance, and it is denied by a number of Gentlemen of honour and probity in Savannah that there were any Deputies for the parish of Christ Church legally appointed. Fourthly, Because had no voice at the said meeting, and because we think the said paper carries with it unnecessary and unjust reflections on the honour and justic of King, Lords, and Commons.

For these and other reasons we do solemnly protest against the

18

proceedings had on the 10th inst. and do entirely dissent from them.

August 26, 1774

James McFarland, J. P. Sanders Walker, Daniel Marshal, John Griffin, Micajah Andrews, Andrew Poull, Aaron Sinquefield, Edward Seed, William Lamar, Charles Jordan, William Love, James Cox, James Young, Charles Hurd, James Hill, John Hill, John Holton, Joshua Hill, Solomon Barfield, John Kely, Giles Tulet [Tillet?], John Bouchanan, William Dorster, Edward Black, John Truman, Moses Powell, William Wilden, John Fouracus, Henry Bruster, Solomon Vickers, William Few, Neil Jackson, George Cowin, Daniel Walker, John Buchanan, David Sidwell, Thomas Mills, Charles Lin [Lea?], John Ratton, John Brady, John Matthas, Dionysious Wright, Robert Story, Henry Golden, John Tarin, Francis Settle, Yohn Howard, John Anderson, John Johnson, Nicholas Mercer, William Standley [Handley?], Frederick Stump, William Wright, Daniel McCanty, Samuel Blair, Jedidiah Smith, James Glaspell, Samuel Smith, Thomas Jackson, Ebenezer Smith, Samuel Morton, William Holliday, Thomas Holliday, John Sruib [Smith?], Thomas Cowing, William Barnard, Fredrick Ashmore, John Loyd, Jacob Jones, Jacob Winfred, Thomas Cussengs, Richard Belaman, George Bagby jun., Nathan Barnett, Frederick Runnals, Mark Jones, John Mitchell, John Fuller sen., John Fuller jun., John Moukly, Rhesa Howard, Benjamin Howard, Thomas Howard, William Satterwoise, George Brown, Thomas Wallace, Zechariah Lamar sen., Micjah Gustans [Custino?], Ralph Cilgore, Robert Mannoran, James Aycock, George Neals sen., George Neals jun., Moses Purkins, Aventon Purkins, Christen Peterson, Jeremiah Cloud, Noah Cloud, Daniel Lulany, Thomas Hooper, Thomas Waters, Thomas Shannon, Richard Aycock, George Simson, Elijah Clark, Andrew Brown, Lewis Clark, William Dicks, Mark Whitaker, James Goolsby, William Thomas, Samuel Whiteaker, Dempsey Hinton, Daniel Safold, Alexander Mills, Archibald Mahon, Richard Woods, Robert Patton, Jacob Colson, Benjamin Brown. [On the version of this petition published in White, dated August 24, 1776, approximately one-third of the names above were omitted. Apparently, White omitted all signatures he could not read from the original petition.]

C. GEORGIA ASSOCIATION, 1775

Georgia was the last of the thirteen colonies to join the American Revolution. So reluctantly did she enter the rebellion that no representatives for the colony, as a whole, were in the First Continental Congress in September of 1774. The colony was moving closer in line with the other colonies, however, and by the following January had adopted a modified version of the Continental Association and had chosen delegates for the Second Continental Congress, to meet in May of 1775. The following is Georgia's modified form of the Continental Association from Peter Force (ed.), American Archives, 4th Series, 1158-60.

Association entered into by forty-five of the Deputies assembled in Provincial Congress, at SAVANNAH, in GEORGIA, on the 18th of JANUARY, 1775, and by them subscribed on the 23d, when they chose NOBLE WIMBERLY JONES, ARCHIBALD BULLOCK, and JOHN HOUSTOUN, Esquires, Delegates to represent that Colony in the Continental Congress, to be held in MAY next.

Whereas a Non-Importation, Non-Consumption, and Non-Exportation Agreement, faithfully adhered to, will probably prove the most speedy, effectual, and peaceable measure to obtain redress of American Grievances: We do, therefore, for ourselves and our consistuents, firmly agree and associate, under the sacred ties of virtue, honour, and love of our country, as follows:

First. That we will not receive into this Province any Goods,

19

Wares, or Merchandises that shall be shipped from Great Britain or Ireland, after the 15th day of March next; or from any other place any such Goods, Wares, or Merchandises as shall be shipped from those Kingdoms after that time, except such as come under the rules and directions of the ninth Article herein mentioned; and except such Goods, Wares, or Merchandises as are absolutely necessary for carrying on the Indian trade, subject, nevertheless, to the control of the Continental Congress, intended to be held at Philadelphia, on the 19th day of May next. Nor will we from this day import or purchase any Tea from any part of the world, nor import any Molasses, Syrups, Paneles, Coffee, or Pimento, from the British Plantations, or from Dominica, nor Wines from Madeira or the Western Islands, nor foreign Indigo.

Second. That we will neither import or purchase any Slaves imported from Africa, or elsehwere, after the 15th day of March next.

Third. That we will not export any Merchandise, or commodity whatsoever, to Great Britain or Ireland, or to the West Indies, after the first day of December next, except Rice to Europe.

Fourth. Such as are Merchants, and use the British and Irish trade, will give orders, as soon as possible, to their factors, agents, and correspondents in Great Britain and Ireland, not to ship any Goods to them on any pretense whatsoever, as they cannot be received in Georgia; and if any Merchants, residing in Great Britain or Ireland, shall, directly or indirectly, ship any Goods, Wares, or Merchandises for this Province, in order to break such Non-Importation Agreement, or in any manner contravene the same, on such unworthy conduct being well attested, it ought to be made publick; and on the same being so done, we will not, from thenceforth, have any commercial connection with such Merchant.

Fifth. That such as are owners of Vessels will give positive orders to their Captains or Masters not to receive on board their Vessels any Goods prohibited by the said Non-Importation Agreement, on pain of immediate dismission from their service.

Sixth. We will use our utmost endeavours to improve the breed of Sheep, and increase their numbers to the greatest extent, and to that end will kill them as sparingly as may be, especially those of the most profitable kind; nor will we export any to the West Indies, or elsewhere; and those of us who are, or may become overstocked with, or can conveniently spare any Sheep, will dispose of them to our neighbours, expecially to the poorer sort, on moderate terms.

Seventh. That we will, in our several stations, encourage frugality, economy, and industry, and promote Agriculture, Arts, and the Manufactures of America, expecially that of Wool; and will discountance and discourage every species of extravagance and dissipation, especially Horse-Racing, and all kinds of gaming, Cock-Fighting, exhibitions of Shew, Plays, and other expensive diversions and entertainments; and on the death of any relation or friend, none of us, or our families, will go into any further mourning dress than a Black Crepe or Ribbon on the arm or hat, for gentlemen; and a Black Ribbon and Necklace, for ladies; and we will discontinue the giving of Scarfs [sic] and Gloves at Funerals.

Eighth. That such as are vendors of Goods or Merchandise, will not take advantage of the scarcity of Goods that may be occasioned by this Association, but will sell the same at the rates they have been accustomed to do for twelve months last past; and if any vendor of Goods or Merchandise shall sell any Goods on higher terms, or shall, in any manner, or by any devise [sic] whatsoever, violate or depart from this Agreement, no person ought, nor will any of us, deal with any such person, or his or her factor or agent, at any time thereafter, for any commodity whatever.

Ninth. In case any Merchant, Trader, or other person, shall receive any Goods or Merchandises which shall be shipped after the

15th day of March, and before the 15th day of May next, the same ought, forthwith, at the election of the owner, to be either re-shipped or delivered to the Committee of the Town, Parish, or District wherein they shall be imported, to be stored at the risk of the importer, until the Non-Importation Agreement shall cease, or be sold, under the direction of the Committee aforesaid; and in the last mentioned case, the owner or owners of such Goods shall be reimbursed, out of the sales, the first costs and charges; the profit, if any, to be applied towards relieving such poor inhabitants of the Town of Boston as are immediate sufferers by the Port Bill; and a particular account of all Goods so returned, stores, or sold, to be inserted in the publick Papers; and if any Goods or Merchandises shall be shipped after the said 15th day of May next, the same ought, forthwith, to be sent back again, without breaking any of the packages thereof.

Tenth. That a Committee be chosen in every Parish, Town, and District, by those who contribute towards the general tax, whose business it shall be attentively to observe the conduct of all persons touching this Association; and when it shall be made to appear to the satisfaction of a majority of any such Committee, that any person, within the limits of their appointment, has violated this Association, that such majority do forthwith cause the truth of the case to be published in the Gazette, to the end that all such fees to the rights of British America may be publickly known, and universally condemned as the enemies of American Liberty, and thenceforth we will respectively break off all dealings with him or her.

Eleventh. That the Committee of Correspondence do frequently inspect the entries of the Custom House, and inform the Committees of the other Provinces, from time to time, of the true state thereof, and of every other material circumstance that may occur relative to this Association.

Twelfth. That all Manufactures of this Province be sold at reasonable prices, so that no undue advantages be taken of a future scarcity of goods.

And we do solemnly bind ourselves, and our constituents, under the ties aforesaid, to adhere to this Association, until American Grievances are redressed.

The foregoing Association being determined upon by the Congress, was ordered to be subscribed by the several Members thereof; and, thereupon, we have hereunto set our respective names accordingly.

In CONGRESS, Savannah, Georgia, January 23, 1775.

John Glen, Chairman.	D. Zubly, Junior,	Samuel Germany,
Noble W. Jones,	James De Veaux,	John Wereat,
Samuel Farley,	Joseph Clay,	Jonathan Cochran,
Ambrose Wright,	Philip Box,	George M'Intosh,
Peter Tondee,	William Ewen,	Raymond Demere,
Thomas Lee,	George Walton,	William Jones
William Young,	John Stirk,	James Cochran,
John M'Clure,	Isaac Young,	Joseph Gibbons,
Archibald Bullock,	Robert Rae,	Francis H. Harris,
John Houston,	Robert Hamilton,	Samuel Elbert,
Joseph Habersham,	Edmund Bugg,	Henry Jones,
George Houston,	William Glascock,	William Lord,
Edward Telfair,	John Germany,	John Mann,
William Gibbons,	L. Marbury,	David Lewis,
Peter Bard,	Hugh Middleton,	George Wyche.

D. PETITIONS, 1777

Georgia did send delegates to the Second Continental Congress. She became an independent state with the signing of the Declaration of Independence in 1776 and adopted her first state constitution in 1777.

Despite this, Georgians were far from united. Many Georgians still sided with the British, and probably many more chose to remain neutral. Even the Patriots were all too often divided into opposing factions. The following abstracts of a series of petitions signed in the summer of 1777 are examples of the factionalism that separated Georgia Patriots throughout the war. The introduction is from a document in the Joseph V. Bevan Papers, Peter Force Collection, Library of Congress. The signatures are taken from the actual petitions in the Georgia State Papers, Papers of the Continental Congress, Records Group 360, National Archives. These petitions are also available on Reel 178-68, Microfilm Library, Georgia Department of Archives and History.

A letter from Colonel John Coleman in Wilkes County to Brigadier General [Lachlan] McIntosh in Savannah dated 31st July 1777 --

Worthy Sir,

Inclosed is a copy of a letter received with a very long petition, addressed to the Hon^{bl} the Cont^l Congress. The letter was sent as an introduction to the petition, -- but on reading the petition, found that the greatest complaints were against your Friends & Relations, therefore was determined to have nothing to do in it. I cannot omit observing to you Sir the deplorable Situation this Infant State at present appears to be in ---- Gentlemen of Abilities, whose Characters are well Established, are the only persons objected to, to govern and manage in State affairs with us. The consiquence [sic] of which I fear, we too soon will see to our sorrow.

> Am Sir with real respect, y^r
> most ob^t Hble Servant
> John Coleman

The following Letter from the Liberty Club, in Savannah was inclosed in the above. vizt.

Gentlemen: (Circular)

The safety of the States, & the good of the American Cause is general, is the sole motive of the present application. At such a time as this when everything that can be dear upon earth to free men is at Stake, it must be the duty of every virtuous member of Society to warn his bretheran [sic] & neighbours of impending danger, that they may Escape, or at least provide against the evils they are threatened with.

The many Encroachments on constitutional liberty & civil government by the corrupt & venal ministry of Great Britain, made it absolutely necessary for the Inhabitants of North America to disolve [sic] their political connection with her, & to Errect [sic] such modes of government as might be most suitable to the genious [sic] of each representative State, & every thinking many must be convinced, that to errect [sic] a constitution calculated to promote the Liberty of the people, & happiness of mankind on the ruins of the former, must be an arduous task -- a work that demands the greatest ability -- but as the civil authority in every new government must necessarily at first be lax, & require the support & countinance [sic] of every lover of order & Society -- so every attempt to oppose & Subvert it must be of the most dangerous Consequences, & tend to the introduction of anarchy, & every evil work. If any man therefore, however high in office, or exalted in Station, shall attempt to weaken, or oppose the civil power of an infant Government, he must be considered by his Country as a dangerous person, whose going at large may be highly prejudicial to the publick welfare--such a person, common prudence will dictate, should be removed from amongst us to prevent the mischiefs that might otherwise be apprehended. Influenced by these considerations, a number of free men, Inhabitants of the county of Chatham, reviewing the conduct of Brigadier General McIntosh, & observing in several instances his aversion to the civil power of this State, have been induced to draw up & Sign the inclosed [sic] memorial, -- addressed to the Honorable the Continental Congress, setting forth the reasons they would aledge [sic] for the removal of the said General McIntosh, & praying, that the same may be done as soon as possible, they being persuaded it is a measure, which would quiet the minds of the greater part of the Inhabitants of this State & be the means of Establishing peace Harmony and unanimity amongst us.

If on perusal, the memorial should meet with your approbation, we request it may be Read to the Inhabitants of your County, & that as many as coinside [sic] with us in sentiments may Sign the same. which being done, you will immediately send it back to his Honor the Governor & council.

We must conclude, with assuring you Gentlemen that we are not led to through any predjudice [sic] or partiality, but from a Conviction of its rectitude & Justice, having no other view but the Publick safety & protection.

William Belcher
Signed /
Presid^t of the Liberty
Society

The following memorial made up in the Liberty Club, to be signed in the several Countys [sic] in the State accompanyed [sic] the above Circular Letter, & were sent by their most inveterate & malicious members, who had most influence in each County that is to say --

(note taken from the secretary of Congress office the alterations & words between, the parenthesis, in a smaller hand were in the Liberty County memo^l alone --

Georgia

To the Honourable the president & the rest of the members of the Continental Congress, now sitting at Philadelphia. The memorial of Sundry Free men, Inhabitants of the County of Chatham, & State afore-said.

Your memorialists anxious for the Safety of the United States, & willing to contribute all in their power to the Support & maintenance of civil Liberty, begg [sic] leave to present their memorial to your Honorable Body which from your known attention to the public peace & the civil rights of mankind, your memorialist flatter themselves will meet with your notice & consideration.

It is with the highest pleasure & Satisfaction yr memorialists are led to mention the great attention your hon^{le} Body have already paid to the safety, & protection of this Infant State in granting us so many Battalions, & other forces, as appeared necessary for our defence [sic]. Your memor^{ts} are sensible [sic], it was with an intention of our further protection that your Hon^{le} Body were induced to appoint Lachlan McIntosh, then colonel of the first Georgia Battalion, to the rank of Brigadier General in the Army of the United States & this with the sufferage & approbation of the Deligates [sic] of this State, then members of your hon^{le} Body -- but your memor^{ts} would begg [sic] leave to represent, that the gentlemen Deligates [sic] were in this instance

23

greatly mistaken, as to the true Interest of their Country, & that they acted without any advice, or Instruction from their Constituants [sic], who never thought M.̇ McIntosh capable of discharging so important a Trust, or remarkable for his warmth, & zeal in the American Cause. Your memor.ᵗˢ cannot but declare, that it is with very great uneasiness they see a man without any merit, or experience whatever, raised to so conspicuous a Station in the army; whose Connections & Relatives, for the most part, are open & avowed Enemies to the United States & have caused great discontent in this State by their Conduct. Your memorialists would take the liberty of mentioning some of them. The generals [sic] Brother, William McIntosh was some time since, intrusted with the Command of the Troops of Horse, raised for the defence of our Frontiers, but resigned his Commission on account of the Clamour of the people. The men under his command were always uneasy, & frequently deserted; so that by some means or other, a large tract of Country on our Southern Frontiers was evacuated, & several thousand head of Cattle were driven by our Enemy a Cross [sic] St. Marys River into East Florida, (whilst he supinely neglected making any attempts to prevent it). Your Hon.ˡᵉ Body are well acquainted with the Traiterous [sic] Conduct of his Brother George McIntosh and not long since a Relation or (Conection) [sic] of his, one Alex.ʳ Baillies was detected in carying [sic] advices to East Florida, & passing to St. Augustine, to appraise our Enemies of an intended attack on that province.

The general has also a nephew Relation of the name McIntosh, now among the Indians, who has been remarkably active against us, & the gentlemen who shipt [sic] the Rice, together with George McIntosh are connected with the general, by the tyes [sic] of consaninity.

As the general abounds with such Connections, your memor.ᵗˢ cannot but labour under the most alarming apprehensions for the safety of this State, & the danger to which our Inhabitants may be exposed through the perfidy of pretended friends, (and many of their notorious Enemies)

Your memorialists, must also remark, that on several occassions, they have observed a great avasion [sic] in General McIntosh to comply with the Executive authority of this State, not to mention his evasive conduct in refusing to call (Join in) a council of war at Sunbury, agreeable to their request, which in the end, was productive of a Duel between him & our late president [Button Gwinnett]; in which the latter received a mortal wound, to the great loss of the publick.

His behaviour, with respect to his Brother George has given us a fresh alarm. Our late assembly ordered, that he should be sent to Philadelphia, with such Evidence as had been procured against him. Mr. McIntosh desired a little time to prepare himself with some Clothes & other necessarys for the journey, which was granted him, through the mediation of the general his Brother, who tampered, & made use of low cunning with the Governor & Council, & even attempted to persuade them, they might chuse [sic], whether they might send his Brother to Philadelphia or not.

The Governor & Council for several weeks past have frequently demanded his Body, to be delivered to the Sheriff, but the General by sundry evasions, hath put it out of the power of the Executive authority to Comply with the order of the Legislature, in sending him to your Hon.ˡᵉ Body, in so much, that we are not without our feard, of being under a military government, & subject to the dictates of a prejudiced & Suspected officer.

Your memor.ᵗˢ must assure your Honorable Body, they have not set forth ought in malice, but entirely from motions of self preservation, & the good of the American Cause. Your memor.ᵗˢ therefore hope your Honble Body will take the premises into consideration & order as soon as possible, the removal of General McIntosh from among them, as your memorialists are thoroughly convinced, it will highly discourage our enemies in East Florida, & be a more deadly stroke to Toryism in this state than any other can be, -- and shall grant them such other relief,

as to your Hon.^{le} Body shall seem meet. Dated at Savannah in Chatham
County the 1st July 1777.

[Chatham County, 1 July 1777]

James Martin
Matthew Stewart
Wm Hornby
Neh. Wade

Nicho^{ls} Neelson
Joseph Farley
John Waudin
Joseph Reynolds
John Brown
Willm OBryen
Ambrose Wright

James Flint

Joseph Dardss [?]

Wm. Wright
Wm Belcher
Wm Evans
Wm Summers
Samuel Spencer

Peter P.[?] Provost
W: F: Chevalier
Thomas Wilson
Henry Bourguin Jnr.
Adden Croget
Benjamin Wilson

Wheywood [?]
John Shick
Mathias Ash
              his
Rudolph   R   Strahaker[?]
          mark
Lewis Giroud
Adn. Loyer
Edwd Davies
Dav: Brydie
Robert Donald
John Newdigate
Jno Langford

John Lyon

Saml Stirk

Frederick Fahm
David Moses Vallotton
Laurence Meitz
Thos: Hamilton
Joseph Strable

Rudolf Fringe [?]
Abraham [?] Gbill
John Wilson
Benja. Mevis
James Papot
Thomas White

John Clarke
Balthaser Shieffer
[illegible]

Saml. Watson
John Richards
Herman Herson
Robert Mann
Benjamin Farley
John Tebeau
Benedt. Bourguin
David Francis
    Bourguin
Frederick Churchwell
              his
Lewis   +   Acord
          mark
Richd. Capers
Joseph Raynes
James Wilson
Robert Harden
              his
John   +   Becket
          mark
Charles Tebeau [?]
John Greene
Peter Pechin
Theodore Gotoars [?]

[Wilkes County, 5 July 1777]

John Lindsay

Geo Bagby
John Heard
Frederick Williams
William Butler
George Reynalds
James McClean

Benj: Mosley
Edwd. Eceles [?]
John Cimbry [?]
Wm Cimbry [?]
Jacob Mcclendon
Henry Duke
Henry Williams
Henry Ware
Nathanel Smith
Daniel Burnett
John Burks
John Hill
Charles Jordon

George Dugles
Charles Hurd

John Phillips

Joshua Hill
Dempsey Phillips
Edward Hill
Davd Holliman
Absalom Holliman
              his
Elijah + Hill
          mark
Thos. Cook
Thos Brantly
Jas. Swords
John Birkord [?]
Joseph Walker
Dred Wilder
Culpeper Wilder
Pulson [?] Bowie
Isaac Cook
Joseph Wilder
Thos Smith
John Carson

Ezekiel Miller

              his
Richard + Holliman
          mark

Joshua Miller
Solomon Banfield
Joseph Miller
Jas. Bowie
Ed. Seeds

James Brantly
Benjamin Braswell
Harris Brantly
Thos. Smith Junr.
Richd. Besley
Natl. Smith
Jams Jones
Jams Bishop
Stephen Bishop
James Davis
William Wilder
William Wiggains
William Wiggains
    Junr.
John Cook

[Effingham County, 20 July 1777]

Jenkins Davis
Ja. Goldwine
Wm. King
Benjn. Richardson
Thos. Mills
Israel Bird
Edward Boykins
Chrisn. Hudson
John Fanly [?]
Ulrich Neidinger
John Sharaus
Jno. C. Cronberger
Mathew Prahm [?]
Johannis Ingel

Richard Scruggs
[illegible]
Robert Hudson
Hillary Butt
J. S. Joulus [?]
John Goldwine
Arthur Ryal
Aaron Moore
Daniel Zetter
Daniel Burgateiner
[illegible]
Michael Mack
Casper Garirard
Samuel Pace

Josau Rrong Fritz[?]
Peter Blyth
Samuel Hudson
[illegible]
Abraham Derocke
John Maurer
Samuel Topp
John Hogins
Andrew Sockinger
George Zeigleer
Andrew Lynch
Frederick Shrempf
Andrew Gnamn

[Richmond County, 25 July 1777]

Sherwood Bugg
Wm Bugg
Moody Burt [?]
George Downs
John Coullenden
Thomas Flandson
John Boyd
Edward Ashton
Robt Bonner
Theo. Davies
Leonard Mobley [?]
Samuel Red
Holland Middleton
[illegible]
Frady Doughtery
John Rainsford
John Heard
Joseph Slayton
William Germany

A Dickey
George Dickey
John Johnson
James Germany
Thomas Hogg
Isaac Skinner
Frd Stallings
Wm Cone
William Sims
Daniel Richardson

Thomas Crittenderz
John Lyon
Philip Higginbotham
John Higgenbotham
Peter Prindess [?]
Samuel Lyon
William Simmery
Daniel Connel
Cors. [?] Wittington
James Willareghby
William Redman
Nath. Richardson
John Gloher
Curtis Low
John Johnson
Samuel Langford
David Harris [?]
Zedeciah Wood
Benjamin Grubbs

Wm Black
Isaac Low
Thomas Smith
John Chambless
William Baylie [?]
Boston Cline
[illegible]
Joseph Higginbottom
Jacob Mercer
Eph.m Ledbetter

Hueeslues Studstill
Charles Atkinson
James Wright
Samuel Bradkit
James Aldridge
John Shackleford
Thos. Chadwick
John Garnett
Eli Garnett
John Germany
John Red
Henry Black
Dan! McNair
William Lucas
John Tindel
William Courson
William Jones
Samuel Walter
Christopher
  Chambless
Samson Creef
Cornelous Smith
William Bryan
Rees Morris
Spencer Kelly
Steven Glover
Thomothy Rickitson
Jordon Rickitson
John Jackson
Timothy Rickitson
MarmaDuke Rickitson

[Liberty County, 3 August 1777]

Permenas Way
John Winn
Samuel Miller
James Taylor
Andw. Way
Palmer Goulding
Saml. Burnley
John Stacy
Lyman Hall
John Roberts
Thos. Morns
Isham Andrews
Lewis McLean

Sorong [?] Adams [?]
Wm Baker
F. Wyatt
William Baker Junr.
Wm. Quarterman
Andrew Maybank
John Mitchell
Fras. Coddington
Theophilus Elsworth
  [?]
John Rogers
James Hamilton
Gilbt: Harrison

James Maxwell
John Sandiford
Robt. Sallens
Peter Sallens
Wm. Way
Moses Way [?]
James Dunwody
Benjamin Towers
Stephen Dickinson
John Yates
John Basdin
John Pubbedge
Richard Hazzard

Benjn. Baker
Bryan Daughtry
Jas. Oswald
Samuel Stevens
Thomas Sturns
Joseph Stevens
Samuel Baker

Lewis Mutteain [?]
Hepworth [?] Cart
Charles Carter
Jos. Bacon
Odni. Way [?]
Robert Sattel
Robert Sattel [Sallet?]
Thos. Shepard
John Winn Jur.
W: Brown
Samuel Sallus
Thos. Elliott
Wm Bennett
F. Graves
Nathl. Bacon
Jeremiah Smith
Parmenas Way Junr.
Joseph Plumer

John Macleod
John Lawson Senr
Thomas White
Alexr. Stuart
Jacob Stobo [?]
Wright Murphey
James Harris

Jone. Holden
Haffd. [?] Tomarsall
Joseph Still
John Dollar
James Johnston
Alexr. Harvie
John Loney
Roger Lawson
John Pinsheere
David Turnerte [?]
James Jeffries
Wm Wallace
William Clark
Nathl. Lacton [?]
Thomas Yates
Joseph Way
John Way
Wm. Girardeau

John Forsteg [?]
Saml. Morcock
Andw. [?] Williams
Dd. Rees
Thomas Recekiel [?]
    his
Joseph J Opeare
    mark
Samuel Helme[Nelme?]
James Cook
Joshahaw Horn
William Woodward
William Warjon [?]
John Carney
Zachariah Ayres [?]
Samuel Strange
Mark Ayres
Peter Maney
Will Bennett Jun.
James Stewart
William Dawson
Chas. Watts

Lazauris Millard
William Bacon Sener

[Wilkes County, 5 August 1777]

Geo Wells
Ben Riden
A Bedell
Robert Day
Edward Black
Jno. Black
John Anglen [?]
William Daniel
William Tiesten [?]
Wm Phillips
John Trevot
James White
John Conner
Richard Johnson
Nathan ONeal
Benj Cathchings
Zachr Phillips
Wm Johnson
Geshem Wood [?]
Zachariah Phillips

Joseph S. Riden
John ONeal
Francis Travick [?]
William Hoollaway
James Nevar
Thomas Luster
William Holley
John Ramsy
Abram Hupam [?]
John Garven
Bollin Luvsy
James Carter
Ambrus Hutcheson
William Lovin
William Eley
Andrew Clark
James Dunkin

Zachr Wheeler
James Bentley
John Folsome [?]
Richd. Gastongne [?]
Richard Whatley
Abr. Prett [?]
Thomas Postess [?]
Sylvane. Johnson
Jacob Iply [?]
Wm Phillips
Willm. Hobbs
John Gray
Jacob Landers
George Neal
David Connard [?]
William More [?]
Jacob Noridike
Wm Downes
William Queen Senr
Robert Harper

Benja Thompson
John ONeal
Thos. Levirer
James Smith
[illegible]
Joseph Laurence
Wm Phillips
Austin Martin
Germany Martin
Joseph Catchings
Gedion [?] Anderson
William Anderson
Meredeth Catchings
Seymor Catchings
Barnard Heard
Edmund Catchings
Saml. Thornton

John Bently
Stephen Pennington
Jesse Webb
Abm. Landers
Thos: Oneal
Moses Stevens
Thos. Brown
Simon Gentery
Charles Parks
Josha. Parkes
George Hoopher
Laird Harris
Joseph Bouchannon
Joseph Brown
Patrick Welch
Matthew Harris
Joel Phillips
Andrew Walcliff [?]
Jseph Hopkins
Benjamin [?]
    Childers
Stephen Maddox
David Jennings
John Webster
Marcus Bowen

27

John Fainbrak [?]	Dennies Hemby
Joel Holland	Liveswill [?] Litz
Isac Refield [Befield?]	Samuel Oliver
Edward Glass [?]	Clemt. Forbes
Jacob Quien	Wm Colwell
Jessy Mills	John Mumford
Benjm Megginson	Thomas Loyd
Ruben Phillips	Saml Wilson
Wm Evans	Joseph Brown
Joseph Rabon	John Banks
Thos. Ellis	Edward Steadvent
Daniel Fosler	John Brown
Julus Dean [?]	Silas Brown

E. ACCOUNTS, 1776 - 1782

1.

The following are the longest of the accounts for payment due for supplies and services rendered the Georgia Patriots that are in the Telamon Cuyler Collection, Special Collections, University of Georgia Libraries. The Cuyler Collection also contains hundreds of papers relating to individual accounts, some listed in the documents reproduced here. Documents used here are reproduced through the courtesy of the University of Georgia Libraries.

Georgia

Parish St. David   The Honble. the Council of Safety

6th. Jany. 1776   Dr. to Sundry Accounts.

To Jessiah Barrington for 5 days service of himself
on the Expedition from Altamaha to St. Simons with
a party of men in order to board Capn. Osburns Sloop
so as to prevent her carrying out a load of Lumber
&c. by order or Request of the Council of Safety Uc.   1.5

To James Read. for 5 days service of himself on Ditto together with Sundrys supplyd the men &c. as pr. his account Rendered &c.	£3..11..8
To William Lain for 4 days Service on Ditto	£2.6..10
To German Knots 4 days . . Do . . . . Do	..2..6..10
To John Houstoun 4 days. . Do . . . . Do	..2..6..10
To Bryan Daughby 4 days. . Do . . . . Do	..2..6..10
To George Arron 4 days . . Do . . . . Do	..2..6..10

14th. Jany. 1776

To German Knotts for 6 days Service of self
& horse from Altahamaha to the parishes
St. Patrick St. Thomas & St. Marys to convey
the Instructions for Election from the Council
of Safety by them sent & Express to the parish
St. David &c.   £1..10

Attested before me   Certified by me   £
/s/ Wm. Carny [?] JP   /s/ J=Barrington   ‾‾‾‾‾‾
                                                                      8.68

```
20th January    The publick to Danl. Bennell Dr.
1776            To Liquour at Thomas Garnetts            Ḅ 0..2..6
  st            To Dist &Liquour had of James Pace          5..6
21              To expenses for victuals & drink
                  with Mrs. Crownberger                    15..0
                To a refreshment at Capt. Waldhairs        11..0
25th            To Expenses with Thomas Garnett            18..8
26th            To Expens. with Jas. Pace                   8..8
27th            To Expens. with Mrs. Crownberger           10..9
28              To Expens. with George Ducker          1...8..6
                To Expens. with Joseph Putney              14..3
                Do. Expens. with Putney                     6..9
```

N.B. The whole of the above being the Expense of Two detachments of
militia marchd. under by Command from the District of Great Ogeechee
in St. Matthews Parish to Savannah. . . .

Certyd. by me . . .

                    /s/ Danel Bonnell

        The Florida Expedition . . . . . Dr.

[There is no date or additional information on this manuscript to
suggest which of the three Florida expeditions this manuscript refers
to.]

```
        Cash paid Ambrose Wright . . . . . . . . Ḅ 100 . . .
        Do:Pd: John Langford . . . . . . . . . .   10 . . .
        Do: John Heard . . . . . . . . . . . . .   40 . . .
        Do:Pd: Joseph Woodruff . . . . . . . . .  150 . . .
        Do:Pd: John Martin . . . . . . . . . . .   15 . . .
        Do: Richard Wylly. . . . . . . . . . . .  250 . . .
        Do: Richard Wylly. . . . . . . . . . . .   25 . . .   590 . .
        Do:Pd: Philo Handley . . . . . . . . . .   10 . . .
        Do:Pd: Geo: Nichols. . . . . . . . . . .   50 . . .
        Do:Pd: John McCluer. . . . . . . . . . .   19 . . .
        Do:Pd: Edwd: Langworthy. . . . . . . . . 1000 . . .
        Do:Pd: Ambrose Wright. . . . . . . . . .  200 . . .
        Do:Pd: Saml. Morcock . . . . . . . . . .   30 . . .
        Do:Pd: Joseph Farley . . . . . . . . . .   30 . . .
        Do:Pd: Edmund Adams. . . . . . . . . . .   30 . . . 1369 . .
        Do: Philip Conway. . . . . . . . . . . .   20
        Do:Pd: Nicholas Neilson. . . . . . . . .   10
        Do:Pd: Ambrose Wright. . . . . . . . . . 1000 . . .
        Do:Pd: John A. Truitland Esqr. . . . . .  180 . . .
        Do:Pd: Colonel McMurphy. . . . . . . . .   50 . . .
        Do:Pd: Josiah Osgood . . . . . . . . . .   18..10
        Do:Pd: John Winn . . . . . . . . . . . .   57 . . . 1335..10
                                                          Ḅ3294..10
```


Georgia   Ceded Lands

    James Aycock, holman freeman Senr. & Thomas Rose Personally
appeared before me and was Duely [sic] Sworn on the Holy Evanjilest [sic]
of almighty god [sic] to Set a true Vallue [sic] according to the best
their Judgmt. on the Several Diffirint [sic] fields corn inclosd [sic]
about fort James Sworn before me this 22d. July 1776.

    /s/ Thomas Wootten   /s/ James Aycock
                                  /s/ Holman Freman
                                          his
                                  /s/ Thos R Rose
                                          mark

Colr. Colemans field	500 Bushels	[illegible]	Ł	50..0..0
Colsons & Wesbrooks	125 Do	Do		12.10..9
Evan Raglens	180 Do	Do		18..0..0
Abram Colsons	25 Do	Do		2.10..0
John F. Tomson	140 Do	Do		14..0..0
Henry Sanders	25 Do	Do		2.10..0
William Walker	50 Do	Do		5..0..0
				Ł104.10..0

1778   The Public of the State of Georgia in Acct. with
        James McFarland.

        no.

July 20.   1   To Cash paid Robt. Bolton freight of
                 300 Barrels Public rice from
                 Ogeechee to Savh.   200

Sepr. 26.   2   To Cash paid Danl. Daniely for Boating
                 up public Rice   225

Novr. 10.   3   To cash paid Jno. Donlery for Storeing
                 & repacking & cleaning 100 Barrells
                 of public rice   250

        12. 4   To cash paid Thos. Lamar for Boating
                 up public Rice to Augusta   90

Decemr 15. 5   To Cash paid Nathl. Hicks for storing
                 repacking & Cleaning public rice   75

            6   To my extraordinary trouble and expense
                 in going four times to Savannah to
                 procure public Rice Boats &c as paid   250
                                                              Ł1090

                 Errors Excepted

                      /s/ James McFarland.

State of Georgia Augusta.   January [page is torn here]
State of Georgia

[1.]   To Elizabeth Johnson For nursing & Cureing
       Francis Traywick & wounded person on the
       27th. Sepr. 1778   Ł25

  2.   To Benedict Hammock for one Three Grass
       Stear as p. Col. Ben. Fews Certificate
       20th Sepr. 1778   Ł30

  3.   To John & Isaack Denniss For Sundry wheat
       & Corn flour delivd. Colo. Ben. Few
       9th Oct. 1778   Ł167.10

[Account number four is out of place on the original manuscript, and
it appears between numbers 13 and 14.]

       United States of America   dollars

  5.   To Thomas Fuzzell for Boardering 13 wounded
       men on the 26th of January 1779. being the
       balance of his account.   2008

  6.   To Humphrey Wells Junr. for Sundry Expenses
       Including Wages Subsistence money &c as pr.

account dated from 28th. June to 4th October
1779.   952

7.   [This account is crossed out on the original
     manuscript.]   27th. Chesnie Bostwick for one
     Mare entry, June 24th certificate of Service
     & Acct. & Receipt. Dated June 24th 1779.   300

8.   To Thomas Carter for Sundry Ferriages as pr.
     acct. 8th April 1779.   178

9.   To Ditto for the use of his Boat and Hands to
     Works at the approach of the British Troops
     in Wilkes County as pr. Acct. dated Feby. 1779   400

State of Georgia

[10.] To Thomas Johnston for rideing [sic] Three
       Expresses as pr. Account dated September
       2d. 1778   [Ŀ] 17.10

11.   To Sherwood Bugg Colo for Sundry Services
      as pr. Account dated April 17th. 1778.   [Ŀ] 106.5

Augusta.   January 28. 1780
State of Georgia

[12.] To John Sharp for apprehendg. and bringing
       to Justice a Certain Jacob Grey & Carrying
       him to the Ninety Six Goal as p. Account
       dated 2d. Novemr. 1779   [Ŀ] 12.10

13.   To Zachariah Lamar for 450 Bushels Corn
      at four Dollars p. Bushel. as p. Account   doll.
      Dated 29th. August 1778   1800

No. 4. To Brigadier Genl. Saml. Elbert for 11
       Months Service   6600

14.   To Col. Geo Wells as pr. Acct.   4864-1/2

               ----------February 3d. 1780---------

       United States of America ----- Dr.

15.   To Docr. Francis Follette as p ser.   [Ŀ?]   8.15

               -----------4th-----------

       State of Georgia ---------- Dr.

16.   To John Benson for 1 Waggon & Hind Geers
      as p acct. dated 22d May 1778   [Ŀ] 150

17.   To John Wilkinson for Sundries as paid   doll   138

18.   To Do. Do. as p. acct. dated from
      May 10th to July 12th 1778   Ŀ 571

               ----------7th----------

19.   To Robert Bonner as p. Account dated
      January 22d. 1780   660

               ----------10----------
                                                                 dollars
20.   To George Walton Esquire as p Account   3750

31

----------12---------

21. To Edward Jones for Subsistence while a
     Prisoner Ten Months & 25 Days as pr. Acct.
     Dated from the 1st. Jany. 1779   2708-1/3

22. To John Stirk Esqr. for Subsistence while a
     prisoner Nine Months & 18 days as p acct.
     Dated from 1st. Jany. 1779   2442-1/2

Augusta. February 15th 1780
State of Georgia   Dr.

[23.] To Moses Tremble for Sundry Rations as pr.
       Acct. dated 1777 & 1778 [Page is torn here.]

----------16---------

[24.] United States of America Dr.
       To Joseph Collins a Capn. of Melitia [sic]
       pay Roll & voucher dated from 1st. day of June
       to 24th. August 1779   [page torn here]

----------17---------

No. 25 State of Georgia   Dr.
        To Nathl. Hicks as pr. acct. & vouchers   Doll
        Dated 1778   306-2/3

26.   To John Lindsay Esqr. for his Subsistence
      during his Imprisonment being 9 months &
      18 days at 300 Dollars pr. Month.   2880

[27.] To John Lindsay Esquire for his attendence
       [sic] as a Councelor [sic] from the 4th
       October to 29th December being 35 Days
       at 4 doll pr. day   3220

----------21---------

State of Georgia   Dr.

[28.] To Robert Phillips as pr. acct. &c Dated   [£]
       from 1778 to 1779   131..6..8

[29.] To Saml. Stirk Esqr. as per acct. &c   [dollars]
       vouchers Dated from 5th feby. to 19th 1780   402-3/4

----------22d.---------

30.   United States of America   Dr.   doll
      Francis Settles as pr. Account Dated
      September 18th. 1779   2770

---------24th---------

31.   State of South Carolina --- Dr.
      To Francis Traywick as pr. Acct. & vouchers
      Dated October 6th & Decr. 1st 1778   332

Augusta February 26, 1780
United States of America   Dr

      [Page is torn here.] Evans for 1 horse pressed   dollars
      service 9th June 1779 as   600

32

33.   State of Georgia   Dr.
        To John Irwins for 1 Waggon & Two Horses as pr.
        recd. & vouchers dated May 16th 1778   Ł 225

No. 34. To Estate of George Rosebrough Decd. for 1
        Waggon Horses &c as pr. acct. dated
        May 20th. 1778   Ł 562.14

No. 35. March 1st. 1780   doll
        United States of America   Dr.
        To Chesley Bostick Esqr. for one Sorrell Mare
        as pr. Acct. Dated May 13th 1779   500

----------7th----------

No. 36. United States of America   Dr.
        To William Candler for 25 Gallons rum as pr.
        acct. Dated 20th Jany. 1780   2000

----

37.   State of Georgia   Dr.
        To Colo. William Candler for Sundries as pr.
        Account dated from 16th Apl. to 13th June
        1778   Ł 194.16

38.   To William Greer Capn. of a Company of Melitia
        [sic] as pr Pay Roll dated from 17th Apl. to
        7th May 1778   21..[?]..4

Augusta March [Page is torn here.]
State of Georgia

[The following five accounts crossed out on the original manuscript.]

[39.]   The 2d. Battalion Richmond County [illegible]
        Pay Roll Dated from 21st October to the
        7th Novr. 1778

[40.]   To Do. Battalion Richmd. Do. as pr. Do. dated
        from 8th Novr. to 21st 1778   [Page torn here.]

41.   To Thomas Wheat for 4 Bushels corn as pr.
        acct. dated 9th September 1778

42.   To Samuel Griffen for 185: prok as pr. account
        dated 16th Oct. 1778   [Ł] 23..2..6

43.   To Siah Dunn for Acting as a Spy 4 Days as
        pr. Acct. dated 16th Octor. 1778   [Ł] 18

44.   To John and Isaack Denis for 1357 lbs.[?]
        flour as pr acct & vouchers. Dated 29th
        Decr: 1779   [Ł] 135.14

----------17th----------

45.   The State of South Carolina
        To John & Isaack Dennis for Ballance of their
        Account Dated October 26th 1778   Ł 60..6

33

[The following account is crossed out in the original manuscript.]

46. The State of Georgia
    To Colo William Candler for Sundries as pr. acct.
    Dated 1777   Ƚ 163.2.7

47. To Ditto for paying John Lencidum [?] a Spy for
    12 days at 8 Dollars pr. Day in October 1778.   Ƚ 24.

48. To Ditto for his Services & Rations from [?]   doll
    April 1778 to 4th January 1777 being 9 months   630

49. To Colo. William Candler for Sundry provisions
    &c a pr. Account Dated 2d. November 1778   Ƚ 61.18

Augusta. March [?]th, 1780
State of Georgia

[50.] Solomon Newsum for Sundries as Account
      Dated September 1778   [Page torn here.]

[51.] Archibald Hatchell Decd. as pr. Account   doll
      [illegible] 1777 from July to Feby 22d 1778   270

[52.] To Ditto of Archibd. Hatchelt Decd. from
      May 1st 1777. to Decr. 28th. of the same year   [Ƚ] 65..9

No. 53. To John Hardey Esquire for his Subsistence
        while a prisoner 2-1/2 Months as pr. acct.
        Dated March 19th 1779   [dollars]   1000

No. 54. To Thomas Johnson for Building a Fort on
        Broad River 100 feet Square as pr. account
        dated.January 3d. 1780   Ƚ50
                                              [illegible]

No. 55. To George Barber for Building a Fort near
        Isiah Goolsby on the Waters of Long Creek
        100 feet Square as pr account dated
        3d. Jany. 1780   [dollars]   2000

No. 56 United States of America
        To Lt. Colo. Robert Rae as pr. Acct. &
        Voucher Dated from the year 1776 & 77   4484

[The following account is crossed out in the original manuscript.]

----------April 14th----------

No. 57. To Andrew McLean Esqr. as pr. acct. & Vouchers
        dated 21st June 1779   Dd.   1136

58. State of Georgia
    To Thomas Avent for one waggon Two Horses Gears
    &c as pr. Account Dated 31st May 1778   Ƚ 210

No. (26th)
59. To Edward Walsh for printing acts of assembly
    &c as per acct. Dated 1778   Ƚ1100

[The following is from a fragment of this manuscript.]

                    May
                 of America
             Johnston for Sundry
         up 3 prisoners &c as pr acct.

May 22d. 1780
State of Georgia
To Doctor John Weitzell for Medicines & attending Francis Traywick
a Wounded person as pr. Acct. Dated October 1778   Doll. 200
May 24th 1780

[The remainder of the manuscript is missing.]

A Weekly Return of Provisions Issued out of the Comisary [sic] of
Issues Store at Augusta Commencing 7th and ending 13th January 1782.

[Actual provisions supplied and their value are shown on the original
manuscript.]

Governors Family	Abm. Jones
Do	Jonathan Bryan
Do	Abm. Ravot
Assembly	Col. Baker
Do	Col. Clark
Do	Col. Martin
Do	Thos. Lewis
Do	Thos. Ansly
Do	John A. Treutlin
Do	Danl. Coleman
Do	Caleb Howel
Do	Saml. Alexander
Do	James McNeill
Do	Robt. Harper
Do	Zachas. Fann
Do	Danl. Howel
Do	Saml. Sert [?]
Do	Charles Craford
Do	George Duly
Do	Saml. Stirk
	Capt. Handly
	Lieut. Hillery
	Lieut. Shick
State Dragoons	Adjt. Hawkins
State Infantry	Capt. Allison
Do	Lieut. Hamilton
Dept. Qr. Mast.	
Genl. Dept.	Joseph Woodruff
Do	Neahmiah Wade
Commissary of	
Purchases Dept.	Jeremiah Oates
Commissary of Issues	
Dept.	John Strong
Governors Guard	Abm. Jones
for Indians	Major Devaux
Sundry Families by order	
of the Council	Abm. Jones Sec't.

/s/ John Strong A.C.I.

2.

The following accounts and other papers are reproduced from the
Military Records Collection, Georgia Department of Archives and History.

The Honble Council of Safety of Georgia

1775
    Marks   To Galphins Holms & Co Dr____
      G H... 500 LD

```
D M... 500        1200 L.D. Gun powder a 10 perCt L 120
G H... 200        4928 L.D. Bullets. . a 40 perLD    82. 2. 8
                                                     202. 2. 8
```

NB 4^ct Shott Pr Reinur which we did receive mark'd Dc.M & G CH

(Reverse)
Account of
Ammunition
Galphin Holmes & Co

Memorandum from Colo. Dunn to his Honor - in granting him, the s^d Dunn,

---

to raise 50 or 60 Vollantears, Ingaged for 3 months under the same
prodicament as Col^o McCoy, by commition, from, his honor, as affor^sd.

---

further in respect of Commitions, for Captain Sabaltans already
elected, in his Regiment

---

also, a post settiled on the fronteers, back of the Richmon Lines, an
officer & 10 men, to provent the Intercores of the Enimy, in our
inhabited lands -

Likewise powder & lead, for the afore^sd. Regiment has not a Round
each man -

---

our Comesary derected by instruction that he may be able to inform his
asistanc in severall posts -

John Kelley, to be licensed as waggon master,

---

the whole above mentioned, desiered to be tollerated, by his Honor
the Governor.

pr me -

Josiah Dunn.

State of Georgia)
)   Personally appeared before me one of the Justics
Wilkes County)   appointed to keep the peace, for S^d County,
                    Nathaniel Smith, and being Duly Sworn Declares
upon his oath, Col^o Midleton & Capt Wright with a party of men, was
at his house, Richmon County and took a quantaty of Corn, and the Day
following - a party more men came, as they Said, ordered by Col^o Few
took away, and wasted what Corn, Suted them and the Next day came
again, and Caried off more Corn, to the amount in all, of one hundred
and fifty Bushels, and has Recevid no pay for the Same.

          provd before me

8th Apriel 1780 --   Nathaniel Smith

          John Hill J. P.

(Reverse)   to
              John Seth Cuthbert Esqr
              Commasary Generall
                 at Augusta

```
```

Shoulder Bone   October 27th 1780
Issue twenty five lbs of Beef for the use of the (Commissioners).
                          Jas. M. Stewart
                          Clk. B.C.

Thos. Porter. C. G. I.

                    (on reverse)

                30 Beef Issued
                       12
                    Commiss[ns]

        Shoulder Bone   October 28th 1780
Issue Sixty lbs. of Beef for the use of the Commissioners. -
                          Jas. M. Stewart.
                          Clk B.C.

Thos. Porter C.G.I.

                    (on reverse)
                       15
                    Commiss[ns]

1781
August 29th   Forage Returns for 5 horses for 1 Days
                  For Col[o] Martin   20   Quarts
               Forage for 9 Horses for 4 Days for
                  Ditto   144   Do
               Ditto for 5 Horses for 2 Days for Do   40   Do
               Ditto for 1 Horse for 2 Days for Do   8   Do
               Ditto for 2 Horses for 5 Days for J. Oates   40   Do
               Ditto for 1 Horse for 2 Days for J. Woodruff   8   Do
               Ditto for 6 Horses for 1 Day for Ditto   24   Do
               Ditto for 2 Horses for 3 Days for
                  J. Stallings   288   Do
               Ditto for Mr Bonner for the use of the
                  Publick   64   Do
               Ditto for Capt. Byus Boyakin   344   Do
               Ditto for 4 Horses for 2 Days for the
                  Governor   32   Do
               Ditto for 1 Horse for 4 Days for Ch[s]
                  Odingsells   16   Do
               Ditto for 7 Horses for Days for
                  General Twigs   56   Do
               Ditto for 7 Horses for 1 Day for Hugh Magee   4   Do
               Ditto for 2 Horses for 2 Days for P. Tarvis   16   Do
               Ditto for 1 Horse for 3 Days Arch[d] Bell   12   Do
               Ditto for Mr Bonner for the use of the
                  Publick   48   Do

                                                          1164   Quarts

                    36 Bushells & 12 Quarts

37

Weekly Return of Forage Drawn by Sundry Pensions Vzt. 8th Novr. 81

To whom Delivered	Number of horses	So many Quarts	So many bushels	The Quantity
Coln Jackson	73	294	9	2/5
Welch & Cooper	30	120	3	24
Hillary	7	28		
Hawkins	7	28		
Jervis	7	28		
Washington	7	38	3	16
Col McIntosh	14	56	1	24
Q M			5	
Jon Bryan			4	
Governor			15	
Escort			17	
G Gard	29	107	3	11
P Thomas			2	
Rt Bonner			2	
C Eustace	4	23		
S Stirk	6	94	1	20 - 3 - 24
				64
			Busl:	67 - 24 Qts

(Reverse)

Weekly Return of Forage at this Post

38

Regulations for the Issuing Commissary

   1st   That all officers and soldiers, on Actual duty, shall be
allowed to draw full rations that the officer making returns shall do
it upon Honer; that himself & those for whom he draws are on actual
duty--

   2nd   That the Governor & family draw Eleven rations, including
Col? Few & Major Deveaux--

   3rd   That each of the Executive Council & Secretary draw Two
rations--

   4th   That Commissary of Purchases draw a full ration for each
white man; that there shall not be allowed more than five men in the
said department at Augusta.

   5th   That the Q. M. Genl draw full rations for himself and two
Assistants, beside artificers & Laboureres - & a Qu^t of meal for each
Negro--

   6th   That all persons who are in the Publick service are to draw
rations for their families on application to the Governor & Council
provided they have no other means of subsistance--they to be accountable.

Note: half rations is to be Issued to Women & Children untill friday
noxt; after that no rations will be allowed them except by a special
order from the Governor & Council--all Objects of Charity will be
allow support by proper application.

                    [On Reverse]

   Returns of Provission Issued &c.

   Recommendations for Rations to Receive d&c.

      N° 14

A Weekly Return of Provisions Issued out of the Commissary of Issues Store at Augusta - Commencing 29th October and ending 4th November 1781

lbs. Beef	Bush. Meal	Qts. Meal	Lbs. of Candles	By whose Order
67½	1	13	3	Jonathan Bryan
21		14		Col. McIntosh for Mrs. Makil
21		14		Col. James Martin for his Family
42		28		Major Walsh
73½	1	17		Capt. Stallings for his Family
21		14		State Dragoons, Lieut. Hicks
979½	20	13	0	State Infantry, Lieut. Hamilton
48	1			Lieut. Hilliry Prisnor of War
220	4	19	3	Q^r M^{st} Genl Dep^t $Rich^d$ Capers
90	1	28		Forage Dep^t, Robt Bonner
196½	4	3		Commissary Purcheses Dept., John Wilkinson
31½		21		Commissary Issues Dep^t John Strong
118½	2	15		Governors Guard, Major Deavaux
56	1	4		For a party of men on Command to Carolina Col. John Martin
96	1			For a Guard going to Genl Greens Camp, Lieut. Camp.
241½	5	1		Sundry Families, Col. Jackson
10½		7		Do Do Col. Euistice
10½		7		Do Do Col. John Martin
84	1	24		Do Do Major Deavaux
108	2	8		Do Do by order of the Gov. & Council, A. Jones, Secy.
			18	For Illuminating Houses, Joseph Woodroof, D.Q.M.G.
2516½	51	26	24	Total

John Strong A.C.I.

Weekly Return

A Weekly Return of Provisions Issued out of the Commissarys of Issues Store at Augusta - Commencing 5th and ending 11th November 1781

lbs. Beef	Bush. Meal	Qts. Meal		By whose Order
94½	1	31	Councellors	Jonathan Bryan
15		10	Do	Daniel Coleman
15		10	Do	Jenkin Davis
7½		5	Commissioner	Archibal Bell
15		10	Col. McIntosh for Mrs. Mahil	
42		28	Major Walsh	
52½	1	3	Capt. Stallings for his Family	
115½	2	13	State Dragoons	Capt. Stallings
21		14	Do	Lieut. Hickes
684	14	8	State Infantry	Nicholas Millar Reg^t Q^r Master
66	1	12		Lieut. Hillary
10½		7	Georgia Militia	Col. Johnson
42		28	For four Prisnors	Lieut. Hamilton
189	3	30	Q^r Mas^t Genl Dep^t	Richd Capers
52½	1	3	Commissary of Purcheses Dept.	John Wilkinson
21		4	Commissary of Issues Dep^t	John Strong
96	2		Governers Guard	Major Deavaux
172	3	19	Sundry Families	Col. Jackson
7½		3	Do Do	Col. Eustice
7½		5	Do Do	Col. John Martin
60	1	8	Do Do	Major Deavaux
243½	5	2	Do Do by order of the Governer and Council, A. Jones Sec^y	
2029½	42	9	Total	

John Strong A.C.I.

Weekly Return

41

A Weekly Return of Provisions Issued out of the Commissary of Issues
Store at Augusta - Commencing 12th and ending 18th November 1781

lbs of Meal	Bush. Meal	Qts. Meal	By whose Order
217½	4	17	Gov. and Family, Col. Martin and Major Deavaux
63	1	10	Jonathan Bryan
21		14	Councellors Daniel Coleman
42		28	Do Jenkin Davis
24		16	Major Stirk
42		28	Major Walsh
18		12	Capt. Handly
93	1	30	Lieut. Hillary
268½	5	19	State Dragoons Capt. Stallings
21		14	Do Do Lieut. Hicks
454½	9	15	State Infantry Lieut. Hamilton
10½		7	Militia Col. Johnson
131	3	7	Q^r Mas^t Genl Dep^t Joseph Woodruff
12		8	Do Do Richd Capers
52½	1		Commissary of Purcheses Dept. John Wilkinson
21		14	Commissary of Issues Dept., John Strong
102	2	4	Governors Guard, Major Deavaux & Col. Martin
297	3	3	For Indians Do Do
42		28	For four Prisonors of War, Lieut. Hamilton
418½	7	29	Sundry Families by order of the Council
			A. Jones Sect^y
2351	45	18	Total

John Strong A.C.I.

Weekly Return

A Weekly Return of Provisions Issued out of the Commissary of Issues Store at Augusta - Commencing 19th and ending 25th November 1781

lbs Beef	Bush Meal	Qts Meal	Qts Salt	Gills Salt	Lbs Candles		By whose Order
181½	3	25		7½	12	Gov. Family, Col. Few & Major Deavaux	
21		14		1		Councellers	Daniel Coleman
49	1	1		2 3/4		Do	Jenkin Davis
6		4		½		Do	Abᵐ Ravot
					6	Do	James Jones
54	1	4					Jonathan Bryan
96	2			4½			Major Stirk
21		14		1	1		Capt. Handly
24		16		1½			Lieut. Hillary
102	2	4		4½		State Dragoons	Capt. Stallings
21		14		1		Do	Lieut. Hicks
145½	3	1	1		1	Do	Lieut. Harvey
97½	2	1		3		State Infantry	Capt. Lyons
37½		25		2		Do	Capt. Harrison
280½	5	27	1	7		Do	Capt. Allison
100½	2	4		5½		Do	Lieut. Hamilton
15		10		3/4		Do	Ensign Lee
88½	1	27		5		State Militia	Col. James Martin
48	1			2½		Do	Major Bostick
167½	4	21	1	1		Dept. Qʳ Masᵗ Genˡ Dept., Joseph Woodruff	
10½		7		½		Do	Richᵈ Capers
103½	2	5		5½	1	Commissary of Purchases Dept., John Wilkinson	
21		14		1	1	Commissary of Issues Dept., John Strong	
69	1	14		3½		Gov. Guard, Col. Few & Major Deavaux	
10½		7		½		For John Anderson, Major Deavaux	
42		28				For four Prisonors of War, Lieut. Hamilton	
656	13	23				Sundry Families by order of the Council, A. Jones Secʸ	
2469	52	22	10	6	2	Total	

John Strong A.C.I.

Weekly Return

A Weekly Return of Provisions Issued out of the Commissary of Issues Store at Augusta - Commencing 26 Nov^mr and ending 2nd Decem^r 1781

Lbs Beef	Bush Meal	Qts Meal	Qts Salt	Gills Salt	Lbs Soap		By whose Order
178½	3	23	1	2	12	Gov. Family	Major Deavaux
54	1	4		3		Councellors	Jonathan Bryan
73½	1	17		4		Do	Abraham Ravot
21		14		1			Col. James Martin
21		14		1			Capt. Handly
86	1	26		5			Lieut. Hillary
132	2	24		7½	8	State Dragoons	Capt. Stallings
64½	1	11		3½		Do	Lieut. Blount
207	4	10	1	3½		Do	Lieut. Harvey
21		14		1		Do	Lieut. Hicks
700½	14	19	5		12	State Infantry	Capt. Allison
33		22		1 3/4		Do	Capt. Morrison
54	1	4		3		Do	Lieut. Hamilton
237	4	30	1	6		Militia	Col. Baker
208	5		1	4		Dept. Qr. Mast.	Genl. Dept. Joseph Woodruff
10½		31		½		Do	Richard Capers
73½	1	17		4		Commissary of Purcheses Dept., John Wilkinson	
21		14		1		Commissary of Issues Dept., John Strong	
9		6		½		Governers Guard, Major Deavaux	
12		8				For Two Deserters	Do
9		7		½		For Two Indians	Do
42		28				For four Prisonors of War, Lieut. Hamilton	
742	15	23				Sundry Families order of Council, A. Jones Sect^y	
3010	64	12	15	4 3/4	32	Total	

John Strong A.C.I.

Return of Provisions

A Weekly Return of Provisions Issued out of Commissary of Issues
Store at Augusta - Commencing 3d and ending 9th December 1781

Lbs Beef	Bush Meal	Qts. Meal	Qts Salt	Gills Salt	Lbs of Candles	By whose Order	
145½	3	1		5½		Gov. Family, Major Deavaux	
36		24		2		Councellors	Jonathan Bryan
18		12		1		Do	Jenkin Davis
6		4		¾		Commissioner	Archibal Beall
21		14		1	1		Capt. Handly
78	1	20		4	2		Lieut. Hillary
201½	4	28	1	3		State Dragoons	Capt. Stallings
76½	1	19		4		Do	Lieut. Harvy
214½	4	15	1	2 3/4		State Infantry	Capt. Allison
322½	6	23	1	4		Do	Lieut. Hamilton
82½	1	23		4½		Regt Qr Master	Nicholas Miller
82½	1	23		4½		Militia	Col. Baker
54	1	4				Do	Col. Cooper
25½		17		1¼		Do	Col. James Martin
286½	5	9	1	3 3/4	2½	Dept. Qr Mast. Genl Dept.	Joseph Woodruff
10½		7		½		Do	Richd Capers
63	1	10		3	1	Commissary of Purcheses Dept.,	John Wilkinson
81		14		1¼		Commissary of Issues Dept.,	John Strong
88½	1	17		3		For Indians and their Guard,	Major Devaux
42		28				Four four Prisnors of War,	Lieut. Hamilton
704	14	29				Sundry Families by order Council,	Abm Jones
2579	53	21	10	1¼	6½	Total	

John Strong A.C.I.

Weekly Return

A Return of Provisions Issued out of the Commissary of Issues
Store at Augusta Commencing 10th and ending 16th Decem^r 1781

Lbs Beef	Bush Meal	Lbs Meal	Qts Salt	Gills Salt	Lbs Candles		By Whose Order
199½	4	5	1	3		Gov. Family	Charles Odingsell
45		50		2½		Councellors	Jonathan Bryan
15		10		3/4		Do	Daniel Coleman
31½		21		1 3/4		Do	Jenkin Davis
21		14		1½		Do	Abraham Ravot
48	1			2½			Major Stirk
21		14		1¼			Capt. Handly
21		14		1½			Capt. Lindsy
45		30		2½			Lieut. Hillary
24		16		1¼		State Dragoons	Lieut Blount
67½	1	13		3 3/4		State Infantry	Capt. Morrison
519	10	26	3	4½	14	Co	Lieut. Hamilton
	5		1	½		Militia	Genl. Twiggs
21		14				Do	Col. Jas. Martin
241½	5	22	1	6½	1	Dept Q^r Mas^t Genl Dept.,	Joseph Woodruff
126	2	27		7½	1	Commissary of Purchases Dept.,	Jeremiah Oates
21		14		1¼	1	Commissary of Issues Dept.,	John Strong
6		4		½		Dept. Barrak Mast. Genl.,	George Embeck
106	1	19		4		For Indians	Charles Odingsell
42		28				For four Prisonrs of War	Lieut. Hamilton
695½	14	23				Sundry families by order Council	Abm Jones, Secy
2316	53	24	12	½	17	Total	

John Strong A. C. I.

A Weekly Return of Provisions Issued out of the Commissary of Issues
Store at Augusta - Commencing 17th and ending 23d Decemr 1781

Lbs Beef	Bush Meal	Lbs Meal	Qts Salt	Gills Salt	Lbs Soap	By whose Order
199½	4	5	1	2½		Gov. Family, Col. Martin & Odingsell
59	1	4		3		Councellors Jonathan Bryan
21		14		1		Do Daniel Coleman
34½		23		1¼		Major Stirk
21		14		1		Capt. Handly
21		14		1		Capt. Lindsy
39		26		2		Lieut. Hillary
27		18		1½		State Dragoons Capt. Stallings
15		10		¼		Do Lieut. Stallings
439	9	5	3		12	State Infantry Lieut. Hamilton
81		18		3		Militia Genl Twiggs
21		14		1		Do Col. James Martin
264	5	1	1	4	2	Dept. Qr Mast. Genl Dept., Joseph Woodruff
118	2	12		6½		Commissary of Purchases Dept. Jeremiah Oates
21		14		1¼	2	Commissary of Issues Dept., John Strong
13½		9		3/4		Governers Guard, Col. Martin
13½		9		3/4		For Men from Col. Carlks Station, Major Deavaux
36		24				For Prisnors going to Savannah, Major Deavaux
82½	1	23				For Indians, Charles Odingsell
695	14	23				Sundry Families by order Councel, Abm Jones Sect
2216½	44	24	9	12	16	Total

John Strong A.C.I.

Return of Provisions

issued

A Weekly Return of Provisions Issued at Savannah Commencing 2nd and ending 8th Feby 1782

To Whom Issued	Lbs Beef	Lbs Flour	Lbs Rice	Qt Salt	Jill Salt
To Honorable Gov.r Hall & Family	175	140			
To Gen.l McIntosh & Commiss Prisoners	70	56			1 3/4
To Supernumery Contl Officers	52½	42			3 1/2
To Dep.t Pervayor L.t Depart.mt	26¼	21			1 3/8
To Virginia Light Dragoons	277½	264		2	5 1/4
To Georgia Regiment	1327½	1062		10	5
To Georgia Militia	70	56			4 3/8
To Purchasing Agents Depart.mt	78 3/4	63			5 1/8
To Issuing Agents Depart.mt	26½	21			1 3/4
To Comm.s Military Stores Depart.mt	52½	36	7½		3 3/4
To Barrack Master's Depart.mt	48	60			5
To Hospital	55	198	21	1	6
To Mr. Higgens Pilot & hands	26½	21			1 3/5
To Mary Muslain Distrissed	8 3/4	7			3/5
Total Issued	2294¼	2047	28½	19	1 1/2

John Strong J.A.

(Reverse)

Weekly Return

Provisions
10th Febry 1783

To his Honor John Howston Esq.ʳ Cap.ᵗ Generall, Governer & Commander in
Chif In and Over the State of Georgia &c -

                         Your Petitioner Humbly Sheweth
that in the year 1781 - my husband John McDaniel through Surprise Joyned
the British at Savanah, and soon after Died with the Small pox, Left
your Petitioner with three Children, to Soport, in a most perishable
Setuation, your Petitioner Remained, with onley a Small Compidence a
few Catle and hogs, which was Soon Wrested from your Petitioner hands,
before any Confiscation took place, these may please your honor - the
Small Subsistance I had was Sold, at Vandue a few Catle and Hogs,
Colonel Daniel Colman, and John Hill Esq.ʳ was purchasers, which the
said Cap.ᵗ Hill, was Gracesush anough to Let me keep what he had pur-
chassed Col.ᵒ Colman Drives off what few Catle I had, all, besides your
unfortunate Petitioner, Go back - there Effects, agreable to Law, Your
Petitioner Prays--

     That Colonel Daniel Colman, and John Hill Esq.ʳ obligations may
be Given up to the Said Gentlemen, or otherwise unavoidable your
Petitioner must become a parish Charge, which if your Petitioner Cold
keep the Small moytiesd her hands wold Strive by her best Indevors to
Live, which Granted, your Petitioner will

                                      her
                  Ever Pray Mary   X   McDaniel
                                     mark

NB - Pleas your Honor the Catle above
mentioned was Captain Bights and clames
bestored to them his and my Children -
a long time before his Decesse, John
McDaniel which can be made appear by
your Petitioner   Mary McDaniel
                                                Petition
             Mary   X   McDaniel

Rob.ᵗ Culpeper
Aley McDanael   Witnises
Mary McDanal
Aaron Burleson   (on reverse)

                              Mary McDaniel   29

                              Posponed

Sir,

     I take the liberty of enclosing my Commission dater the 23.ᵈ
January 1780, the day on which it was renewed on parchment - the
resolution of Congress 7th November 1777 obtained me a Commission
by brevet (in Consequence of my intention to visit the southern Army
where it would prove a better step to establishment in the line,
than the rank before given me) my appointment to Genl. Lee's suite,
early in 1776 with the full rank of Major, happens to be with my
Papers at the N.ᵒWard, but as the resolve of Congress expresses the
motives on which the Brevet was granted, by relating my services with
the General's Lee and Sullivan, the date of his capture by the enemy
in Jersey will include three years alone before the renewal of my
Commission in february 1780.

     You did not particularly inform me of the mode presented by the
act, except the certificate by the Commanding Officer of the State -
as the Generals, Macintosh or Elbert, can have no other than the
vouchers enclosed I did not concieve it essential to make application
for their Certificate.

     In matters of this nature the most official vouchers are

required but as my case is a matter of public notoriety, and can be moreover attested by Majors Lucas or Pierce it may perhaps induce the Governor of council to wave the more formal method.

I thought this a more easy mode than by Memorial, and by you would communicate its contents.

                    I am sir,

                            respectfully your fr.

                            John Skey Eustace

        (On Reverse)

John Skey Eustace Pass'd as Major - 29th March 1784

John Skey Eustace, 10

        David Rees, Esquire

"This is to certify that John osbell william osbell william Jones and Charles Frances was soldiers under my Command in the Continental Regment of Light horse belonging to the state of Georgia and served the time of their Inlistment and is therefore Intitled to a bounty of two hundred and fifty acres of land agreeable to Law given under my hand this 24th day of Decr 1785.

                    /s/ Leod. Marbury L.C.C."

/On the reverse, this document reads:/

"Your petitioners pray the Within Land granted in the Name of Leod. Marbury

            /s/   Jno. Asbell
                   William Asbell
                   William Jones
                   Chas. Frances"

State of Georgia   Daniel Gunnell & George Barber
Wilkes County   Being Sworn to Value Two Certain Horses
                      The property of John Clark, One a Grey
Horse about 5 years Old 14 Hands Hy's-- The Other a Sorrell about
6 years Old 14, Hands Hy's. We Say on there oaths that according to
the Best of their Judgment the Grey Horse is Valued @ L 25 Speice
                    The Sorrill @   L 30   Do

                    Sworn to
                    this 21 Feby 1782   55

Barnard Heard J.P.   Danl Gunnells
                            George Barber

State of Georgia   John Clark Being Sworn sayeth that the Above
County of Wilkes   Mentioned Horses was his property when Lost &
                      That they were both Lost in the field of Battle

Sworn to before Me   John Clark
This 22nd Feby 1782

M Manadue J.P.
    I do certifye that the above mention'd Horses were Lost in Action
                              E. Clark, Col^o.
(Reverse) John Clark   Am^{ts}

50

State of Georgia)
)
Wilkes County)

Fort Martin 1st febr. 1782

John Hill A. C^d. to George Walton Esqr.
Commissary General of sd State Derected to Nehemiah Wade Esqr.
quartermaster Generall, of the State affor^sd.

Name	Drivers	Wagons	Fodiridge to Spys & Horses	Horses	Value horses	Horses lost in service	Commencement of time
Ambrose Holliday	1	1	6 Bu. Corn	2	0	0	1th feb^r. 1782
Joshua Hill	1	0	6 Dito	2	0	0	7 months 1782
William Mims	1	0	2 Dito	1	0	0	2 m^o. 1 Feb^r. 1782
John Mims	1	0	2 Dito	1	0	0	2 m^o. 1 Feb^r. 1782
John Hill	0	0	2 Dito	1	16	1	5 m^o. Jarvis 1782

proved before me

James Bowie J P

John Hill

REVERSE

Comesary

        accoump^ts of Hill

Capt. John Hill

51

State of Georgia

John Hill, A. C. D. To Colo Woodrow Esq. Quartermaster Generale, of sd State,
Colonel Dunn Regment July 1st 1781 &c Second Devition, Richmon County

Names	Drivers	Waggons	Fodarin to Spies & Wagon Horses	Horses	Value of horses	Horses lost in service	Commencement of time
Joseph Avent	1	1	3 bu corn	4	0	0	to 11 Days Octr. 1781
John Kelley	1	1	3 "	"	"	"	to 10 Days 30th 1781, Octr.
Michal, Wagon man	1	1	3 "	"	"	"	to 11 Days 1st. Novr. 1781
Lucy Cook, widow	0	0	6 bu corn	1	10	1	7 months Survis before
Jabus Evans	0	0	6 "	1	0	1	Stole, 31st Decembr. 1781
Reson Bowie, Spie	0	0	10 "	1	0	0	7 months survis before
James Bridges, "	0	0	10 "	1	0	0	Stole 31st. December. 1781
							7 months each 1781

Ordered and received pr me, sd. services, of Different persons above named, and do Certifie
Likewise, the sd. horses was stole out of the publick sarvis belonging to the persons as afford.

Josiah Dunn Col.

The within amount, certified before me, by Capt John Hill to be just and true.

James Bowie, J. P.

16th June 1782

State of Georgia)
)
Wilkes County   )
                    Publick to Saml. Alexander Sen. Dr. for
Sopling Capt. John Hill Company Commanded by John Dooly Esqr. Col^n.
of the Militia in sd County, Fort Dooly.

Commenced the 15 of October 1779, Continued to the 18th Apr. 1780
to 10 men kept up, by proper Devitions at sd fort to 12th of Janr.
1782 from thence 25 privates Inroled Novr. 3 Sergents Drummer &
fifer, 2 Spies, with 3 officers

To my Sarvises 6 months & two Days	Ration
Decem. 1st as Commasary for sd Company &c	<u>50 men 12 Days</u>
Jan. 12th to Sopling 50 men at Rearing sd fort	600 Dollars
12 Days	902 Do 1
to 25 privates 3 Sargt. 2 Spies, 3 officers	3960 Do.
Apr. 17th 4 months & 2 Days	500
to a wagoner, wagon & horses 3 months	
to hiering man & horse to mill	
9 Days	
to Bringing Salt 4 Days	
to bringing Salt again two Days	
to hunting & Driving up Cattle Sunday	
time 12 Days	
to the total Sum of Ration, of the whole	54.62

I do Certify that I believe the abouve Amo^t. to be Just and True.

                    John Dooly Col^o.

Recd. the above mentioned provitions or Rations for use of sd.
Company, Recd. pr. me.
                    John Hill Capt.

                    17th Apr. 1780

State of Georgia Wilkes County

fort Martein 1st feb. 1782

Beves, and Pork Purchased for use of sd fort Cap^n John Hill Company
Commanded by Elijah Clark Esqr Colonel Commandant of sd State

by John Hill A. C^d.

Names	Pork	Beves	Wait	Mark & Branded	Value	Commencement of time
John Mims	Pork	0	60		16	10th febr 1782
John Hill	Do	0	100		20	15th febr 1781
Sarah Golden	Do	9	100		20 1	20th febr 1781
John Smith	Do	0	225		2 5	1th march 1782
Saml Alexander	Do	0	200		2 0	10th march 1781
John Oneal	Do	0	200		1 10	20th march 1781
Sarah Golden	0	1	200		1 10	1th apr 1781
John May	0	1	200		1 10	16th apr 1781
Rich Courton	0	1	200		1 10	23d apr 1781
No Claim	0	1	250	a trap in the Rite	1 15	30th apr 1781
William Lemar	0	4	1200	Ear & whole in	9 10	2d may 1781
Isaac Green	0	1	200	the Left Brand	1 10	16th may 1781

James Simpson a private man in the Militia of my Company in Colo^l
Martins Redigment Who is a Good friend to his Country has had the Mis-
fortune (Caused by the Publick Calamity of the times) to miss makeing
Bread for his Family and his low Sircumstance in the World will not
admit him to Procure a Necesary Subsistance for them I would there fore
recommend Him to Your Clemancy

Thos Greer Capt

To

The Honourable John Martin Esqr
Governor General and Commander in Chief
of the State of Georgia and his Council

January 29th 1782

[Reverse]

Capt Greer
29th Jany. 1782

This is to certify that the Revd Silas Mercers in the Beginning of these Times was very active and usefull in convincing the People of the Justice of the Cause of America and after the Brittish took possession of Savannah he spent much of his Time in preaching to the armies and obtained an Excellency Recommendation from Col^o Hammond's to General Lincoln in order that he might preach to his army and as he was on his Way to purishburgh he Came to Burk Jail to preach to my Regiment and was there in the Time of a very warm Engagement and behaved himself exceeding well in time of the Action and soon afterwards he left the State at the expenes of chief of his property rather than to surrender to Brittish Government and I have been Creaditably informed that he has behaved himself honourably during the Time of his absence and has spent much of his Time in preaching to Armies and has at all Times supported the Caractor of a good Whigg.

Therefore I believe that he is intitled to as much Land as any Gentl^n of his Rank

B^n Few Col^o

of Richmond County

[On reverse]

We the Subscribers do certify that the within mentioned Certificate is just and true--

Daniel Coleman

Zacha^s Fenn

Silas Mercer   5
Allowed to pass as the of Chaplain
to that of Major
            Silas Mercer
               Chaplain

I Certify that Major Edward Welch, immediately after Savannah was taken by the British Troops, on my being sent to Augusta by General Lincoln, Joined my Command and Acted as Brigade Major to the Militia & Troops that were then Embodied, to the time of my being made a prisinor, after which I have been informed he joined General Williamson and was in service under him

Given Under my Hand Savannah
15th March 1784
S. Elbert Brig^r Genl.
    Cont. Army -

I do hereby certify that, after the Capture of genl. Elbert at Bryar Creek, Major Walsh joined the Command under Genl Williamson & acted as an assistant to him until about the middle of June 1779, at which time I left the General's family at Stono.

Seth W. Cuthbert   15th March 1784

	State bounty	Continental	Total
Colonel	500	500	1000
1st Colonel	450	450	900
Major	400	400	800
Captain	300	300	600
Lieutenant	200	200	400
Ensign	150	150	300
Private	100	100	200

[On reverse]   16 March. 1784   Maj Edward Walsh

Following the British capture of Savannah and Sunbury and their victory in the Battle of Briar Creek, their haul of American prisoners-of-war totalled close to 1,000 men. Many of the Patriot officers were eventually granted paroles but for the rest of the prisoners, their stay in British hands was aboard prison ships. Georgia Historian Hugh McCall wrote that the survivors of this imprisonment:

> complained highly of the ill-treatment which they had experienced on board these filthy floating dungeons, of which their countenances and emaciated bodies exhibited condemning testimony. They asserted that they had been subsisted on condemned pork, which nauseated the stomach, and oat meal so rotten, that swine would not have fed on it; that the staff officers, and the members of council from Savannah, shared in common with soldiery; even the venerable /Jonathan/ Bryan was obliged to partake such repasts, or die of Hunger. The Jews of Savannah were generally favorable to the American cause, and among this persuasion, was Mordecai Sheftall, commissary-general, and his son, who was his deputy: they were confined in common with the other prisoners, and by way of contempt to their offices and religion, condemned pork given them for the animal part of their subsistence. In consquence of such food, and other new devices of mal-treatment, five or six died daily; whose bodies were conveyed from the prison-ships to the nearest marsh and trodden in the mud; from whence they were soon exposed by the washing of the tides, and at low water, the prisoners beheld the carrion-crows picking the bones of their departed companions.

Such was how many of the continentals ended their service in Georgia.

The following records from The Gazette of the State of Georgia tell of men who suffered aboard these ships. The author would like to thank Gordon B. Smith of Savannah and Mary B. Warren of Danielsville for bringing these articles to his attention.

The Gazette of the State of Georgia, 13 May 1784, p. 1 c. 1:

HOUSE OF ASSEMBLY

Augusta, Thursday, July 31, 1783

THE House then proceeded to take into consideration the report of the committee on petitions reported on last session of Assembly, viz. No. 106, Memorial of Col. John M'Intosh, on behalf of Dr. Donald M'Leod, and the petition of sundry inhabitants of county of Chatham, charging a certain Dr. M'Leod with sundry crimes towards the American Prisoners whilst on board the prison ships in the river Savannah, and particularly of having mixed fine, broken, or pulverized glass, in a parcel of medicines sent by him on said prison ships for the use of said prisoners, which memorial is accompanied by sundry affidavits, to wit, that of Dr. Rehm, that of Mordecai Sheftall, that of Hepworth Carter, and that of John Rogers, tending to the proof the said charges on the said Dr. M'Leod, the said memorialists praying, that, in consequence of said charges, the said Dr. M'Leod may not be admitted to become a citizen of this state.

And the committee have also taken into like serious and impartial consideration a number of affidavits and other testimonials produced to them in favour of the said Dr. M'Leod, to wit, the written testimony of Col. Walton, setting forth the great care and attention paid him by the said Dr. M'Leod when he lay dangerously wounded in Savannah, and to whose skill and humanity the Colonel does in a great measure attributes his cure and recovery; also the written testimony of Gen. Elbert, setting forth the Doctor's care of and attention to him and his servant when prisoners and sick in Savannah, and attributing the salvation of the said servant's life to the same; the affidavits of Judith [illegible], Jane Watts, Matthew Roche, Peter Henry Morel, and William Harris, Capts. William McIntosh, Edward Cowen, Peter Henry Morel; and the petition of Col. John McIntosh; all setting forth Dr. M'Leod's humanity and attention to the sick, wounded, and distressed American prisoners and families whilst under the British domination at or near Savannah, and his general good character in said town of Savannah; also a letter from Edward Davis, Esq. a member of this House, and an annexed affidavit, setting forth, that, during his confinement on board one of the prison ships aforesaid, he never heard any thing of the charges against the said Dr. M'Leod, as exhibited in the memorial and affidavits aforesaid, and that the Doctor had nothing to do on board said prison ships, at least on board the ship where he (Mr. Davis) was, except to inquire the sta-e of the prisoners, and report thereon to his superior; also an affidavit of William Roche, setting forth the doctor's care and humane treatment of him whilst a prisoner and sick in Savannah; also the affidavit of Col. William M'Intosh, setting forth the Doctor's attention and humanity to him and his family when he was a prisoner, and his family when he was a prisoner, and his family labouring under accumulated distresses; also the affidavit of James White, a soldier in the continental army, setting forth the Doctor's care of, attention, and humanity to himself and another soldier when prisoners, having not only recovered them from dangerous and grievous wounds, but had also clothed them from their nakedness at his own expence; also the verbal testimony of Col. Robertson, a member of this House, setting forth the Doctor's patient care and very humane treatment of the wounded and sick American prisoners in the hospital where he lay when a prisoner in Savannah, and that the said prisoners were always rejoiced to see Dr. M'Leod come in the hospital, being comforted and revived by his kindness to them, but that they dreaded the sight of the other doctor who superintended the hospital, for that he was continually endeavouring to get them sent on board the prison ships, from which Dr. M'Leod frequently screened them; also the affidavit of Dr. Beecroft, a surgeon in the British service during the time aforesaid, setting forth that Dr. M'Leod never had the compounding or mixing up of medicines for the prisoners on board the prison ships aforesaid, but that this business was ordered by Dr. Hill, and performed by Mr. Atkinson the acting apothecary, and further, that, at the particular instance and representation of Dr. M'Leod of the distresses that the American prisoners labored under, in being crowded sick and well together in the same ship, a vessel was furnished and sent down for the accommodation of the sick. From all which circumstances, the committee are of opinion that the charges set forth in the memorial and affidavits aforesaid are not sufficiently found to enforce the prayer of the said memorial, but seem to have originated in a keen and jealous sensibility of the sufferings of the said deponents, and an over hot and misguided zeal for the honour of the country; and the committee beg leave to observe, that, with reference to the glass being mixed with the medicine, such a thing is far from being improbable, as it may frequently happen, but from accident only; but, as Dr. M'Leod appears to be a man of considerable professional abilities, they cannot believe that, even admitting his heart was wicked enought to prompt him to the destruction of the unhappy prisoners, he would have made use of glass as the instrument of his wickedness, when he might have made use of many other means more effectual and much less subject to detection.

And the committee are further of opinion, that the said Dr. M'Leod is worthy to be admitted a citizen of this state, and particularly recommend to the House to enter into a speedy and dispastionate investigation of the several matters set forth at above, upon which the committee have solemnly founded the opinion, which passed in the negative.

The yeas and nays being called to by Mr. Carter are as follows:

Yea. Mr. Jackson, Mr. John Houstoun, Mr. William Houstoun,

Mr. Deveaux, Mr. William Gibbons jun., Mr. Habersham, Mr. Cuthbert, Mr. M'Intosh, Mr. Heard, Mr. Lamar, Mr. William Few, Mr. Robertson, Mr. Middleton, Mr. Lee, Mr. Telfair, Mr. Williamson. 16.

Nay. Mr. Burnet, Mr. Cunningham, Mr. Harper, Mr. Ware, Mr. Alexander, Mr. Fort, Mr. Burke, Mr. Benjamin Few, Mr. Emanuel, Mr. Clements, Mr. James Jones, Mr. Davies, Mr. Carter, Mr. Johnson, Mr. Lanier, Mr. Pugh, Mr. Palmer, Mr. Crawford. 18.

The Gazette of the State of Georgia, 17 June 1784, p. 1 c. 3:

Mr. Printer,

In your paper of 13th May I observe you have inserted, as the Journals of the Assembly at Augusta on the 31st July last, a report of the committee on the memorial of Col. John M'Intosh in favour of Dr. Donald M'Leod. The Committee speak of a number of affidavits against and in favour of said M'Leod, but I am surprised no mention is made of the affidavit of Major John Lindsay, which I think makes very materially against the said M'Leod has acted with the same humanity to the poor suffering prisoners on board the prison ships as to those gentlemen on shore whose affidavits are in his favour. These gentlemen being on parole, and of high rank in the army and state, could have got assistance from other hands had the said M'Leod refused it them, and no doubt, as the fate of war was uncertain, the Doctor thought any politeness shown to gentlemen of rank, in case he should fall into the hands of the Americans, would be returned him; but the poor prisoners confined on board those ships of destruction could never return him any kindess; therefore those unhappy men received none, but were doomed to make the numbers of the Rebels less--The Subscriber wishes to acquaint the publick, that he never acted with any misguided zeal or individual resentment, nor did he ever deviate from the true principles of an American.

HEPWORTH CARTER.

14th June, 1784.

State of Georgia,) Personally appeared John Lindsay, of the state
Richmond County.) aforesaid, who, being duly sworn, saith, that he
was taken a prisoner, on the 29th of December, 1778, by the troops under the command of Col. Archibald Campbell at Savannah, and put on board the ship Whitby, a prison ship at Cockspur; and that the prisoners were visited by one Dr. M'Leod, in the British service, who brought medicines for the use of the prisoners; and that Drs. Davenport, Rehm, Wells, and M'Kennie, were prisoners likewise on board said ship; some of the aforesaid gentlemen examined said medicines that was delivered by the aforesaid M'Leod for the use of the prisoners, and finding that a mixture of fine glass was in it, they made experiment of the medicines by extraction; which deponent saw the glass that was extracted, and it was carefully wrapped up in paper to shew the said M'Leod when he should come down again to visit; and, on his coming aboard again, the extracted glass (as I understood) was shewn to him, and told him such medicines would kill all the prisoners; his answer made all the prisoners within hearing cry out directly. We are deprived of all assistance of medicine but such as is destructive to us-- which was this, in case the medicine did kill, shrugging up his shoulders, it was only so many Rebels dead. And further this deponent saith not.

JOHN LINDSAY.

Sworn before me, this
  25th July, 1783.
    ZACH. FENN, J.P.

I certify that the above deposition is a true copy of the original lodged in my office. JNO. WILKINSON, C.G.A.

The Gazette of the State of Georgia, 1 July 1784, p. 2 cols. 1-3:

Mr. Johnston,

As you have published an affidavit in your paper relative to my conduct, (although that matter has been already sufficiently investigated by the Honourable the House of Assembly) you will likewise please to insert the following on the same subject, and let the impartial world judge.

Sir, your humble servant,

DONALD MACLEOD.

Savannah, June 28, 1784

G E O R G I A.

Personally appeared before me, Samuel Beacroft, of Savannah, in Georgia aforesaid, Surgeon, being duly sworn, deposeth and saith, That he, this deponent, hath been personally acquainted with Donald Macleod, Surgeon, for the term of five years last past: That, in the course of said time, he invariably found him a very attentive humane man, both in his profession and otherwise: And respecting the crime alledged against him by Dr. Rehm, to wit, that of mixing powdered glass in the bark sent on board the prison ships for the American prisoners in the year 1779, must be totally without foundation of truth; for that he, Mr. Macleod, never had the compounding of medicines or the putting up of drugs, sent on board for the aforesaid prisoners. Mr. Macleod's report of the sick (which he received from the American Surgeons) was always given to Dr. Hill, who gave directions to the acting Apothecary, Mr. Atkinson, and he made them (the medicines) up. The deponent further saith, That, in the absence of Mr. Macleod, he, at the instance of said Macleod, used to dress the wounded in the American hospital in Savannah, and hath frequently heard them express themselves fully satisfied with the attention and care he took of them, that they could not experience better treatment in their own hospitals. And further, That in consequence of the representation of Mr. Macleod of the distress the prisoners labored under, from being crowded sick and well together, they had a vessel furnished for their reception and convenience. And deponent further saith not.

SAML. BEECROFT.

Sworn before me, this 8th day of January, 1783,

DAVID MONTAIGUT, QU.

I certify that the above is a true copy from the original lodged in my office.

JOHN WILKINSON, C. G. A.

To Dr. DONALD MACLEOD.

Savannah, 9th November, 1782

SIR,

On hearing that you was accused of giving poisonous medicines to the prisoners on board the prison ships at Cockspur, one of which I was from December 30th to the 18th March, and as I was called upon to give such information on that head as ever had come to my knowledge, this is to inform you, and all the world, that I never heard, during my confinement, any such thing, or ever heard any matter of the kind hinted; nay, in fact, you had not any thing to do with us American prisoners, at least aboard the ship Whitby. Capt. John Lawson, where I was, but inquire about the state of the prisoners, and make a report

59

to where it might be your duty so to do. As D. Davenport and
D. M'Kinney, Doctors, taken in the American service when I was, were
appointed to attend us, it is thus far true, their application to you
was for medicines in my hearing, and very little, God knows, they got,
as I saw. I have heard you excuse yourself by saying there was not
much in town or garrison, but you will use your endeavours with the
Doctor General to assist them. After the people grew sickly, I well
remember a ship came down to Cockspur, commanded by one Capt. Ryburn,
or somewhat like the name; I believe she was called the Eleonora, and
was called the Hospital Ship, and as fast as the people were taken ill
they were immediately removed on board her, where the American Doctors
resided, and they made their business to attend each prison ship every
two or three days, and when you came down, perhaps once a week or longer,
I have seen them reporting to you. Whatever mode was used after my
departure can easily be told by many people who live in town that
staid longer than I did.--I am, Sir, your's,

                                        EDWD. DAVIES.

G E O R G I A.

        The above Edward Davies appeared before me, and maketh oath the
above is a just and true relation of facts above written.

        Savannah, 9th November, 1782.

        Sworn before me, DAVID MONTAIGUT, J.P.

I certify that the above is a true copy from the original lodged in
my office.

                                JOHN WILKINSON, C. G. A.

STATE OF GEORGIA

        Personally appeared before me, Charles Francis Chevalier, Esquire,
one of the Justices of the Peace for the said state, Matthew Roche, of
Savannah, citizen, who being duly sworn maketh oath, That he was near
four months a prisoner on board the Whitby prison ship in the year
1779, in the course of which time he frequently observed a certain Dr.
Macleod come on board, and heard him at one time in particular express
his sentiments and feelings for the situation of our unhappy prisoners much in their favour; and to the best of his, this deponent's
knowledge, never heard any accusation against him for administering
poisonous drugs to any one on board the said ship Whitby. And further
this deponent saith, that although he had no personal acquaintance with
Dr. Macleod, he always looked on him as a gentleman of honour, dis-
creation, and humanity. And further this deponent saith not.

                                MATT. ROCHE.

Sworn before me, this 13th January, 1783

        CHS. FRS. CHEVALIER, J.P.

I certify the above to be a true copy from the original lodged in my
office.

                                JOHN WILKINSON, C. G. A.

G E O R G I A

        Personally appeared before me, Samuel Stirk, Esquire, Attorney
General of the Said state, James White, formerly a soldier in the
second continental battalion belonging to this state, who being duly
sworn, saith That the day the British forces landed and took the town
of Savannah the deponent was one of the unfortunate soldiers who was
wounded by the British, when he lost his arm, and was put into the

60

American hospital, the charge of which was committed to Dr. Macleod: That, during the time the deponent was under the care of the said Dr. Macleod, he experienced every kin of attention and humane treatment towards himself, as well as to the other continental soldiers who were under his care: That, at the time his arm was to be amputated, Dr. Macleod informed him, if he chose to have any of the American surgeons to attend the operation, that they should, and have such medicines as they might demand; that during the time the deponent lay in the hospital, he was greatly in want of a shirt and a pair of overalls, and that John Newman was also in the same condition. Dr. Macleod seeing the wretched situation they were in, unasked, went and purchased necessaries to cover their nakedness, and endeavoured all in his power to tender their situation as comfortable and as agreeable as possible

his
JAMES X WHITE
mark

Sworn this 12th July, 1783, before

    SAML. STIRK, Att'y. G'l.

I certify that the above affidavit of James White is a true copy from the original lodged in my office.

JOHN WILKINSON, C. G. A.

Extract from the Report of a Committee of the House of Assembly on the Petition of sundry Inhabitants of the County of Chatham respecting Dr. Macleod, taken up by the House on the 31st July, 1783.

"ALSO the verbal testimony of Col. Robertson,* a Member of the House, setting forth the Doctor's great care and very humane treatment of the wounded and sick American prisoners in the hospital where he lay when a prisoner in Savannah; and that the said prisoners were always rejoiced to see Dr. Macleod come into the hospital, being comforted and revived by his kindness to them; but that they dreaded the sight of the other Doctor who superintended the hospital, for that he was continually endeavouring to get them sent on board the prison ships, from which Dr. Macleod frequently screened them."

Extract from the minutes.

JOHN WILKINSON, C. G. A.

* At the time above alluded to Col. Robertson was a private militia man.

THE underwritten having been dangerously wounded on the 29th day of December, in the year 1778, in a conflict with the British light infantry on the plains of Savannah, got from the field to Mrs. Watts's at Yamacraw, where he remained for his recovery. Early the next morning he was attended by the Doctors Irvine and Trail, who extracted the ball and dressed the wound with attention and humanity. Soon after Doctors Hill and Macleod attended, and said they were directed so to do by the commanding officer Col. Campbell. About a week after, as well as he recollects, he applied for an extension of Dr. Brydie's parole to Mrs. Watts's, to attend him at night, which was granted. Some time after Dr. Trail, who had been sick a long time, grew worse and died, having been particularly attended, during his illness, by Dr. Irvine and Dr. Brydie, had obtained permission to stay in his own house in town. These circumstances gave greater opportunity for the other Doctors to discover their willingness and disposition to serve. And this much the underwritten feels himself under the strongest injunctions of conscience to declare to the world, that Dr. Donald Macleod, during the course of a tedious and critical cure, in addition to his professional skill, manifested the most sincere humanity. Without intending the most distant reflection upon the Doctors Irvine, Trail, and Brydie, each of whom attended in the style of, and with the tenderness becoming fellow citizens, it is but justice to mention a circumstance respecting Dr. Macleod: A small vessel having built into the wound discharged much blood, threatening speedy death, the Doctors were sent for, but only Dr. Macleod was to be found; and it was upon that occasion that he most particularly discovered his great abilities and the goodness of his heart--feeling and participating, as he most surely did, in the danger and distresses of an unfortunate stranger. In that crisis of the wound, it was to his being in the way, to his skill, and probably, above all, to his sympathy and comforting manner and address, that he ascribes his life; and to that purpose he afterwards wrote to him while a prisoner at Sunbury.

The underwritten has heard a report, that, in the medicines administered to the prisoners in the prison ships, was mixed powdered glass, or other noxious article. Without being able to contradict such report, he cannot forbear to express disbelief of the fact being chargeable upon the Doctor, admitting the medicines had been corrupted; because in general his conduct with him evidence a very different disposition; and because, in particular, he used to inform him from time to time, upon his return from the ships, of the situation of the prisoners, and appeared to lament that it was not better.

Given at Savannah, in the state of Georgia this 25th day of January, 1783.

GEO. WALTON.

I certify that the above testimony is a true copy from the original lodged in my office.

JOHN WILKINSON, C. G. A.

G. BURKE COUNTY, 1778 - 1782

Under Georgia's first official state constitution, in 1777, colonial St. George Parish was renamed Burke County. The British completely retook Georgia in 1780 and Burke County reverted again to St. George Parish. After the fall of Augusta in 1781, the area fell into Patriot control for the last time and was once more Burke County. Several surrounding counties have since been created from what was St. George Parish/Burke County during the Revolution.

The list of officers of the Burke County Patriot militia in 1778 is reproduced from Commissions Book B, pp. 227-28, Georgia Department of Archives and History and is used here through the courtesy of that department. Paul Leicester Ford (ed.), Proceedings of a Council of War Held at Burke Jail (Brooklyn, 1890) is the source for the minutes of the militia council of January, 1779, that preceded the Patriot victory at the Battle of Burke County Jail. The 1782 petition is reproduced from the Telamon Cuyler Collection, Special Collections, through the courtesy of the University of Georgia Libraries.

Officers of the Burke County Patriot Militia, 3 February 1778

Colonel John Thomas, commander.

1st Company

Joseph Atkinson Esq. Capt.
Joseph Reeves Gent. 1st Lt.
Anthony Bonnett Gent. 2nd Lt.

2nd Company

John Conyers Esq. Capt.
James Roberts Gent. 1st Lt.
Gilshot Thomas Gent. 2nd Lt.

3rd Company

John Duheart Esq. Capt.
Thomas Lewis Jr. Gent. 1st Lt.
Amos Whitehead Gent. 2nd Lt.

4th Company

James Lambert Esq. Capt.
Fredrick Odom Gent. 1st Lt.
John Bonnett Gent. 2nd Lt.

5th Company

Moses Davis Esq. Capt.
William Underwood Gent. 1st Lt.
Thomas Ford Gent. 2nd Lt.

6th Company

John Warring Esq. Capt.
Battle Jones Gent. 1st Lt.
William Fulsam Gent. 2nd Lt.

7th Company

John Adam Neisler Esq. Capt.

8th Company

John Roberts Esq. Capt.
David Marren Gent. 1st Lt.
Charles Goletely Gent. 2nd Lt.

9th Company

John Patterson Esq. Capt.
John Foil Gent. 1st Lt.
Matthew Marshal Gent. 2nd Lt.

10th Company

Blissingame Harvey Esq. Capt.
Jesse Warmack Gent. 1st Lt.

11th Company

Charles Harvey Esq. Capt.
Robert Morgan Gent. 1st Lt.
John Twitty Gent. 2nd Lt.

12th Company

David Steward Esq. Capt.
Thomas Alexander Gent. 1st Lt.
John McNeily Gent. 2nd Lt.

13th Company

Robert Henderson Esq. Capt.
William Godby Gent. 1st Lt.
Robert Jarret Gent. 2nd Lt.

14th Company

Francis Hancock Esq. Capt.
Charles Williams Gent. 1st Lt.
James Red Gent. 2nd Lt.

15th Company

John Sharp Esq. Capt.
Jarrett Hendley Gent. 1st Lt.
James Hall Gent. 2nd Lt.

16th Company

Andrew Johnson Esq. Capt.
James Martin Gent. 1st Lt.
John Anderson Gent. 2nd Lt.

17th Company

Nicholas Cavannah Esq. Capt.
William Livingston Gent. 1st Lt.
Zebulon Cox Gent. 2nd Lt.

At a Council of War held at head Quarters at Burk [sic] Jail Jany.
14 -- 1779, for the Purpose of considering the most expedient method to
reclaim the disaffected that has been influenced to Assemble in consequence of the proclamation signed by Hyde Parker & Archibald Cambell
[Campbell] dated Savannah 4th. of January -- 1779 ----

Present Colo. Francis Pugh Lt. Colos. Jams. Ingram, & Samuel
Lanier, Majrs. Jams. Martin, Capts. Andrew Burney, Benjm. Mathews,
Charls. Crawford, Danl. Walikon, John H. Wilkinson, George Wyche,
Joseph Atkinson, Moses Davis, John Sharp, Thoms. Lewis, Joshua Hinman
[Inman], John Warren, John Murrey, --- Lts. Robt. Clark, Thoms. Townsend,
Matthia Gray, Thoms. Ford, Shadrick Hinman (Inman], Jams. Castilo,
Saml. Holton, Jams. Lewis, Fre-erick Wommach ----

It was agreed Nem: Con.----That a Proclamation be issued by Colo.
Ingram giving the disaffected three Days time to come in (Colo. [John]
Thomas, David Russel, William Tucker, Willm. Belfair [Telfair?], John
Bonell, John Robison, Henry Overstreet, Valentine Hollingsworth, &
Parson Ranoldson, All the above persons having forfited [sic] their
Recognizance being excepted. It was likewise agreed that the above
persons be took as prisoners & those of them that was not to be taken
their Estates to be seized for the use of the State & all that fail
coming in are to be deemed as Enemies & dealt with accordingly -- It
was agreed that Colo. Pughs Officers take each a Party of light horse
& apprehend all their leaders & deluders of the people & bring them
into Camp.

[This same publication also includes Ingram's proclamation and letter
to the Georgia state government, both dated 15 January 1779.]

To the Honorable John Martin Esqr. Governour [sic] and Commander in
Chief of the State of Georgia and the Honourable Executive Council of
the same. The Petition of us the Subscribers Inhabitants of Burke
County Living on Ogeecha [sic] & Rocky Comfort Being Capt Alexr Irwins
District ----

Humbly Sheweth

That your Petitioners Being frontier Setlers [sic] and But fiew
Psic] in Number and Consequently too fiew in Number to admit any
Division, Iff [sic] we mean to Remain Inhabitants of the Said District
and as thear [sic] Has Very Lately Been Considerable Damage By the
Indians in our Neighborhood, and some in our District By Indians or
others, which has Alarmd [sic] us in such Amaner [sic] as that Iff we
have Not assistance We must Remove from our Homes Towards Savannah
River which will make anew frontier of the other Inhabitans [sic] ----
We Pray that the Honourable Council Will Order that the whole of their
own District and to act in Conjuction [sic] With any other Scout that
may be ordered to our assistance to Prevent Inroads of Indians or
others. The Scarcity of grain that takes Place in the State Will Be
augmented If we must Remove our familys [sic], as We With good economy
may support them where we are, and as there is Not grain in our Settlement to feed Horses on Constant Duty, We pray that two men out of this
Company may Be kept out as Spies on the frontier which we apprehend
will Be of Benefit and Safety to this Settlement, and your Petitioners
as Duty Bound Will Ever Pray -----

March 2nd. 1782 --- [All names below are from signatures.]

John Clemence
Hugh Irwin
John Lawson
Roger Lawson
William Fleming
John Fleming
Samuel Fleming
John Allen

William Beatty
Daniel Mheil
Samuel Clemence
Wm Clemence
Wm. Little [?] Jr.
Archd. Little
Hugh Wilson
James Martin

John Martin
Wm. Hadden
Hugh Mc Neely
Robert Darnuch
John Patterson
Jarret Irwin
Willm Irwin

In colonial times, St. George Parish was the largest parish in land area and, possibly, in population in Georgia. Because of religious differences between the Irish Presbyterians in the south and the English Anglicans in the north, it was subdivided into two districts. A civil court was later established in each of these two areas.

When the British retook Georgia in 1780, all of the old colonial institutions were reestablished, including the courts, colonial militia, and royal governor and council. The following are two petitions by the people of the restored St. George Parish and a list of the officers of one of the restored royal militia regiments. The petitions are from the Telamon Cuyler Collection, Special Collections, courtesy of the University of Georgia Libraries. The militia officers list is reproduced from Collections of the Georgia Historical Society, Vol. X, and is used here through the courtesy of the Georgia Historical Society.

To His Excellency Sir James Wright Baronet Captain General Governor and Commander in Chief in and Over his Majestys Prov- of Georgia Chancellor and Vice Admiral of the Same

The Humble Petetion [sic] of his Majestys faithfull [sic] and Loyal subjects Inhabitants of Queens = Bourough and with a few of our fellow subjects in the Ajacent [sic] Settlement of Brier = Creeck

May it Please your Excellency we His Majestys faithfull [sic] subjects and your Suplicants [sic] Beags [sic] Leave to Return our hearty thanks for the favour we had Received. During your Excellency Residing with us in the Government, We now Petetion your Honourable Authority for the Priviliges [sic] we formerly enjoyd. to wit that of his Majestys Court of Conscience to have a place in our Destrick [sic] as their [sic] is now nothing but Disorder and fraudes [sic] Comitted [sic] by Lawles [sic] vagrants as allso [sic] for militia Officers we have had none During this summer and the Late Seige untill [sic] your Excellency Granted Commissions for Captain Morison and Lieutenant Ronaldson for the same, we Return your Excellency our Gratefull [sic] thanks.

The maxon [sic] we Bound our Selves by our Nomination is to Chuse [sic] from such as Like Loyal Subjecks [sic] Lay in Confinement as Prisoners of war Rather than Comply with the terms offered them by Rebells [sic] or such as Left there [sic] familys [sic] and their all and Actted [sic] under arms within the British Lines During the time of the Seige of his majestys Provine and town of Savannah, The Persons we petition for as our majors is Matthew Lyle for the lower Destrick [sic] and Gavin Ronaldson for the upper Districk they are men of Descresion [sic] Activity Good Conduct who hath suffered Persecution and Confinement for Loyalty sacke [sic] as allso [sic] David Russell we Desire as Captain the persons we Petition [sic] for as majastrates [sic] is the above Mathew Lyle and Samuel Montgomery as being persons of known fedelity [sic] Disseation [sic] and Eaquity [sic] with Every other mark of subjescon [sic] and Loyalty to British Government in all of them within Saint Georges Parish in hopes of your Excellency approving of the persons your Long Presidence [sic] in Government with a Restoration of British Laws your Prosperity here and hapiness [sic] hereafter your Excellencys Humble Petitoners [sic] are Bound to Pray This 22d of November 1779

John Morison Capt. Militia

William Reed	John Flimang	Vinson Carter
James Robinson	Robert Simms	Jese Carre
John Brown	Robert Boyd	Thos. McCroan

John Robinson	Willm Simpson	Jorge Sloan
John Rgger [?]	Thomas Fox	Alex Carter
Jeremiah Rodes	Josiah Spurs	

Officers of Lieutenant Colonel Mathew Lyle's Loyalist Militia, St. George Parish, 4th Regiment, Colonial Georgia Militia, 1780

William Corker, Capt. John Johnson, Lieut. and Edward Corker, Ensign, in the 1st Company, or the District from Walker's Mill Creek, up Brier Creek to the Line in St. George's Parish.

John Morrison, Capt. John Ervine, Lieut. and James Archer, Ens., in the 2nd Company or District from Livington's Fording to the Head of Buckhead and in a direct Line from that to Richard Burney's on Lambert Big Creek.

Edward Pilcher, Capt. Benjamin Brantly, Lieut. and Edward Caswell, Ens., in the 3rd Company or the District on the north side of Briar Creek from Raes Road and upwards.

Daniel Howel, Capt. Jerry Atkinson, Lieut. and Jonathan Wood, Ens., in the 4th Company or the District from the Lower Part of the Parish of St. George, up Ogeechee to the Mouth at Bark Camp, and from thence to the old Indian Road on Buckhead.

William Read, Capt. Robert Woolfington, Lieut. and Thomas McCoon, Ens., in the 5th Company or the District from Sandy Run up the New Road to Rocky Creek to the head thereof, and to Walker's Mill Creek.

James Lambert, Capt. Jacob Thompson, Lieut. and Peter Oglevie, Ens., in the 6th Company or the District on the Southside of Briar Creek from the Beaverdams to Sandy Run.

John Wilson, Capt. John Montgomery, Lieut. and David Cavanah, Ens. in the 7th Company or the District from the Mouth at Bark Camp to Livingston's Fording on Buckhead, with a direct Line to the Head of Black Jack Branch.

John Fleming, Capt. John Brown, Lieut. and John Martin, Ens., in the 8th Company or the District from Lambert's Big Creek to the Fork of Rocky Comfort.

Henry Ferguson, Capt. in the 9th Company or District in the Fork between Savannah River and Bryar [sic] Creek.

Georgia

To His Excellency Sir James Wright Barronett Captain General Governour [sic] and Commander in Chief in and over His Majestys Provine of Georgia Chancellor and Vice Admiral of the Same. ---

The Petition of the Inhabitants of the Upper district of the Parish of Saint George. ---

Humbly Sheweth that your petitioners are liable to many Inconveniences on Account of the Atendance [sic] they are obledged [sic] to give at the Court of Consience [sic] of this Parish, it being settled in the Lower districk [sic] by which many of them are obledged [sic] to ride Forty Miles, and often Attend Five Successive days, sometimes Three or four Seperate [sic] Courts before they can get any business done, which is a great Grivance [sic], running into unnecessary Expences [sic], breeding Confusion and Turmult [sic] on Account of the Multitude of people that are obledged to attend on various Accounts.

This parish was formerly laid out in Two districts, and a Court of Concience held in both districts, by which the[y] got their business done with the one fourth less trouble, Cost and Time. --

They therefore humbly conceive, if your Excellency would Allow them to hold a Court of Concience [sic] as usual, in the upper district it would remove many causes of Complaints in both districts as they are a burden to the people in the lower part of the parish, while they are detained at Court. --

We therefore Humbly pray that your Excellency would allow us to hold a Court of Conscience in the upper district of the Parish of Saint George, and grant a Dedimus [?] to Qualify Isaac Lorimore gent. Gavin Ronaldson gent. as Majestrates, as we believe they are proper Persons for such office. We are Induced to make our Grivances known to your Excellency being convinced of your Goodness and readiness to redress or remove all the Complaints of his Majestys Loyal Subjects. -- And your Petitioners a in duty bound will ever pray &c &c

Queensborough 15th
Feby. 1781 ---

[All names below appear on the original manuscript as signatures.]

William Ronaldson M:A	George Donaldson	Capn. Morrison
David Alexander	Wm. Baduly	Addam Morrison
Wm Little Senr.	John Wilson Capt milt.	Jon. Ingram
Samuel Gordon	Samuel Irwin	Robert Donaldson
John McCanliss	Andrew Minecy	George Donaldson
Jon. Cagil [?]	John Gibson	Samuel Gibson
George Spiers	John Brianes	John [?] Martin Jur.
James Beaty	Samuel Little	John Manson
Jas. Finly	Robert Haththorn	David Hogg
Saml. Fleming Junr. [?]	Saml. McBride	James Breckenridge
Gavin Ronaldson	Ths. McBride	Zebulon Wethesup[?]
Robert Boyd	John Kennedy	James Robson
Archd. Little	Robert Brison	William[?] Pherrson
Josiah Spires	Capn. John Fleming	Richerd Fleeting

I. GEORGIA TREASON ACT, 1780

In the first session of the restored royal assembly of Georgia, an act was passed by both houses to attaint 114 Georgia Patriot leaders and confiscate their property. Later, another act was passed to disqualify 151 Georgia Patriots from any political or civil office in the restored colonial government. Unlike the latter act, the first listed the Georgia Patriot leaders occupations. It is reproduced here from the Joseph V. Bevan Papers, Peter Force Collection, Library of Congress. The second, or Disqualifying Act, has been published in Allen D. Candler (ed.), The Revolutionary Records of the State of Georgia (Atlanta, 1908), Vol. I, pp. 348-63, and in George White, Historical Collections of Georgia. . . (New York, 1855) pp. 98-105.

An Act to attaint of High Treason the several Persons herein after-named who are other absent from this Province or in that part of it which is still in Rebellion against His Majesty and to vest their real and personal Estates in his Majesty his heirs and Successors in manner herein aftermentioned Subject to the lawful debts and Claims thereupon

Whereas a most desperate and bloody Rebellion hath been levied and raised against his Majesty in this Province in which a Number of His Majesty's Subjects contrary to their Duty and Allegiance have been wickedly and traitorously engaged and amongst others the several persons herein after-named. We therefore pray your most Sacred Majesty

that it may be enacted And be it enacted by His Excellency Sir James
Wright Barronet Captain General and Governor in Chief in and over this
His Majesty's Province of Georgia by and with the Advice and Consent
of the Honorable The Council and Commons House of Assembly met and by
the authority of the same That John Houstoun late of the Province of
Georgia Esqr. John Adam Truetland late of the same Esqr. John Glen late
of the same Attorney at Law Richard Wylly late of the same Esqr.
Lauchlane [sic] Mackintosh [sic] late of the same Esqr. John MacKintosh
[sic] Junr. late of the same Esq. James Houstoun late of the same
Surgeon George Walton late of the same Attorney at Law William Stephens
late of the same Attorney at Law James Habersham late of the same
Planter Joseph Habersham late of the same Planter John Habersham Planter
John McLeur late of the same Carpenter Raymond Demare late of the same
Planter John Milledge Junr. late of the same Planter Joseph Clay late
of the same Planter Noble Wimberly Jones late of the same Surgeon
Mordecai Sheftal late of the same Shopkeeper Levi Sheftal late of the
same Butcher Philip Jacob Cowen late of the same Shopkeeper John
Sutcliffe late of the same Shopkeeper Jonathan Bryan late of the same
Planter William Obrian late of the same Merchant Joseph Reynolds late
of the same Bricklayer John Spencer late same Cabinet maker John Wereat
late of the same planter Rawlins Loundes late of the same Esqr. George
Abbot Hall late of the same Merchant Stephen Bull late of the same
Esqr. Thomas Bee late of the same Esqr. Pierce Butler late of the
same Esqr. The Revd. John Holmes Clerk Edward Langworthy late of the
same Schoolmaster Rodolph Strohaker late of same Butcher Edward
Telfair late of the same Merchant William Gibbons Senior late of the
same Merchant Philip Minis late of the same Merchant Edward Davis late
of the same Merchant Samuel Elbert late of the same Merchant Coshman
Pollock late of the same Shopkeeper Benjamin Lloyd late of the same
Gentlemen Robert Hamilton late of the same Attorney at Law Sheftall
Sheftall late of the same Shopkeeper James Alexander late same Fidler
John Jenkins late of the same planter John Stirk late of the same
planter Moses Bernard late of the same Shopkeeper Samuel Stirk late
of the same writing Clerk John Turner Junior late of the same planter
Philip Damaler late of the same planter Henry Cuyler late of the same
writing Clerk John Martin late of the same Rebel Provost Marshall
Joseph Gibbons late of the same planter Seth John Cuthbert late of the
same Shopkeeper Ebenezer Smith Platt late of the same Shopkeeper
Mathew Griffin late of the same planter William Holzendorff late of the
same planter Henry Laurens late of the same planter Peter Deveaux late
of the same planter Charles Odingsele late of the same planter Benjamin
Odingsele late of the same planter John Gibbons late of the same
planter Edward Howley late of the same writing Clerk Joseph Wood Senior
late of the same planter Joseph Wood Junior late of the same Attorney
at Law William Moore late of the same Shopkeeper John Smith late of the
same planter The Revd. William Piercy late of the same Clerk Daniel
Roberts late of the same planter Lewis Gable late of the same Butcher
Charles Gable late of the same Butcher William LeConte late of the
same planter Charles Francis Chevalier late of the same Dancing Master
Washington late of the same gentleman Thomas Savage late of the same
planter William Butler late of the same planter Adam Fowler Brisbane
late of the same planter Thomas Stone late of the same planter Elisha
Maxwell late of the same planter William Gibbons Junior late of the
same planter William Baker late of the same planter Francis Brown late
of the same planter Nathan Brunson late of the same Surgeon William
Davis late of the same planter John Graves late of the same planter
John Hardy late of the same Carpenter John Braddock late of the same
Mariner Gilbert Harrison late of the same Mariner Charles Kent late of
the same Merchant Thomas Morris late of the same Mariner Samuel Miller
late of the same Merchant Thomas Maxwell Senior late of the same
planter Josiah Maxwell late of the same planter Thomas Maxwell Junior
late of the same planter Joseph Woodruff late of the same planter
Jonathan Bacon late of the same Mariner Joseph Oswall late of the same
Planter Thomas Palmer late of the same Planter William Peacock Senior
late of the same Mariner William Peacock Junior late of the same
Mariner Josiah Powell late of the same planter Job Pray late of the
same Mariner Nathaniel Saxton late of the same Tavern keeper Samuel
Saltus late of the same planter Charles Spencer late of the same
Mariner John Saniford late of the same planter Peter Faarling late of

the same planter John Winn late of the same planter Samuel West late
of the same planter Josiah Dupont late of the same planter Oliver Bowen
late of the same planter Lyman Hall late of the same planter Shall be
and they the said several Persons above named and each and every of
them is and are hereby Attainted of High Treason and is and are declared
to be Subject to all the pains penalties and forfeitures by Law inflict-
ed on Persons guilty of High Treason to all Intents Constructions and
purposes whatsoever as if they the several persons above named were
and each and every of them was convicted and attained of High Treason
in a Court of Justice having jurisdiction therein according to the Law
of the Land

And be it enacted by the Authorities aforesaid that the several
Persons above particularly named Shall not in the first instance be
subject to the pains of Death but are hereby banished from the Province
for ever and in case any or ether [sic] of them shall return into any
part of this Province he shall be lyable [sic] to be punished with
Death as a Traitor and Execution may and shall be awarded against the
person so returning as in the case of a Traitor convicted and attainted
of High Treason by the due course of Law

And be it further enacted by the Authority aforesaid that all and
every the lands and Tenements Goods Chattells [sic] and Effects and
other real and personal Estates of what nature and kind so ever they
be in this Province whereof the several Persons above named or any or
ether [sic] of them at the time afterward hath or have been or now is
or are seised [sic] possesed [sic] of interested in or intitled [sic]
unto in trust for them or any or ether [sic] of them in which the said
Persons above-named or any or ether [sic] of them can or may forfeit
by this Attainder now stand and are hereby forfeited to his Majesty
His Heirs and Successors and shall be deemed vested and adjudged and
are hereby declared and enacted to be in the actual and real possession
of His Majesty his Heirs and Successors without any office on Inquisi-
tion thereof now or hereafter to be taken or found and without any
other process whatsoever to be had or obtained Subject nevertheless to
all Actions Attachments Suits and other process now depending [pending?]
in his Majestys Courts in this Province and also to all Claims and
demands whatsoever of His Majesty's leige Subjects which shall be made
and prosecuted within twelve months from the date herein as if this Act
had never been made and [illegible] said real and personal Estates
shall be lyable [sic] to be levied the payment of all Just Debts and
Demands or are due to any of His Majesty's leige Subjects in the same
manner as other real and personal Estates are by the Laws of this
Province lyable to be levied or extended and sold for the payment of
just Debts and Demands provided always and it is hereby declared that
if after any Levy and sale made by the acting Provost Marshal for the
time being or other proper officer an overplus shall remain in his
hands after deducting the Debts Damages and Costs that may be recovered
in any action now depending or hereafter to be brought within twelve
months as aforesaid the Said acting Provost Marshal or other proper
officer shall forthwith pay such Overplus into the hands of the persons
who shall hereafter be appointed Commissioners of Forfeited Estates in
this Province or one or more of them upon pain of the said acting
Provost Marshal or other proper officers being proceeded against with
the utmost severity as for a [illegible] of that Court out of which
such Writs of Execution shall issue and the Receipt of such Commissions of Forfeited Estates or any one or more of them shall in every
instance be a sufficient discharge to such Acting Provost Marshal or
other proper Officer for the sum of money he shall really and bona fide
pay to such Commissioners or Commissioner

A Bill intituled [sic]

An Act to attaint of High Treason the several Persons herein after-
named who are ether [sic] absent from this Province or in that Part of
it which is still in Rebellion against his Majesty; And to vest their
Real and personal Estates in His Majesty, his heirs and successors in
manner herein after mentioned; Subject to the lawful debts and claims
there upon.

Upper House of Assembly

Read the 1st Time 23d. May 1780
Read the 2d Time 24th May 1780.
Read the 3d Time 25th May 1780.

                    Geo: Dervage A.C.C.

Commons House of Assembly

Read 1st Time   26th May
     2d Time   1 June
and ordered to be committed
     3d Time   7th.
and ordered to pass.

J. GEORGIA LOYALIST PETITIONS, 1780 - 1782

     The restoration of royal rule in Georgia from 1779 to 1782 did not
bring a halt to the war in Georgia or, apparently, even a slowing down
of the fighting. Bandits robbed Georgia citizens on land and sea.
Some of the robbing and killing was done by Patriots and Frenchmen,
but much of it was also done by former Loyalists and by bandits of no
particular allegiance. Probably the worst was Daniel McGirth, who,
actually used the restored colonial political system and his former
service to the king to aid in his robberies and cattle-rustling, and to
prevent his arrest. In the last days of the war, Patriot raiding parties drove Georgia Loyalists from their homes in the backcountry to
within the British lines around Savannah. The fighting and killing
among Patriots, Loyalists and Idnians at that time was so terrible that
in the South, the murder of unarmed prisoners of war was being called
"granting a Georgia parole."

                              1.

     The following Loyalist petitions from this period are reproduced
from the originals in the Sir James Wright Papers, Telamon Cuyler
Collection, Special Collections, University of Georgia Libraries.

     To His Excellency Sir James Wright Baronet Captain General
     Governor & Commander in Chief of the Province of Georgia,
     Chancellor & Vice Admiral of the same.

The Petition of the Merchants of Savannah & other the Inhabitants of
the said Province.

Sheweth

     That the Coast, rivers & Inlets of this province are infested by
a number of men consisting of French & Rebels, in gallies & armed
Boats, who lately have captured several vessels, as well loaded with
Goods & Effects coming into this province, as going out; and have also
robbed & plundered several plantations on the Sea Islands of the same,
of Negroes & other Effects, the property of your Petitioners, & other
His Majesty's faithful Subjects therein, to their great Injury &
oppression.

     That your Petitioners have great Reason to laiment [sic] it will
be daily the Case, having no vessel of war, galley, or armed Boat in
the Province, so as to protect their trade & Property, which will
unavoidably be their ruin, unless some immediate Steps are taken to
prevent the same.

That your Petitioners are ready & willing to advance as much money
as they can possibly afford towards purchasing a Boat or Boats, to be
armed & mann'd for the purpose of protecting the trade & property of
the said Inhabitants; but your Petitioners find from Information
received of the force of the Enemies Galleys & Boats now on the Coast
& in rivers of the Province, that such your Petitioners Intention will
not fully answer the purpose designed without further assistance.

Your Petitioners therefore pray your Excellency will be pleased
to take the Premises into your serious Consideration and call the House
of Assembly, so as to lay before the same the present distressed
Situation of the Province, Province, that provision may be made for
getting of gallies & other vessels to protect the trade & Sea Islands
thereof. And in the mean time you will also be pleased to signify the
present alarming Situation of the Province to the Commanding Officer in
Charlestown, & request him to send some armed vessels to our immediate
assistance; and also to Sir Henry Clinton & admiral Arbuthreot in New
York, by which means your petitioners and other the loyal Inhabitants
of the Province may be relieved
          and your Petitioners will ever pray &c

Savannah Decr. 2nd 1780.   [The following are all from signatures.]

James Mossman	David Zubly Junr.	John Mac Iver
George Baillie	John Starr [Storr?]	Thos Mills
Willm. Telfair	Ben Wilson	Alexr. Gay
Samuel Douglass	Patk. Crookshanks	Geo: Macaulay [?]
Alexander J. Speirs	Wm. Wallace	James Belcher
Owen Owens	Tho. Tallewrath [?]	Jas. Herriot
George Ker	S. H. Jenkins	Peter Henry Morel
Wm Thomson	Alexr. McGown	John Morel
Hy. Keall	Hy. Keall for	Peter Dean
Ross & McCricky	Willm. Struthers	Wm Jones
John Wood	John Wallace	

To his Exelency [sic Sir Jams [sic] Wright Esqr. Baronet Capt. and
Comander [sic] in Chief in an [sic] over his majestys said province
of Georgia Chancelor [sic] and vice admiral of the same   The petition
of some of the inhabitants of the uper [sic] parts of Saint phillops
[sic] parish humbly sheweth
That By Reason of the want of Magistrates in these parts of the parish
The inhabitants sufers [sic] grately [sic] by Reason these parts is
Cheafly [sic] settled with ill Desposed [sic] persons that Dont want
Law nor Civell [sic] government to take place and the parish being very
Long near fifty miles from the mouth of Deep Creek to the flay ford at
gregors
We your Excelencys [sic] humble petitioners Do Represent that three
Majestrates [sic] to act in that Destrict [sic] would be much to the
permotin [sic] of good Deciplane [sic] in these parts We therefore
humbly Represent That Joseph Johnston David gains and Benjamin Richard-
son being filly [sic] qualified would ad [sic] much to the peace and
satesfaction [sic] of all well Desposed persons in these parts and your
Excelencys Humble petition[ers] shall Ever pray   March 14th 1781

[All the following are from signatures.]

Charlton Mizell	John Mizell	John Nivell
Wm. Mizell	David Mizell	Wm Still
Luke Mizell	Archd patterson	Samuel Cradock
Jams Mizell	Robert Dixon	Drurey Shorter

Ebenezer 21st June 1781

Sir

Being Informed that a Doctor or Surgeon to be appointed by the
Govournor [sic] and Council for to attend the Militia on this present

71

occasion and being Informed that Doctor Folliott is not Engaged and that
he may be pursuaded [sic] to take upon him that Charge and from the
knowledge and good opinion we have long since Experienced in that
gentleman beg you will use your best endeavours to get him appointed
to that Trust and you will Much oblige.

your Hble Servants

To Col Rogers Comdt Militia at Ebenezer

[All of the following are from signatures.]

John Goldwire Capt.	Joseph Reaves Lt. ____
John Morke [?] Captn.	John Wilson Capt.
John Thomas	Jeremiah Rogers Lt.
David Russell	Robt. Carr Capt.
William Corker Capt.	Benja. Lanier Leut. [sic]
William Read Capt.	Anthony Bounell Capt.
John Morrison Capt.	Thomas Mills Capt.
John Brown Lt Militia	Joel Walker

His Excellency Sir James Wright Barronet and Governor of Georgia &c &c

We his Majestys Loyal subjects of the Parish of St. George being sensible
of your Excellencys indulgent goodness towards us at every period and
in every circumstance We look upon ourselves as in duty bound from such
indulgence to present to your Excellency every circumstance that may be
injurious ether [sic] to [the] British government or faithful subjects.
We do therefore recommend to your prudent consideration the following
things all of which we look upon as detrimental both to government and
subjects.   first mr mc gerth [sic] with many others (some of whom have
even left our stations here) are employed in driving down Cattle from
our upper settlements whereby not only rebel cattle which properly
belong to government but also the property of Loyal subjects who are
now upon actual duty here [illegible word] destroyed and becomes the
prey of men distinguished so often for taking advantage of subjects
distress to inrich [sic] themselves. We recommend to your Excellencys
consideration the expences [sic] attending the giving Depositions against
and prosecution of rebels and as our own substance is now mostly
exhausted. We hope something will [be] allowed to supply the expences
of those who look upon themselves in conscience bound to give information against ether [sic] before Magistrates in publick Courts or
bound by solemn obligations. We recommend to your Excellencys Consideration our not having a superior officer over us whereby an open [opening]
is left to our treachrous [sic] though Clandestine enemies to practice
their evil designs and have endeavoured to blacken the Character of men
actuated by gracious principals [sic] & have evidenced themselves from
the beginning most firm friends of government and men whom your Excellencys prudence most Judiciously thought worthy of the principal trust
amongst us we therefore hope your Excellency will take into your prudent consideration Colonel Lyles Case and if evil affected and under-
ming [sic] persons for sinister ends misrepresent his Conduct to your
Excellency we hope you will of your goodness grant him a hearing which
we verily Believe will turn to his honour and we assure your Excellency
we know of no other person in the parish St george so fit in every
respect as is Col. Lyle for the Commission in which he for a considerable time has acted both with Courage and Conduct amidst many diffi-
culties and inconveiences [sic] and we believe his restoration to his
former Command over us would be a very acceptable privalege [sic] to
every Loyal subject of sd. Parish some other things that effect [sic]
us we might recommend to your Excellencys prudent consideration such as
want of the Laws of the Province to walk [?] by as also the Craving
necessity of men now a long time on duty here in respect to Cloathing
[sic] But that we may not to [illegible] we should conclude with earnest
prayer that the Lord may bless your Excellency with long life and protection with Strength and wisdom suitable to the important duties you
are Called to in your Eminent station in the Critical juncture and that

He make you a blessing to this Province &c

August 17th 1781

[All names below are from signatures.]

Samuel Montgomery JP
Robert Irwin
John Wilson Capt.
John Morrison Capt.

John Irwin Lieut.
William Reed Capt.
Edw Caswell Lieut.

To His Excellency Sir James Wright Governor of Georgia
The Petition of Thomas Rutherford Capt. Thomas Beaty Fredrick Jones
Jeremiah Rodgers William Black Gabriel David Thomas Whitehead Many
Duick Jones John Welche and others

Humbly Sheweth

That being drove away from our habitations Destitute of money cloths
[sic] and Provisions by the Rebells [sic] and are Come here for shelter
under the British standard We humbly Implore your Excellency to Order
us your Petitioners Rations as we cannot subsist at this time without
your assistance and we shall always be in Readiness at your Excellency
command to go upwards to Distress our enemies and in hopes that your
Excellency will grant us our Request we shall be obliged and for your
Excellency shall Ever Pray

August 28th 1781

[All of the following are from signatures.]

Gabriel Davis
Mamy Duick Jones
John Welch
Thomas Rutherford Capt.

Frederick Jones
Thomas Beaty
Jeremiah Rodgers
William Black

Georgia: To His Excellency Sir James Wright Baronet Captain General
          and Governour [sic] in Chief in and over His Majesty's
          province of Georgia Chancellor and Vice Admiral of the same,
          and to the Hourable [sic] the Council of the said Province.

The Humble Petition of us the subscribers for Ourselves and Others.

Shewth

     That your Petitioners for their Attachment and Loyalty to his
Majesty hath lately with their Wives and Children been by the Rebels
drove from their Habitations near Wrightsborough, and are now near
Ebenezer where they are under considerable difficulty to find Shelter
for their Families to defend them from the inclemency of the Weather

     Your Petitioners therefore begg [sic] leave to lay before your
Excellency and your Honourable Board hoping for such Support and
Assistance as the nature of their Case may require, in as much as they
have lost their all for their steady attachment to their King they
therefore crave such protection as his subjects, as you in your Wisdom
may think proper.

[All names shown below are from signatures.]

I believe these men to be Subjects
and have Suffered Considerable
Joseph Maddock
September 22d. 1781

John Hockens
Abraham Johnson
Joell Sanders
Joell Sanders Junr.

                    Joseph Williams
                    John Embre
                    George Struthers
                    Reuben Been
                    John Carson

Georgia To his Excellency Sir James Wright Baronet Governor and
         Commander in Chief of his Majesty's Said province of Georgia
         and to the members of his Majesty's Honourable Council.

The memorial of divers of that Christian People Called Quakers.

                    Respectfully Sheweth

That your memorialists having reason to believe, that the Ill will and
prejudice [sic] which prevailed against them at the time of the reduction of the province by the Rebels on account of their Political attachment to the British government when they were forced from their Homes
has now subsided or greatly abated. And their situation here being no
ways serviceable but Burthensome [sic] to Government, themselves now
generally Languishing Thro, sickness and Infirmities, are therefore
desirous and respectfully request, if it be consistent with the sence
[sic] of your Excellency and council, That permission may be allowed
them to return to their respective homes. And that your Excellency and
council, would be pleased to use your Endeavours to obtain a Flag, or
by some other means assist them preparatory thereto, to Treat with the
Americans, the incitements to this, our request are far different from
those of disaffection or discontent. They greatly [sic] acknowledge
the attention show their distress, while under the British government
which they have in the most perilous times manifested. Your memorialists
now apprehend from the change of the temper of their enemies. And con-
scious of their inoffensive and pacific disposition their situation may
be bettered by returning without Injury to the British Interest.

       Your memorialists beg leave to Submit their Case to your Excellency
and Honourable council hoping that you will take the premises into
consideration and grant such redress as you in your wisdom shall soon
meet and your memorialists as in duty bound will pray.

Savannah first day of the fifth Month 1782 ---

[All names below are from signatures.]

          Joseph Maddock   Joel Sanders
          John Stubbs   John Earcy
          Abraham Johnson   Joseph Stubbs
          Isaac Stubbs

A List of Owners Names Whose Negroes are Drafted on the Publick Service
by order his Honr. the Governor [1782]

          ___ Spencer   Jas. Mosman
          Doctr. Irwin   Mathias Ash
          James Parker   Joseph McLane & Croaton
          Wm. Bulock   Doctor Rem
          Wm. Butler & Children   Mrs. Jones
          Orphan house   Henercy Real
          Thos. NetherCliff   Peter Farling
          Joh. Morell   Wm Fox
          Wm. Sruthers

[The number of slaves owned by and the number drafted from each
individual is shown on the original manuscript.]

                              74

[The petition below is reproduced from the original in the Miscellaneous
Manuscript Collection, Library of Congress.]

"To His Excellency Sir James Wright Bart. Capt. Genereral [sic]
Governour & Commander in Chief in & over his Majestes Province of
Georgia Chancelor & Vice Admiral of the Same.

The Petition of us the Subscribers Inhabitants of Queensborough and
Places adjacent on Ogeecha river.

Humbly Sheweth that your Petitioners Being on the frontiers of this
Province, and the Creek Indians having made Several Incursions & Killed
four Families in this Place So that We are in Constant Danger of our
lives and the Present Situation We Cannot See any Prospect of Assistance from your Nor dare We take up arms in our Defence for fear of
offending the other Partie; Nor Cann We in our Present Distressed
Situation move our helpless Families to any Place of Safety as all our
Horses are Carrued off Either By Sculking People from Below or Plundering Parties from above. Your Petitioners Do therefore Humbly Pray that
your Excellancy Will take our Present Situation into your Imediate
Consideration and as you cannot Send to Assit us, that you would be
Pleased to use your influence with the Indians to prevent their further
Cruel & Savage Barbarities Against the Distressed & helpless Inhabitants of this Place, & Consider us A Neutral People, and Sir Order to
your Scouting Parties Not to Molest us or our Remaining fiew Horses
that yet remain amongst us, So that We may use Endeavours to Suport
our helpless & Almost Perishing Families and that you would be Pleased
to assist us With a Small Supply of ammunition to defend ourselves
against the Indians or Horse theives that doth infest us--& your Petitioner as in duty Bound Will Ever Pray.

[All names below are signatures.]

Queens^{gh}
March 19th. 1780

Roger Lawson   Thomas [?] mountain   Archibald Woods
John Allens   Frances mountain   Robert Benson[?]
Joseph Scott   William Bois   Wm. Little Senr.
Joseph Beatty   George Mc maghan   Samuel C Gnnens[?]
James Martin   John Sharp   George Speres
Samuel Fleming   Hugh Irwin   Robert Ronaldson
                                              John Corker

3.

    The following Loyalist petitions and other papers are from the
Military Records Collection, Georgia Department of Archives and History.

Georgia

    John Murray of Christ Church parish Esquire being duly sworn saith,
That on or about the 8th day of September last the Deponent was taken
prisoner on his passage from St. Augustine by water; That he was then
sent as a prisoner on board of the Languedoe, a French Man of War
commanded by the Count D'Estaign, where amongst many others the deponent saw John Glen formerly of Savannah Attorney at Law: that the
deponent being particularly acquainted with the said John Glen entered
into conversation with him; and amongst other things upon Mr Glen's
declaration and assurance of meeting with success on the expedition
against Savannah the deponent expressed his wish to him that as he the
said Glen expected to be powerful, he hoped he would be also merciful,

75

by using gentle & lenient measures towards the friends to Government, to which Mr Glen replied, "that it was not now a time to sue gnetle & moderate measures, but to make reprisals and to retaliate for the injuries which had been done to their persons and their properties," or words to that effect, And further saith not.

Sworn to this 6th   John Murray
June 1780 before

    A Stokes
       A true Copy from the Original
       John Simpson Pa CC

      The Affidavit of John Murray   No 14
        6 June 1780 Military
              Prisoners

Minute of Council,

His Excellency having ordered the case of Sir P. H. to be considered the Petition of the said Sir Patrick Houstoun to be relieved from the Disqualifying Act [which was presented on the 20th Sept. and then postoned] was read. and in Support thereof was read an Affidavit of Andrew Maclean of Augusta, Merchant: Also by his Excelly's permission was read a letter to him from Lt. Coll. Cruger, Commandt. of the King's Troops at Ninety six, in Favour of Sir Patrick; for the Alacrity & Zeal he showed in joining the Troops, and acting with them, at the relief of Augusta & the Garrison there under Lt Coll. Brown, when lately attacked by the Rebells:

On which, His Excelly desired the opinion of the Board, whether Sir Patrick in consideration of the zeal he had shown in support of Government, as set forth by Coll. Cruger's letter, as well as the whole of his conduct before, being such, as manifested a disposition to leave the country, and detach himself from the Party in Rebellion, should not be restored to the Rights and priveleges of a Loyal Subject.

The Board was unanimously of opinion, that in consideration of Sir Patrick's past conduct, throughout; & particularly in this late instance, mentioned by Coll. Cruger; Sir patrick deserved to be relieved from the whole of the Disqualifications & Incapacity imposed on him by the Disqualifying Act, and that he should be forthwith restored to the Rights & privileges of a Loyal Subject. It was therefore ordered, clerk, should prepare an Order of Council for that Purpose in Behalf of Sir Patrick, agreeably to the Form, and insert therein the following State, as deduced from the petition & several proofs now read, ___ and whereas Sir Patrick Houstoun.

[Reverse:]   Minutes of Council

           On The Petion of
           Sir Patrick Houstoun
           to be relieved from the
           disqualifying Act

MAY IT PLEASE,
     Your Excellency
                Agreeable to your order in Council, I have considered the memorial inclosed- signed "John Houstoun" I have also searched the Crown Office, and by Information on Oath there lodged, I find that person, is charged with having been very active- in the Rebellion, which lately prevailed in this province and particularly, that he acted within the same, - in the capacity of a Governor; and further, that he-was before the Town of Savannah, associated with the

Rebels, when the French beseiged the Town; and by the papers alluded
to in his Memorial, I find he did not submit himself to his Majestys
Authority, till some day after the reduction of Charles Town, Notwith-
standing- Georgia, the proper place of his residence, and Savannah the
capital, had been Eighteen months before in-His Excellency Sir James
Wright Bart.-possession of the Majestys troops, and Twelve Months, at
the Kings Peace, as declared, by proclamation of the Majestys-Commis-
sioners, for restoring peace in America;-So circumstanced, I humbly
concieve, the Kings pardon, only, - can afford the protection sought
after, and that your Excellency cannot, grant the Indemnity prayed for.

> I have the honor to be
> Your Excellency's
> Most Obedt. hble Servt:
> James Robertson Atty Genl.
> Sava: 20th Decr. 1780

[Reverse]   Attorney Genl's Report
            on the memorial of Mr. John Houstoun - 20th Dec. 1780
            Copy sent to Mr. John Houstoun
                            Rept.

We the Subscribers beg leave to recommend to His Excellency the Governor
and Council Mr. William Stephens as a Person whose good Conduct and
Attachment to Government renders him worthy to have the disqualification
under which he labours, removed, so that he may be restored to the
Benefits and Immunties enjoyed by his Majestys loyal Subjects; His
readiness and activity to oppose the rebel- Gallies which lately
alarmed our Costs, together with the whole tenor of his Behaviour since
his return to his allegiance should be an Example to all others who are
desirious to reap a like advantage.

> Sam Farley
> B. Cowper
> John Simpson

Savannah
June 4th 1781

        [on reverse]

        Recommendation in favor of William Stephens to
        relieve him from the operations of the disqualify
        Act of 1781

K.   OATH OF ALLEGIANCE (Not Dated)

    Exactly when or why the following document was signed by more than
150 Georgians remains unknown. Perhaps Georgia Patriots in 1783
required Georgians of questionable loyalty to sign this document in
order for them to remain in Georgia temporarily. The original document
is four pages long and made of silk. It is filed under "Georgia
Declaration of Independence" in the Keith Read Collection, Special
Collections, University of Georgia Libraries. All names on the original
document are signatures. The editor would like to thank Dr. Kenneth
Coleman of the University of Georgia for his ideas concerning this
oath.

    We and each of us do truly and sincerely acknowledge, profess,
testify, and declare that the State of Georgia is and of right ought
to be, free, Sovereign, and Independent and do swear to bear true faith
and allegiance to the said State and defend the same against traitors,
conspiracies, and all hostile attempts whatsoever, and that we do
renounce objure, all Allegiance subjection, and obedience to the King
of Great Britain. And that no foreign prince, person, prelate, state

or potentate hath or ought to have any jurisdiction, superiority, pre-
eminence, authority and power which is or may be vested by their
constituents in the Congress of the United States. And I do further
testify and declare that no man or body of men hath or can have any
right to absolve or discharge me from the obligation of this oath,
declaration and affirmation and that I do make this acknowledgement
profession, testimony, declaration, denial, renunciation and abjuration,
heartily and truly according to the common meaning and acception of the
foregoing words, without any equivocation mental evasion or secret
reservation whatsoever. So Help Me God!"

Jacob Wisenbaker
Philip Densler
John Herb
Michael Densler
Jacob Readick
Thos Sims

Benjn Lavinder
John Gilbert
  his
James I Davis
  mark
(John Marage)
  Yohun [Marage]
Nathal. Adams
Edmund Adams
Thomas Innes
George Nungezer
Henry Fisher
John Ring
Nicholas Hanner
  his
John X Exley
  mark
Peter x Dowel
John x Dowele
Wm: H: Spencer
James Parker
Richard T___ard

Smith Clarendon
Laurance Watson
Jonah Bulow
Peter Karr
peter Chambers
Thomas Dowell
Abattor Gabriel [?]
Jonathan Norton
Wm Watt
Wm Roches
Herman Herson
Frederick Fahm
Ulric Tobler
Matt Roche
John Shaw

Jno. Simpson
Isaac Young
  his
Robert RB Brady
  mark
Jno. Lawrey
Thos Norton
Saml Watson
James Simpson
David Snook
Robt. Patterson

James Galache
Francis Caviz [Davis?]
Powell Griggs
Thomas Palmer
W Leden
Philip Ulmar

Isaad Lovoch
David Bundy
  his
John 3 Warnoch
  mark
Daniel Giroud

James Milledge
James Hogg
Alexander Moor
George Keller [?]
Emanuel Kieffer
John X Williams
William Phillips
David x Kieffer
Valintine Kinsy
James Papot
Jacob 11 Warbach
Henry 11 Herbach
John 11 Timmons
Nathan Riesser
Joelalaken

Elijah Norton
John Clarke
Ratthaser Shaffer
Wm Hackell
George Richardson
James Kirk
Henry Clark
James Vallatton
Jas. Storie
Elisha Elon
David Maxwell
James Meyers
Jos. Farley
  his
Simon x Kender
  mark
De Moses Vallotton
Alexander allison
James Douglass
Wm Platt [?]
  his
Jacob /// Myers
  mark
Richd. D. Murray
Wm. Andrews
John Newdigate
Daniel Saxe

W Spencer
Sam Beecroft
John Glanin
John Rentz
  his
Jacob I Thyss
  mark
Matthew Salsner
Benjn. Wright

William Gilbars [?]
George X Basclay
William + Triplett

William Bisset [?]
Petr. Taarling
Thomas Polhill
Thos. Johnston
Wm: Barnard
Banister Winn
John Tebeau
Solomon Shad
John Barnard
Robt. Gibson
Robert Barnard
William beur [?]
Cospar Mock
  his
Lucas x Lucena
  mark
Aaron Moore
John Dickinson
John Riley
Wm. Maxwell
John Hammett
James Weatherford
John Vauchier
John Keowin
Hezekiah Wade
Frederick Keiffer
Charles Boyd
Recherd floyd
Charles L. Murrino
  his
David F Fisher
  mark
Peter Theiss
James Gwin
Joseph Huchinson
Jas. Whitefield
  Junr.
Robt. Thos. Hornby
Geoe. Rolfes
Henry Bourguin
Richd. Leake
Godliss Miller
John Millen

his
Thos. TS Sullivan
mark
his
John HS Rentz
mark
Thomas Taylor
Wm. Haskins
Richard Dennistoun
Jonathan Fox

Frane. Begbie
Thomas Moore
In English John
   George Hikes
Richard Whitefield
Geo: B. Spencer
Wm. Harris
Leonard Cecil
his
William w Stedman
mark
his
Peter + Lambeth
mark
Peter Ihly

David Fox

Jno. Campbell

A. Haskins [?]
Thomas Gibbons Junr
Willm. Fox Junr.
his
John x Exely
mark
John George Heisler

James Porte
Andrew Cunear [?]
Thos. Mills
Peter Henry Morel
Henry Nungezer

William Finden

W. Coales
his
Samuel x Pelbon
mark

Thos Triplett

B: Wilson

Thos. B...Kett
Alexd. Downer
John Ruppert

Thos. Fringe

John Stewart

James Thompson
T Netherclift
Wm. Horigan [?]
Thomas Shandly
Owen Owens

Jas. Merrilies

David Duhlan

L. WILKES COUNTY LOYALISTS, 1783

Georgia Patriots began taking legal action against Georgia Loyalists as early as 1777. Apparently there were some Loyalists who succeeded in avoiding being named on any of these numerous acts, as shown by these presentments of the Wilkes County grand jury in The Gazette of the State of Georgia, 20 November 1783, p. 1, c. 3. For more information on actions taken by Georgia's state government against Loyalists, see Allen D. Chandler (ed.), The Revolutionary Records of the State of Georgia, 3 vols. (Atlanta, 1908) and Heard Robertson (ed.), "Georgia's Banishment and Expulsion Act of September 16, 1777," Georgia Historical Quarterly, LV (1971), 274-82. The editor would like to thank Mr. Gordon B. Smith of Savannah for contributing the following.

STATE OF GEORGIA,

Wilkes County.

At a Superior Court, begun and holden [sic] at Washington, in the County aforesaid, on Tuesday the 4th day of November, 1783, before the Honourable George Walton, Esquire, Chief Justice, and the Honourable William Downes, Stephen Heard, Absalom Biddle, and Benjamin Ketchins, Esquires, Assistant Justices.

We the Grand Jury for the Body of the Country of Wilkes upon our oaths present as a great grievance, that his Honour the Governor and Executive Council have refused to sign grants for lands in this county belonging to the distressed inhabitants thereof, only because they had not been able to cultivate the same, when it was well known that it was altogether owing to the incursions of the enemy.

We also present as a very great grievance, the want of a publick buildings, in this county; and also that spirituous liquors are retailed without license.

We also present as a grievance, Indians and Indian Traders passing through this county without legal authority.

We also present as a grievance, that the citizens of South Carolina are allowed to keep publick ferries on Savannah river, and landing men in this state, without license from the same.

We also present as a grievance, the want of publick patrols to guard and scout on the different roads leading from places of trade into this country, as the great interruption given to the passing of carriages with goods tends in a great measure to keep up their price to a very extravagant [sic] heighth.

We present also as a very great grievance, that the under mentioned persons are not included in the Bill of Attainder and Confiscation of this state, that is to say, Samuel Tillet, Henry Summerline, John Wilkey, William Cain, Sampson Caudle, Richard Caudle, Andrew Stevens, Job Bowers, Joseph Williams, Little River, Charles Collins, John Bollinger, Joseph Sharp, Abraham Coleson, John Doolan, Thomas Stewart, Little River, Robert Cunningham of South Carolina, Mark Whitaker, Edward Crawford, James Bynam, Luke Bynam, Daniel Murphy, and Thomas Hoofsen.

We return our sincere thanks to his Honour the Chief Justice for his excellent charge given to us, and request that the same, together with these presents, be published in the Gazette of this state.

George Alton, Foreman	(L.S.)
John Rutherford,	(L.S.)
Thos. Ansley,	(L.S.)
Drury Rogers,	(L.S.)
Wm. Black,	(L.S.)
Alex. Awtry,	(L.S.)
Daniel Gunnels,	(L.S.)
James Little,	(L.S.)
Drury Cade,	(L.S.)
John Huchens Johnson,	(L.S.)
Richd. Woods,	(L.S.)
William Bailey,	(L.S.)
Thos. McDowel,	(L.S.)
Dionactous Oliver,	(L.S.)
Thos. Carson,	(L.S.)
Nathl. Howell,	(L.S.)
John Awtry,	(L.S.)
Jesse Johnston,	(L.S.)
Lesly Coats,	(L.S.)
James Starlett,	(L.S.)

In COURT, 5th November, 1783.

The Attorney General having no farther [sic] business to lay before the Grand Jury, their presentments were received, and, together with the charge of the Chief Justice, ordered to be published. Extract from the Minutes, John Freeman, C.W.C.

M. PETITION OF THOMAS YOUNG, 1783

Those who tried to stay on the middle ground in Georgia during the American Revolution are probably the least remembered and least understood of the population. Many of these Georgians left the state during the war to live in the comparatively safer areas in the North or in Florida. One of these who chose to stay behind was Thomas Young. Although he was a Loyalist, the following petition reveals that he also did a great deal of service for the Patriot cause, inadvertently, through his humane efforts on behalf of his Patriot neighbors and of the American prisoners held by the British at Sunbury, Georgia. This document makes appropriate end to this first part, because of the statement by John Wereat in this petition, "I agree to forgive every

80

body now the War is at an end." All names on this petition are reproduced from signatures. The original document is filed under "Revolutionary War" in the Keith Read Collection, Special Collections,
University of Georgia Libraries, and is used here courtesy of the
University of Georgia Libraries.

Georgia

   To the Honble. Joseph Habersham Esqr. Speaker and to the other
members of the Honble. the House of Representatives of the State
aforesaid.

   The petition of the subscribers, officers in The army of The
United States of America; and others whose names are Hereto Subscribed.

   Shewth

   That your petitioners are informed Thomas Young is by Act of your
Honble. House, restored to his family & friends, and relieved from the
penalties of the Act of Confiscation and banishment.

   That as a number of the Neighbours, and persons acquainted with
the conduct of Said Thomas Young, in Liberty County during the war, had
by petition to your Honble. House urged divers facts, in favor of the
Said Thomas Young, your petitioners were in hopes, that the Estate of
the said Thomas Young would have been free from tine for Amercement.

   Your petitioners, feel themselves impelled to state some further
matter to your honble. house. it appears from good proof, that in
march 1776 the Said Thomas Young was appointed, a commissioner to
negoeiate [sic] and did effect the exchange of Mssrs. Demere, Roberts,
& Rice; then prisoners at cockspur on board a British prison ship,
under the command of Capn. Barclay; and also pursued Verry [sic]
decided measures in behalf of Sundry Merchants, Inhabitants of this
State, in Adducing [sic] proofs, which Secured to the Said persons
Considerable Sums of money, on account of rice taken by said Barclays
Orders from the Shipping in Savannah River.

   That the Said Thomas Young found a substitute in the Georgia line
of Continental Troops, Was, and Still is a Cityzen [sic] of So. Carolina,
and did actual duty as a militia man at purysburgh, when the American
Army lay there.

   That the Said Thomas Young sustained heavy loss and damage In his
property by having the Same apply'd to public use, and taken by
Individuals, as appears by a number of vouchers.

   That the Said Thomas Young, when the British Troops crossed
Savannah river, returned to his family in Chatham County, and There
remained, without taking any active part whatever against America.

   That your said petitioners are well informed, the Said Thomas
Young, Used every means in his power at the Evacuation of Savannah
& Charleston, to Secure Such Negroes as had run away from their lawful
owners, and That he did actually take up and Send from Charleston to
this State; Upwards of forty negroes, belonging to differint [sic]
Cityzens [sic] Thereof.

   That during the Imprisonment of many of your petitioners at Sunbury, they experienced every hospitable mark and attention of the said
Thomas Young & his family. were often at his house, and Shewn every
mark of respect as prisoners. a conduct, in those days, not verry [sic]
Common. and which make a strong impression on the minds of your
petitioners, who, from these facts, take the liberty to apply, to your
Honble. House on behalf of the said Thomas Young.

   Wherefore your petitioners pray, that the estate of said Thomas
Young, may be freed from the amercement, intended to be levied, In as

much as the Services of the said Thomas Young in a public capacity. His
attention to your petitioners, and the acts of friendship received in
Their hours of adversity, ought to weigh with your Honble. House, as
circumstances strongly favor of the Said Thomas Young, Especially when
it is considered; that the Said Thomas Young has Suffered a verry heavy
loss of property. exile of person from family and friends, which your
petitioners trust your Honble. House will consider as punishments,
adequate for any political delinquencys [sic] charged against the said
Thomas Young.

And your petitioners &c &c &c

John McIntosh Lt Colo G.L.
John Berrien [?]
John Eustaus
James Field
Arthur Hayes
Edw: Cowan
John Lucas
Wm. Jordan
Jno. Jenkins
Alexr. Danl. Cuthbert
W. Day
Wm. Pierce Jr.
Lachn. McIntosh Junr.
F. O Neal
Frederick Shick
Mich. Rudolph

Ray Demere
James Wood
David Douglass
Wm. Maxwell
Samuel Stiles
Banja. Stiles
Seth Cuthbert
George Cubbedys
Geo: Handley
Thomas Glascock
James Merewether
Z. Dulerns [?]
H. Wagnon
Ben. Fishbouch
Thos. Washington
Joseph Forsterll

I agree to forgive every body now the War is at an end
John Wereat

PART II: GEORGIA PATRIOT SOLDIERS

"She recollects some of her own relations joined the British, or consented to remain neutral, accepting the terms of a Proclamation made by
the British Governor or commander at Savannah. Her husband said he
wished no other protection--but his Rifle; he so acted & joined Genl.
Clark. . .as a soldier in all his campaigns."

                              Margaret Strozier
                              Revolutionary War Pension Claim
                                 of Peter Strozier, Ga. R. 10,279

Dedicated to Gordon B. Smith of Savannah, Ga., and Arthur Gross of
Palm Harbor, Fl., for their kind help and constant encouragement.

A. GEORGIA MILITARY UNITS IN THE AMERICAN REVOLUTION

Georgia had military problems in the American Revolution that were unique. On every side, the Patriots in Georgia were confronted with real or potential enemies. The long, western borders faced the Creek and Cherokee Indians, whom British Indian agents attempted to lead against the Georgians. East Florida was used as a base by British troops and ships to raid Georgia's southern border and coast while to the north, in the back country of the Carolinas, thousands of settlers retained a loyalty to the British in Florida and in Savannah after the British captured that city in 1778.

To defend the scattered settlements on this long border, Georgia had only about 2,300 able-bodied men who could be formed for militia service. Even these comparatively few men, however, were so poorly trained and disciplined that Royal Governor Sir James Wright had once complained that there was "not one in five or ten that would face an Enemy." Had all Georgians eagerly joined the Patriot cause, they would have been able to defend Georgia from so many enemies for very long. In reality, many Georgians were actively loyal to the British and probably many more were neutral, adding the dangers of counter-revolution and indifference to further weaken Georgia's defences. From early in the war, Georgia Patriots sought to effectively organize what militia they had and to recruit additional soldiers from outside of the state.

Georgia's first formal state constitution, adopted in 1777, authorized one militia battalion in each country for every 250 able-bodied men therein. In counties with fewer than 250 men, independent militia companies were to be formed.

The Georgia militia had numerous shortcomings. Usually, only from one-third to one-half of the militiamen in each unit could be drafted for active service in the field at a time and then only for short terms of no more than a few months. Some men avoided militia service by hiring substitutes, although some would volunteer to continue serving when their time was up. Even in times of an immediate danger that cut across political questions, the militiamen insisted on being paid for their time, for any of their provisions that they consumed, and for any property losses caused by their service. The political differences of the militiamen and the poor quality of their equipment, training, and discipline made desertions and defections to the British common, even among militia units that had been successful in battle.

Despite this, the Georgia militia was far more than just an armed mob. Militia officers were usually chosen by election and often were capable men aided by staffs that included waggonmasters, paymasters, chaplains, surgeons, commissaries, adjutants, and other men with special duties or skills. Paperwork for these units was extensive, even for routine orders, as well as for keeping accounts, drafting men, procuring supplies, and constructing fortifications. Properly led by such men as John Dooly, John Twiggs, John Baker, Benjamin Few, and Elijah Clarke, the Georgia militia won impressive victories in Georgia and South Carolina, notably at Kettle Creek, Burke County Jail, and Musgrove's Mill. They were a part of the Patriot forces at King's Mountain, Cowpens, and Augusta.

The most important full-time troops that Georgia had were her
Continentals, whose officers were usually Georgians, but whose enlisted
men were recruited from the Carolinas and Virginia. Some even came from
Connecticut, New York, and Pennsylvania. Among these Continentals,
there were also a few French officers and some British and Hessian
deserters. At its height, the Georgia Continental Line numbered more
than 1,500 men organized into four battalions of various types of
infantry, a regiment of horse, three artillery companies, and a small
navy.

Both the Continetal Congress and Georgia failed to keep their
promises to provide these men with pay and even the most basic neces-
sities of food, clothing, blankets, and shelter. Disease, desertions,
and low morale were always major problems. Brigadier General Lachlan
McIntosh wrote in 1779, as he watched the last of these men returning
to their home states, "it hurts me to see them go away almost naked,
& in arear [sic] for several months pay, & the state unable to make
good their engagements of Land to them." Despite their shabby treatment,
the Georgia Continentals did Georgia a great service and left a record
of herioism in battles on land and sea at Fredrica, Midway, Sunbury,
Savannah, Charleston, Stono, and Brier Creek, under Samuel Elbert,
Robert Rae, John White, Francis Henry Harris, the McIntoshes, the
Habershams, and others.

The State of Georgia organized two minuteman battalions, two
legions, several independent companies, and other regular units as the
State Line of Georgia, chiefly from men recruited from outside of the
state. These units were created to give Georgia troops that, unlike the
Georgia Continentals, would be under state control and not the control
of the Continental Congress. Critics claimed, however, that these
units were often formed chiefly to create military positions for
political hacks. Georgia state units suffered from the same problems
as the Continentals, but usually did not last as long. One notable
exception was James Jackson's Georgia State Legion, which did a great
deal of service in the last days of the war. This unit was composed
partly of British deserters and former Georgia Loyalists required to
serve in atonement for past loyalties.

One unit in Georgia that defies normal classification was William
Candler's Regiment of Refugees. During Elijah Clarke's unsuccessful
attack on the British outpost at Augusta in September of 1780, this
unit was created from Richmond County Patriots, most of whom were
paroled prisoners of war who risked being hung by the British for
violating their paroles. When the Patriots were forced to retreat from
Augusta, Candler and his new regiment went with them and served with
distinction in several battles in South Carolina, notably at King's
Mountain and Long Cane. Augusta was retaken by the Patriots in 1781,
allowing for the reestablishment of the Georgia state government and
the Patriot militia. When this happened, Candler's regiment, which had
been one of the units responsible for retaking Augusta, was disbanded.

The following rosters provide the names of a fraction of the
thousands of men who served in the Georgia Patriot forces during the
American Revolution. Each of the three basic types of units--militia,
Continental, and state regulars--are represented. This brief explana-
tion of the differences in these Georgia units has been included to
provide researchers with a clearer understanding of the nature of their
ancestors' service in Georgia, particularly when a researcher is
relying on a Revolutionary War pension statement, in which an ancestor
might describe service that he did in any, some, or all of the units
described above.

The author would like to especially thank Mr. Gordon B. Smith
of Savannah for his help in preparing this introduction and the various
lending organizations for their permission to publish these rosters.
For more detailed information on these various units, the reader is
advised to consult Mr. Smith's excellent series on Georgia military
units of the American Revolution in <u>Georgia</u> <u>Pioneers</u> <u>Genealogical</u> <u>Maga-
zine</u>, beginning with Vol. XIV, No. 4 (November, 1977).

B.   PATRIOT MILITIA

(1)   Rosters from the Telamon Cuyler Collection, Special Collections,
      University of Georgia Libraries.

A List of the People who Engaged under the Command of Capn. Thomas Pace
to assist in the Execution of the measures adopted by the Congress for
the Preservation of that Liberty which every American Has a Just Right
to

[This was the company of early Patriot militia of the Augusta Committee,
30 August to 19 September 1775. The length of service of each man is
included on the original manuscript.]

Thomas Pace Captn.	Danl Richardson
Edward Ashton 1st Lieutenant	Enoch Richardson
Marmaduke Ricketson 2 Do.	Zedekiah Wood
John Lyons	Danl Connell
Jordon Ricketson	Reas Morris
John Grubbs	Thos Williams
Ephraim Ledbetter	Isaac Cloit
Timothy Ricketson	Theophilus Davies
Thos McCrary	Nathl Young
Ths Wright	Ben Grubs
John Hammond Junr. Sergeant	Edwd Burke
Saml. Lyons Do.	Saml Bradket
John Shadsdill	Peter Kinder

State of Georgia   1778

To Jenkins Davis's Company of Melita [sic] for duty done at the Magazine at Ebenezer from ye. 5th to the 12th March and Rations

[The length of duty for each man is shown on the original manuscript.]

Godleib Neidlinger Sergt	Jacob Buhler
Jonathan Fetzer	Godhilf Smith
John Rentz Senr	

State of Georgia   1778

To Jenkins Davis's Company of Melitia [sic] for duty done at Magazine
in Ebenezer from the 11th to the 21st March and Rations

Saniel Weitmann Sergt.	Thomas Schweigopfor
Veit Lechner	Jacob Buhler
Christian Heit	Samuel Neidlinger
John Rentz Junr.	Jonathan Sechinger
John Waldaver	James Welch
Christopher Hinds	Jonathan Earnstdorf
John Maurer	

State of Georgia

To Jenkins's Davis's Company of Melitia [sic] for duty done in Ebenezer
from 6th to 14th April 1778

Francis Vauchea	John Remshardt
Ulrich Neidlinger	John Heinly
John Phloger	George Earnstdorf
Frederick Lachner	Joshua Helfenstine

State of Georgia

To Danl. Burgsteiners Company of Melitia [sic] for duty done at Magazine at Ebenezer from ye. 9th May to the 17th May 1778

Daniel Weitmann Lieut
John Phloger Private
Veit Lechner
John Waldhauer
Samuel Neidlinger
Christopher Gugel
George Schele

George Gruber
John Maurer
Christian Heit
Benjamin Glaner
Thomas Schweigopfer
Frederick Lechner

State of Georgia

To Daniel Burgsteiners Company of Melitia [sic] for duty done at Magazine in Ebenezer from the 16th to the 21st May 1778

Israel Leinberger Lieut.
Christopher Cramer Private
Veit Lechner
John Phleger
Samuel Neidlinger
John Rentz Junr.
Christian Heit

John Rodenberger
John Waldhauer
Christopher Gugel
George Schele
George Gruber
Christian Seiplven

State of Georgia

To Daniel Burgsteiners Company of Militia for duty done at the Magazine in Ebenezer from the 25th of July to the 2d. of August 1778

Daniel Weitman Lieut
George Zigler Private
John Rentz Senr.
Daniel Helfenstine
Frederick Lechner
John Rentz Junr.
Christian Heit

Godleib Schneider
Christopher Rodenberger
Veit Lechner
Jacob Gnann
John Phleger
Christian Shuptrine

A List of the Officers and Soldiers Who fled the Protection of the
British and took Refuge in Other States and did their Duty faithfully
Under the Command of Collo [sic]Wm Candler from the 15th Septm 1780
Untill [sic] the Reduction of the British Troops in Augusta

1st Company

1.	Fredreck Stallions	Capn.
2.	Jas. Stallions	Lieut.
3.	Edmond Martin	Lieut.
4.	Henry Candler	Private
5.	Jno Shackelford	do
6.	Wm McKinney	do
7.	Marshal Martin	do
8.	Mathew Martin	do
9.	Philip Hornby	do
10.	Thos.Greer	do
11.	James Culbreath	do
12.	Richard Johnston	do
13.	Edmond Bugg	do
14.	John Maddox	do
15.	Obedia Son [?]	do
16.	Isaac Fuller	do
17.	Wm Hyrne	do

18.	Saml Hyrne	Private
19.	Daniel Joslin	do
20.	George Downs	do
21.	Thos Johnston	do
22.	Isaac Skinner	do
23.	Wharton Watley	do
24.	Willm. Thompson	do
25.	Edward Boyd	do
26.	Daniel Evans	do
27.	Archabald Mcneil	do
28.	Ezekiel Stallions	do
29.	Downs	do

3rd Company

| 1. | Ezekile Offutt | Capt. |
| 2. | Jacob Linn [Ginn?] | Lieut. |

3.	Jas Martin	Lieut.		13.	Abner Roundtree	Lieut.
4.	Jessey Offutt	do		14.	Job Roundtree	do
5.	William Hatcher	do		15.	Jessey Roundtree	do
6.	Jeremiah Hatcher	do		16.	Henery Day	do
7.	Robert Hatcher	do		17.	Abraham Pierce	do
8.	Nathaniel Offutt	do		18.	George Hammond	do
9.	Blanford Davis	do		19.	Simon Martin	do
10.	Vachal [?] Davis	do		20.	Abner Hammond	do
11.	William Brewer	do		21.	John Hatcher	do
12.	Charles Hammond	do		22.	Henry Hatcher	do

No. Total officers & men: 1 Collo [sic] 1 Majr 3 Captains 5 Lieuts
65 Privates This is to Certify that Colo William Candler was Unanimly.
Chosen & Elected to that Rank by the Refugees that fled from Richmond
County that Year 1780 and faithfully Did his Duty in that Command
Untill [sic] the Reduction of Augusta 1781

Certified By

/s/ Elijah. Clark
Colo. Commandant of Refugees

Return of the Militia belonging to the upper Counties of the State of
Georgia, serving with the army under the command of General Wayne. Hd.
Qrs. Ebenezer, 22d. April, 1782

[From Burke County]:

Captain William Darey
Lieutent. William Ryals
Serjt. Maj. Levi Emanuel
Qr Mr. Serjt. James Young
Serjteant William Marshal

Priv.
1. Mathew Jordan
2. James Bruton
4. Robert Allen
5. Benja. Maxley
6. Henry Elliott
7. Zebulon Cox
8. Jonathan Coleman
9. Elijah Fapp
10. Thomas Hannah
11. James Wiere
12. John Everet
13. Peter Wynne
14. John Farmer
15. Henry Todd
16. Samuel Buxton
17. Grosse Scruggs

[From Richmond County]:

Captain William Kemp
Lieut. Jonathan Jones

Waggoners
    Joseph Brown
    James Brown
    Daniel McKewn
    Henry Anglin
    Thomas Vicars

Priv.
1. Joseph Beezly
2. Daniel Runnels
3. Darby Riggens
4. William Hunt
5. Robert Walden
6. John Grotehose
7. James Swords
8. John Curtis

[Deserters from the Richmond
County militia]:

1. Adam Shows
2. Abraham Perkins
3. Edeard Ickles
4. John Saunders
5. Moses Hill
6. James Scott
7. Benjn. Cooper
8. James Hogg
9. Jordan Wells
10. Alexr. Angely
11. William Perrit
12. Abraham Greason
13. Burrel Beezly

[Deserters from "Reclaimed Citizens
Capt. Marbury's Compy.," Burke
County militia]:

1. John Hicks
2. Josiah Nobles
3. Oliver Martin
4. Thomas Jones

[Deserters from the Burke County militia]:

5. John Nelson
6. John Howell
7. Benjn. Powell

8. George Lewis
9. Lewis Deshager
10. Jacob Young

2. Rosters from the Military Records Collection, Georgia Department of
Archives and History.

[Muster] role of Captain Burrell [Burwell] Smith's Company of Volunteers
in State of Georgia in wilkes [sic] County Commanded by Col. John Dooly
the first of June 1778 to the first of august 1778

mith Capt.
   Lieut.
     ergant
   tt
   ps
  phillips
   ps
    Pester
hn___ parks
hn McClain
nery anglin
  et McBurnitt
   huett

pson
mes Stewart
Richard Graves
Shadrack Mimms
  lliam Camp
mas Littleton
lliam Brooks
 ilkins
 heard
Smart [Stuart?]
Reaction
mon Warters
Daniel Corner

hal hindsmond
iam anderson
n Dardin
eph kitchens
hn Wilson
James linsley
 ences Crain

sworn before me this Day December 1778

   Ba.d Heard JP

I do Certify the abouve [sic] Accot [sic] to be Inst and True and that
the Duty was Done by my orders /s/ John Dooly Colo.

P.S. in order that there be no Mistake in This Said acct. I have
Certified our acct. for this money before and I am Informed it is
lost So I Desire that if the other should be found not to be paid
/s/ J. Dooly [Note: Amount paid has been omitted, although shown
on the remnant of the original manuscript.]

[Source: Wilkes County, Military Records Collection, Georgia Department
of Archives and History.]

Militia Roll of Captain Robert Carr

State of Georgia Dr to Robert Carr for Ranging as Captain of the Militia
in Wilkes County by Order of Coln. John Dooly

John Owtry first Lieut.
George Runnals Second Lieut.
Zachariah Henderson Sergn
Lambeth Hopkins
Robert Trapp
Saunders Walker
John Coats
Black Sanger
Alixr Owtry Ser
John P Fling
Robert Hammett Ser.
Robert Hammett Jnr.
Wm. Philips
Wm Ellis
Fedrick Runnals

Jacob Owtry
Wm. Morgan
Wm. Hopkins
Tunstall Roan
Wm. Jackson
Henry Summerill
Moses Trapp
Luke John Morgan
Asa Morgan
George Bagby
Jonathan Riggan
Robert McNabb
Thomas Norton
Alixr Owtry Jur.
John Philips Ser.

Edwd. Hammett
Jacob Wilkins
Isaac Wilkins
Dennis Maddin

Benjamin Philips
Wm Young
Daniel Young

From the 15th of September to the 15th of October 1778 this Acct.
Proven before me this 9 day of Janr. 1779
                                          his
                             Robert (X) Carr
                                 mark

/s/ Wm. Downs   /s/ John Dooly Colo.

I do Certify the above Amt.

[The original manuscript includes number of days and pay.]

State of Georgia Dr To Robert Carr for Ranging as Captain of the Militia
in Wilkes County by Order of Coln. John Dooly

John Owtry First Lieutend.
George Runnals Second Lieut.
Jacob Wilkins
Thos. Norton
Jacob Owtry
Wm. Morgan
Dennis Madden
Benjamin Philips
Wm. Jackson
Wm. Hammett
Edwd. Hammett
Lambeth Hopkins
Jonathan Riggan
William Ellis
Robert McNabb
Abraham Smith
Henry Summerill
William Thompson
Benjamin Thompson, Sr.
Robert Hammett

Tunstall Roan
Robert Trapp
Isaac Wilkins
Fedrick Runnals
John Philips Sr.
John Phlips Jur.
Wm. Philips
Zachariah Henderson
Joseph Trap
Moses Trapp
Alixr. Owtry Jur.
Asa Morgan
Alixr. Owtry Ser.
John Norton
David Philps
David Madden
Luke John Morgan
Benjamin Thompson
Wm. Lachey
George Bagby

From the 15th of Augst. to the 15th of September 1778

[Original manuscript includes number of days and pay.]

Colonel Robert Middleton's Battalion, Richmond County Militia

A Pay Roll of Cpatian [sic] Charles Crawford Company of Militia in
Colonel Robert Middleton's Battalion.

Captain	Charles Crawford	Private	William Maddox
Lieutenant	David Harriss	"	John Youngblood
"	David Walker	"	William Bryan
Sargent	William Barnett	"	John Dyas
Private	Nathaniel Barnett	"	John Maddox
"	James Alderridge	"	Samuel Pounds
"	Benjam Daniel	"	William Tindol
"	Isaac Low	"	William Bolus
"	John McKinneah	"	Daniel Conel
"	David Barnett	"	Marmmerduk Rickerson
"	Joel Barnett	"	Robert Baley
"	Jesse Barnett	"	James Greene
"	William Barnett	"	John Tripplett
"	Benjamin Grubbs	"	Anderson Crawford
"	Christopher Chambers		

Certified by me   Sworn Before /s/ John Jermany

/s/ R. Middleton Col.   10-15 April 1782

[The original manuscript showed the time served and pay for the period
19 August to 18 November 1779.]

A Pay Roll of Capt Jeremiah Bugg Company of Militia in the Lower
Battalion, Commanded by Colonel Robert Middleton

Captain	Jeremiah Bugg	Private	Mathew Hopson
Lieutant	Sherod Bugg	"	John Webster
Lieutant	Nathaniel Hickel	"	Archi Ball
Private	Charles Simmons	"	Daniel Danielly
"	Richard Johnson	"	Andrew McLean
"	Samuel Bugg	"	Edmond Bugg
"	James Weatherford	"	Jesse Winfrey
"	Isaac Eveans	"	Aug^s Bagners
"	Stephen Eveans		
"	Samuel Hicks		
"	Daniel Wallihom		

Certified by me   /s/ R. Middleton Col.

[Original manuscript showed the pay owed each man from 8 September to
18 October 1779.]

A Pay Roll of Captain Jeremiah Beall Company of Militia of Georgia,
Commanded by Colonel Robert Middleton

Lieut.	Zefen^h Beall	Private	El^a Woard
Lieut.	John Hatcher	"	Benj^a Woard
Sergeant	Thomas Beall	"	Robert Jones
Private	Hugh Megee	"	Benj Davis
"	Luis Megee	"	William Shurly
"	Hillery Philps		

Certified by me   /s/ R. Middleton Col.

[The original manuscript included pay owed each man for the period
8 September to 18 October, 1779.]

A Pay Roll of Capt. James McNeals Company of Militia in the Lower
Battalion of Richmond County State of Georgia, Commanded by Colonel
Robert Middleton.

James McNeal	Captain	James Culbreth	Serjeants
James Simpson	Lieutenant	Bengamin Waller	ditto
William Lucous	Lieutenant	William Greer	ditto
Thomas Smith	Serjeants	Benjamin Hart	ditto
John Crawford	ditto	John Shackleford	ditto
Abner Webster	ditto	John Bugg	ditto
Joseph May	ditto	Strong Ashmore	ditto
Thomas Greer	ditto	John Garnett	ditto
John Johnson	ditto	Samuel Lomous	ditto
Arche McNeal	ditto	Alexander Fraser	ditto
Liles Messer	ditto	John Peek	ditto
Jeremiah Warren	ditto	Hustons Studstill	ditto
John Maddox	ditto	Michel M Neal	ditto
William Barnett	ditto	Moses Marshal	ditto

Sworn two [sic] before me this 4 day of May 1782
/s/ Zachas fenn J.P.

Certifyed [sic] by me
/s/ R. Middleton Col?

[Original document included service from September 8, 1779, to October
25, 1779, and amount of pay each one received.]

A Pay Roll of Capt. John Peake, Company of Militia in the Lower Battalion, Commanded by Colonel Robert Middleton.

Capt.	John Peake	Private	William Loucous
Lieut	John Garnette	"	Thomas Holladay
Sergt	William Greer	"	Leonard Marbury
Lieut	Benjamin Howard	"	John Larvin
Private	John Maddox	"	Alexander Fraser
"	William Barnette	"	Isaac Fuller
"	Owen Watley	"	Jeremiah Duck
"	Wharten Watley	"	Randol Ramsey
"	Robert Eimerson	"	William Ramsey
"	Willis Watley Sen.	"	Sherod Watley
"	Joshua Fuller	"	Willis Watley Jr.
"	John Greer	"	John Johnson
"	Mikel McNeal	"	John Wilson
"	Joshua Greeff	"	Ely Garnett
"	James Hogg	"	John Fuller
"	Joel Barnett	"	John Tindol
"	John Hogg	"	Jesse Barnett
"	Luis Powell	"	Benego Wright
"	John McKineah	"	John Ramsey
"	Richard Dowdy	"	John Irvin
"	Jurdin Wilsher	"	Edward Cartledge

Certified by me
/s/ R. Middleton Col

[Original manuscript included the pay owed each man for the period
1 June to 2 August, 1779.]

A Return of the Wilkes County Reg^t--4th Oct^br 1781

Coln.	Majr.	Captn.	Lieut.	Adjt.	Serjt.Majr.	Sergt.	Rank & File	Without Arms
2	1	10	20	1	1	20	227	62

Total 202

on Comand at Cap^tn Gunnels Station   )
1 Cap^tn 1 Lieu^t. 2 serj^ts. 17 Men   )
at Cap^tn Littles Station 1 Cap^tn.   ) E Clark (Col)
2 Lieute. two spies 2 serjt. and 20 men)
on Comand with Col^o. Cunningham to   )
Gen^rl Twigs Camp 75 Men   )

A List of the Captn. Names

1	Zachria Philips	6	William Walker
2	Daniel Gunnels	7	Alexander Alexander
3	James Little	8	Alexander Autry
4	John Autry	9	Saml Harper
5	Richard Herd	10	Peter Rockimore

Captain John Hill's Company

A Pay Roll of Capt. John Hill's Company of Militia at Fort Martin
Commanded by Colonel Elijah Clark of Wilkes County Duty Done at sd
Garrison two months, Commenced first of March to first of Mary 1782.

John Hill	Capt.	Simon Salter
Stephen Bishop	1st Lieut.	John Mims
Joseph Mims	2nd Lieut.	William Mims
John Whatley	Sergt.	William Bishop
Ezekiel Miller	Sergt.	Samson Wilder
Joshua Hill	Sergt.	Richard Barfield
Malichi Miller		Malbery Simons
Edward Hill		James Crismas
James Davis		Henry Castleberry
Remey Philips		Joab Brooks
John Bugg		Thos. Branham
David Holliman		Ezekiel Cobb
Mark Holliman		James Crismas
Bolling Courton		
John Castleberry		
John May		Sworn before me the above Duty was
Joseph May		performed at sd Garison
Martin Mims		
Joseph Cobb		/s/ Jas. Bowie J.P.
Richard Courton		

I do here by Certify that the above
duty was performed by sd Capt. W M

/s/ E Clark Coln.

A Pay Role [sic] of Capt. John Hill Company of Militia Commanded by
Josiah Dunn, Colonel of the uper [sic] Devition [sic] of Richmon [sic]
County, for duty Don [sic]-brought over from the tweenty [sic] Six
of June 1781, to the twenty Six of Janr. 1782.

John Hill	Captn.	Saml. Bloodworth
Joshua Hill	1st. Lieut.	Mark Holliman
Edward Hill	2d. Lieut.	John Evans
Demey Philips	Sergt.	Thos. Whight
James Davis	Sergt.	William Cowin
John Whatley		Richd. Holliman
Malichi Wilder		Reson Bowie
Rich. Courton		
Ezekiel Miller		
Malbery Simons		
Richard Barfield		
David Holliman		
Simon Salter		I do Certifie [sic] the above Duty Don [sic]
John Ilands		by the Sd. officers and men proved before me-
Richd. Whatley		
Davis Criswell		Josiah Dunn Colo.
John oneal		
James Bowie		
Henry Castlebery		6th of may 1782
		/s/ James Bowie J.P.

[The original manuscript also included
arms and accountrements.]

A Pay Role of Capt. John Hill Company of Militia at fort Martin, Commanded by Coln. Elijah Clark of Wilkes County, Duty Don at sd. Garison, four months, Commences first of May, to the Last of August 1782.

John Hill	Capt.	Ezekiel Coob
Stephen Bishop	Lieut.	Thos. Branham
Joseph Mims	2nd Lieut.	Moses Powell
John Whatley	Sergt.	Silas Motes
Francis Grubbs	Sergt.	Simeon Motes
Joshua Hill	Sergt.	Levi Motes
Edward Hill		William Motes
Malichi Wilder		William Brooks
James Davis		John Castleberry
Henry Castleberry		Joab Brooks
John May		William Kelley
Joseph May		Thomas Kelley
Martin Mims		Drury Mims
Joseph Coob		John Kelley
John Mims		William Donoho
William Bishop		
Samson Wilder	proved before me	
Richd. Barfield	J A Bown J P	

REVERSE

I do Certify that the Within duty was performed by sd. Capt. John Hill

E Clark Coln

Capt. Hill
1st May to 31st Augt. Capt. John Hill pay Role
1782

Head Quarters   Augusta

ye 31st May 1782

Dear Sir,

Whereas Col. Martin has resigned the Command of ye. 1st. Battallion of Richmond County on Act. of his being one of the Commissioners of Confiscated Estates & Lt. Col. Bostick being under an arrest the said Battallion is left intirely without a Commander, & I find that is is wish of both officers & Men that you should take Command of the--- I now therefore be glad you'd come to Augusta Immediate-y in order to Consult with you on that head. --- Interim
I am Dr. Sir.
Yr. Mo. Obt. Sevt.
J. M.

C O Neal.

[J. M. must be Governor John Martin. Louise F. Hays]

"1776 The publick of the province of George
To Mathew Marshall Lieutamant Dr

	L	s	d
For Scouting on Ogeetcha at the Rate of Seven Pounds Sterling 8 Days from the 15th to the 23rd of September and for Rasshings 1s10] per Day	2	12	4
Jeremiah Rodgers Sargant 8 Days at Ł 3 rs per month and Rasshings 1s9 per day	1	7	4

	Ł	s	d
Robert Crummey 8 Days at Ł2 10s per month and Rashings 1s3 per Day	1	3	4
John Cuning 8 Days at Do per month Rasshings 1s3 per Day	1	3	4
Robert Boyd 8 Days at Do per month Rasshings Do per Day	1	3	4
John Mathews 8 Days at Do per month Rasshings Do per Day	1	3	4
William Penson 8 Days at Do per month Rasshings 1s3 per Day	1	3	4

Total Sum Ł9 16 4

The above acct. sworn to &c just and due Before me /s/ Dal. McMurphy
J.P.   17th Sept 1776"

"November the 19th 1782 a List of the men that wrought at Brier Creek
Bridge

Jas. Lambert	Keleb Sapp	Lewhue Thompson
John Crozier	Shedrick Sapp	Petter Hawthorn
John Scot	Abraham Sapp	Jas McConkey
George Slown	Jas. Handcock	Henery McConkey
George Carter	George Turner	John Lowery
Jonathan Hobbs	Frederick Roberts	Moses Mcneekon
John Clark	Charls Hedgon	William McColagh
Jas Clark	Drury Sharp	Samuel McColagh
William Reves	Henery Brasell	Charles Golikley
Joseph Reves	Jesey Wigons	John Thornton
John Tealer	Abraham Lott	Drurey Roberts
Jas Juardon	Simon Sheret	Philip Thomas
Henery Sapp	Samuel Brasel	John Manson
Isey Sapp	Kindred Brasel	Jas Cohram
	Isock Thomas	William Allen"
	John Moses	
	Joseph Floyad	

[The above is filed under Wilkes County in the Military Records Collection although the names on this list appear to be men from Burke County.]

"A pay Rool of officers & privates in Capt. Patrick Carr's Company of
Rangers in Burke County & State of Georgia for the year 1781 and 1782.
Col James Mackays Ridgment.

Names	Officers & Privates	Commencement of Time		To what Time	
Patric Carr	Capt.	1 Octr 1781		1st Jany. 1782	
Michl. Jones	1st Lieut	16 sept		16 Jany	
Josiah Hatcher	2nd Lieut	Do	Do	Do	Do
Wm Paterson	Private	Do	Do	Do	Do
Wm Moore	Do				
Andw Berryhill					
John Murrey					
Timy Rickerson					
Zephrh Bell					
Daniel Evans					
John Hatcher					
John Leith					
Theodk Goodwyn					
Archd Hatcher					
John Mannin					

Names	Officers & Privates	Commencement of Time	To what Time
Hillery Phillips			
Nathl. Bell			
Charles Burch			
Edwd Burch			
Edwd Bugg			
John Davis			
John Hix			
Wm. Jones			
Peter Beason			
Epperson			
Wm. Coletrap			
Henry Doolin			
Patric Mologr			
Isaac Ardis			
Ezekiel Oxford			
Ezekl. Harris			
Thos. Galphin			
Wm Holmes			
George Galphin			
John Milleoge			
John Millheny			
Wm Collins			
Wm Hatcher			
Wm Stewart			
John Kitts			
Lud Outlaw			
Edwd. Outlaw			
Ballard			
John Talley			
Luke Durbin			
Hill [Hillyer?]			
Martin Shirley			
Saml. Griffin			
James Harris			
Wm. Hunt			
Patric Connaley Serjt."			

[The original manuscript also shows the amount of money owed to each man.]

[According to a note on a card in the Vertical File, Main Search Room, under "Williamson, Micajah," the following is a list of Revolutionary War soldiers. Perhaps this is a list of Revolutionary War Bounty Certificates.]

Jno. T. Duke		Moody Burt	
Jno. McLain		do do	
ditto do		Richard Leven 30	
James Roan		George Williams	
William Morgan	5	do do	
David Anglin		do do	
James Duke		Anthony Metcalf	
James McLair		Wm. Sullivant 35	
John Awtry		do do	
Willm. Duke	10	Chas. Williamson	
Willm. Adair		Do Do	
John T. Duke		Ephraim Bowin	
Benja. Petit		do do 40	
Gideon Patterson		Micajah Williamson Junr.	
do do	15	David Shaffer	
do (minute) do		Joel Bowins	
Robert Harper Senr		Bentley Stocks	
George Harper		John Seay 45	

97

```
Alexr. awtry             Abram. Hammond
David Philips    20      Leonard Philips
Isaac Atwood             Philip Guize
John Bankston            Priscilla Jennings
Willm Harper             Jacob Trash [?]   50
Saml. Harper             Chas. Dean
Robert Harper    25      John Dean
Erasmus Brewer           Peter Williamson
David Anglin             Richard Philips   54
```

Augusta 12th April 1784. Ten days after date hereof for value received
I promise to pay or cause to be paid unto David Rees or Order Eight
Pounds fourteen shillings specie the Dolls at 4s8. also short pay in
Certificates Eight shillings and two pence /s/ M Williamson"

3.   Roster of Captain Abner Bickham's Company, Burke County Militia,
     Records Group 93, National Archives.

[This roster was originally part of the Revolutionary War Pension
Statement of Abner Bickham, Ga. S 30274, Military Service Records,
National Archives, but was later removed and incorrectly filed under
"Georgia Continentals" in Records Group 93.]

A Pay Role [sic] of the Commissioned and none [sic] Commissioned
officers and Privates of Capt. Abner Bickham Company of Malitia [sic]
of Burk [sic] County in the State of Georgia Commanded by Colonel Asa
Emanuel from the 15th. august 1781 to 5th February 1782 with the
Subsistence Monie [sic].

[Amount of money paid to each soldier and length of service are also
included on the original manuscript.]

```
 1.  Abner Bickham     Capn.        19.  [illegible]       Private
 2.  Willm. Young      1st Lieut.   20.  Moses Davis          do
 3.  Wm Darcy          2nd Lieut.   21.  Petr. Young          do
 4.  David Emanuel     Privates     22.  John Wodkins         do
 5.  [illegible                     23.  Robt. Barrow         do
        Patterson      do           24.  Jacob Young          do
 6.  [illegible]                    25.  Robt. Allen          do
        Bowling        do           26.  John Bryan           do
 7.  [illegible] gamble  do         27.  Benjn. Moxly         do
 8.  Joel Darcy        do           28.  Robt. Boykin         do
 9.  [illegible]                    29.  Chas. Birch [?]      do
        Patterson      do           30.  Edwd. Birch          do
10.  Thos Ford         do           31.  James Darcy          do
11.  Wm Underwood      do           32.  John Canady          do
12.  James Davis       do           33.  [illegible]          do
13.  John Peal [Qeal?]  do          34.  [illegible]          do
14.  Jacob godoin      do
15.  Benjn. Darcy      do
16.  John Farner [?]   do
17.  James Braiton     do
18.  [illegible]       do
```


4.   Military Commissions in Commission Book B, Georgia Department of
     Archives and History.

pp. 229-30

Matthew Stewart - 8 February 1777 - Lieutenant, Grenidier Company.
Abraham Ravot - [no date]*- Major, Effingham County Battalion.
Henry Cuyler - 20 October 1778 - Captain, Light Infantry Company.
John Lyons - 20 October 1778 - Second Lieutenant, Light Infantry Company.
  * [Probably 20 October 1778]

John Landeford - 19 July 1777 - Colonel of Battalion of Militia, Liberty County.
John Elliott - 9 July 1777 - Lieutenant Colonel.
James Maxwell - 9 July 1777 - Major.
Moses Way - 9 July 1777 - Captain.
Lewis Matture - 9 July 1777 - First Lieutenant.
Joseph Lewis - 9 July 1777 - Second Lieutenant.
Francis Brown - 10 July 1777 - Captain, Company of Militia, Liberty County.
Jonathan Bacon - 10 July 1777 - First Lieutenant.
Peter Goulding - 10 July 1777 - Second Lieutenant.
John Bacon - 11 July 1777 - Captain, Company of Rifle Men, Liberty County.
Thomas Bacon - 11 July 1777 - First Lieutenant.
Edward Ball - 11 July 1777 - Second Lieutenant.
Joseph Oswald - 12 July 1777 - Captain, Company of Rangers, Liberty County.
James Carter - 12 July 1777 - First Lieutenant.
William Middleton - 12 July 1777 - Second Lieutenant.

George Wells - 20 August 1777 - Colonel, Fourth Battalion of Militia, Wilkes County.
Zachariah Lamar - 20 August 1777 - Lieutenant Colonel.
Absolom Bedell - 20 August 1777 - Major.

Philip Howell - 26 July 1777 - Colonel, Effingham County Battalion.
Andrew Elton Wells - 26 July 1777 - Lieutenant Colonel
Daniel Bonnell - 26 July 1777 - Major.

John Martin - 24 February 1777 - Lieutenant Colonel, First Battalion, First Regiment of Foot Militia.
Richard Wylly - 24 February 1777 - Major, [same unit].

William Stephens - 17 June 1776 - Captain, Volunteer or Grenideier Company.
Benjamin Loyd - 18 February 1777 - Second Lieutenant, [same company].

John McCleur - 22 June 1776 - Captain, First Company of Foot Militia, Town of Savannah.
William Evans - 5 July 1776 - Lieutenant, [same unit].

Daniel McMurphy - 30 July 1776 - Lieutenant Colonel, Battalion of Foot Militia, Queensborough District.

Ambrose Wright - 26 February 1776 - Commissr., German Fuziliers.
James Gallache - 4 April 1776 - First Lieutenant, [same unit].
Thomas Dowle - 4 April 1776 - Second Lieutenant, [same unit].
James Flint - 4 April 1776 - Third Lieutenant, [same unit].

Jenkins Davies - 16 July 1776 - Captain, Company of Militia, Ebenezer District, Effingham County.
Daniel Zettler - 16 July 1776 - First Lieutenant, [same unit].
Daniel Burgesteiner - 16 July 1776 - Second Lieutenant, [same unit].

John Gasper Greiner - 19 July 1777 - First Lieutenant, Bethany Company, Effingham County.
Jacob Cranberger - 19 July 1777 - Commr. and Captain, [same unit].
Frederick Schuemph - 23 July 1777 - First Lieutenant, [same unit].
Benjamin Mieser - 22 July 1777 - Second Lieutenant, [same unit].

Richard Gnnyn - 4 March 1777 - Captain, Cherokee Hill Company.
William Brack - 27 September 1777 - First Lieutenant, [same unit].
Nathaniel Langley - 4 March 1777 - Third Lieutenant, [same unit].

John Sharp - 10 October 1777 - Captain, Burke County.
Jared Handley - 10 October 1777 - First Lieutenant, Burke County.
James Hall - 10 October 1777 - Second Lieutenant, Burke County.

Thomas Alexander - 3 August 1776 - Lieutenant, Queensborough District, Company Commanded by Captain Hugh Alexander.

John Poutell - 24 October 1777 - Captain, Grenidier Company, Effingham County.
Martin Dasher - 25 October 1777 - First Lieutenant, [same unit].
Christopher Cronberge   25 October 1777 - Second Lieutenant, [same unit].

Daniel Gunnel - 28 May 1777 - Captain, Second Company, Fourth Battalion.

Charles Odingsell - 8 July 1776 - Lieutenant, Sixth Company of Foot Militia, Little Ogeechee District, Commanded by Captain Stephen Dean.

John Thomas - 17 November 1777 - Colonel, Burke County Battalion of Militia.
John Jones - 17 November 1777 - Lieutenant Colonel, [same unit].
Francis Pugh - 17 November 1777 - Major, [same unit].

John Adam Nessler - 8 November 1777 - Captain, Militia Company, Burke County.
Joseph Shoemack - 8 November 1777 - First Lieutenant, [same unit].
James Montgomery - 8 November 1777 - Second Lieutenant, [same unit].

William Bailey - 28 May 1777 - First Lieutenant, Second Company of Militia, Commanded by Daniel Gunnel.
Elijah Goolsby - 12 January 1778 - Second Lieutenant, Second Company Fourth Battalion. Commanded by Daniel Gunnel.

[Other military commissions from this volume are abstracted in Part I: F. Burke County.]

C. STATE TROOPS

1. Roster from the Telamon Cuyler Collection, Special Collections, University of Georgia Libraries.

The State of Georgia Dr To: Lieut. Colo. William McIntosh 1776 For the payment of the first Troop of Light Horse From the time of Their Different Enlistments up to the 16th June at 40g pr month. . .

[Actual amounts owed to each man are shown on the original manuscript.]

Apl 25th	Ebenezr: Callender Doctr. to 1st November
20th	Lachlan McIntosh Qr. Master to 1st November
	Hugh Matthewson, as a private, 22nd April to 16 June
	From 16 June appointed Serjt.
Apl 25th	Robt. Wilson, Serjt. 2 months
30th	William Cain Enlisted Serjt. to Last of October
Do 30th	David FitzJarrell as private, 1 month 17 days
June 16th	appointed Corpl:

--- Privates ---

Apl. 22nd	William Lain, to 1st Novr.	
	Pierce Lain, as William Lain	
	Abner Eilands	Do.
	John Hoover	Do.
	Joseph Baisdon	Do.
Apl. 25th	Richd. Stevens to 1st Novr.	
	John Weeks as Richd. Stevens	
	Jams. Cherry	Do.
	Randle Ramsey	Do
	Francis McKinnie to 24th June when he went to Capt.	
	Havenden of the 4th Troop	

```
July              deserted Patk. Kelly
25th April        deserted Michl. Chandler
27th              Robt. Brown, to 1st Novr.
                  Jams. Houston, as Robt. Brown
                  John Finley  Do.
                  Thos. Bryan  Do.
                  Thos. Clark  Do.
                  Stephen Clark  Do.

5th May           John Crooks to 1st Novr.
                  George Ruminer as Jno Crooks
                  John Malpress  Do.
                  Ezekiel Malpress  Do.
                  Willm. Forsyth  Do.
                  John Arnold  Do.

5th Do.           Andrew Russell 3 months one day
                  John Bates [Bales?] 20 days
                  Willm. McCalphin 3 months five days

7th               Jno. Gray to 1st Novr.
                  Moses Bennett 20 days

13                Jacob McCullough to 1st Novr.
                  John Elliot 26 days

5th June          John Canty to the 1st Novr.
6th June          James Murphy to the 1st Novr.

11th              John Keen to the 1st Novr.

12th              Ephraim Vanzant to the 1st Novr.
                  Saml. Mason as Ephn. Vanzant
                  Willm. Pringle  Do.
                  Charles Pringle  Do.
                  James Pringe     Do.
                  David Pringle    Do.

13th              Jacob Sourjournor to 1st Novr.
                  Elijah Peters as Jacob Sourjourner
                  Mark King        Do.
                  Philamon Walters  Do.

8 July            John Hill        Do.
10th              Arthr. Sykes     Do.

30th              John Gorden      Do.
                  Miles Raleigh    Do.
                  Thos. Coleman    Do.
```

Pay Roll of the Guard at the State house from the 8th day of January
to the 8th day of April 1777 both days inclusive

[Actual amounts owed to each man are included on the original manuscript.]

Thomas Johnson	Captn	91 days
Michael Schley	Private	do
George Johnson	do	do
Jacob Peterson	do	do

A Pay Roll of Capt. John Lamar's Company of Light Horse, enlisted for
the Defence [sic] of the State during the Florida Expedition in 1777.

[Actual amounts owed to each man for the period of 9 June to 12 August
1777 appear on the original manuscript.]

John Lamar   Captn.
Geo. Philips   Lieut.
William Barram
John Palmer
Sherwood Bugg Junr.
John Hicks
John Ely
Samuel Bugg
Nathaniel Hicks Junr.
Edward Prather
Simon Cushman

Phillip Higgenbottom
James Jackson
John Magae [McGee]
John Fanner
Roger Quarles [Quailes]
John Farvin
Daniel Daniely
Thomas Smith
Martin Shirley
John Stratford
John Winn

2. From 19th-Century Copies of Original Rosters in the DeRenne Collec-
    tion, Special Collections, University of Georgia Libraries.

1778 Major Jacks Battalion of State Troops
David Dickson Capt receipt to Wm Martin DQm of Sam Jack Batt
DEramine Wilson [?] major comdg the five independent companies to
Chas Laslie Commissary for Issue

John Farley, Lieut - Provision return - for 1 Capt
                                            1 Lieut
                                            4 Segn
                                            28 Priv   Trice Blue Company
                                            1 Fife
                                            1 Drummer
John McCleaur Capt of [illegible word] - on Mr. Stiles   do
David Waters Lieut   do
Joseph Dunlap - draws ration in connection with   do

Cherokee Company
Richd Gunn signs register on Saml Stikes for 18 men Cherokee Comp
Wm Ross Lieut.   do

Abram Rawoth Sign as Major registers for men belonging to the
County of Effingham doing duty at Cherokee Hill.

Wm Baker Capt makes requisition for Capt Baker's volunteers
                    1 capt 1 Lt 2 sgts & 15 privts

Thos Dowell - Lieut 17 men at Coffee Bluff

Jas Galach 1st Lieut with 13 men at Bewly

Abraham Gay makes rations return for Militia under his command at
Fort McIntosh.

3. Bounty Land Certificates, Telamon Cuyler Collection, Special Collec-
    tions, University of Georgia.

Below are abstracts of bounty certificates issued by the State of
Georgia, after the Revolution, to her soldiers, sailors, citizens, and
refugees of the war. These are from Box 68, Telamon Cuyler Collection,
Special Collections, University of Georgia Libraries. Other such
certificates are on file in the Georgia Surveyor General Department.

GEORGIA STATE MINUTE BATTALIONS, 3 June 1777 - 1 March 1778

The Certificates below were issued to the men who served in the 1st and 2nd Georgia State Minute Battalions. Officially, these two units only existed from 3 June 1777 to 1 March 1778 but evidence has been found that they were continued long enough to serve in the third and last invasion of British East Florida in the summer of 1778. Enlisted men for these units appear to have all been recruited from outside of Georgia, particularly from South Carolina.

Name	Rank	Certified By
File Ba - Ha		
Anthony Cooper	Soldier, Minutemen	Elijah Clarke, lt. col., 19 Oct. 1784
Benjamin Chisolm	Lieutenant, Minutemen	Saml. Jack, col., 5 Apr. 1784
James Magen	Soldier, Minutemen	Elijah Clarke, lt. col., 2 Feb. 1785
James Hall (of S.C.)	Private, Minutemen	Saml. Jack, col., 13 Mar. 1784
William Ham	Sergeant, Minuteman	Saml. Jack, col., 5 April 1784
James Hambleton	Soldier, Minutemen	Elijah Clarke, lt. col., 25 Jan. 1785
Joseph Harper	Sergeant, Minutemen	Elijah Clarke, lt. col., 25 Feb. 1784
George Hart	Soldier, Minutemen	Saml. Jack, col. 29 Jan. 1784
Henry Hartley	Soldier, Minutemen	Elijah Clarke, lt. col., 21 June 1784
Peter Harris* (Catawba Indian)	Private, Minutemen	Saml. Jack, col. 25 Mar. 1784
Cesar Hawkins	Soldier, 1st Bn. Minutemen	Elijah Clarke, lt. col., 7 Apr. 1784

* State of Georgia.
This is to certify, That Peter Harris Cutaba Indian was Enlisted--to ferve as a private--in the ___ Battalion of Minute-Men, raifed for the Defence of this State, by Refolve of Affembly, paffed the 3d June, 1777; and that the faid Peter Harris Cutaba Indian was not, at the Time of his Enlistment-an Inhabitant of this State, nor had he refided in any Part thereof for Twelve Months preceeding his Enlistment And furhter, That he was in Service at the Time the faid Battalion was reduced by a fubfequent Refolve of March 1ft, 1778.

Given under my Hand at Augusta this
25th Day of March 1784.
Saml Jack Col

Name	Rank	Certified By
James Hawkins	Captain, 1st Bn. Minutemen	Elijah Clarke, lt. col., ,7 Apr. 1784
Richard Haylewood	Soldier, Minutemen	Elijah Clarke, lt. col., 16 Nov. 1784
File He - Ho		
Robert Heatley (of Camden Co., S.C.)	Minutemen	Saml. Jack, col.
Edward Heil	Private, Minutemen	Saml. Jack, col., 26 Apr. 1784

Name	Rank	Certified By
William Henderson	Lieutenant, Minutemen	Saml. Jack, col., 8 Apr. 1784
Zachariah Henderson	Lieutenant, Minutemen	Elijah Clarke, lt. col., 2 Mar. 1784
Nicholas Higgins	Soldier, Minutemen	Elijah Clarke, lt. col., 25 Jan. 1785
James Hill	Soldier, Minutemen	Elijah Clarke, lt. col., 3 Apl. 1784
James Hogges	Soldier, Minutemen	Elijah Clarke, lt. col., 6 May 1784
Saml. Hogg	Soldier, Minutemen	Elijah Clarke, lt. col., 3 Apl. 1784
Thomas Holland	Soldier, Minutemen	Elijah Clarke, lt. col., 25 Jan. 1785
Francis Holton	Private Soldier, Minutemen	Elijah Clarke, lt. col., 6 Apl. 1784
Thomas Hopkins	Soldier, Minutemen	Elijah Clarke, lt. col., 25 Feb. 1784
Wilder Housley	Sergeant, Minutemen	Elijah Clarke, lt. col., 29 Mar. 1784
Henry Houston	Private, Minutemen	Saml. Jack, col., 13 Mar. 1784
James Houston	Private, Minutemen	Saml. Jack, col., 13 Mar. 1784
William Houston	Private, Minutemen	Saml. Jack, col., 13 Mar. 1784
Charles Howard	Soldier, Minutemen	Elijah Clarke, lt. col., Jan. 1785
David Howard	Soldier, Minutemen	Elijah Clarke, lt. col., 18 Feb. 1785
Henry Howard	Soldier, Minutemen	Elijah Clarke, lt. col., 4 Jan. 1785
John Howard	Soldier, Minutemen	Elijah Clarke, lt. col., 16 Nov. 1784
Caleb Howell	Major, Minutemen	Elijah Clarke, lt. col., 2 Feb. 1784
Robert Heatly	Private, Minutemen	Elijah Clarke, lt. col., 14 May 1784

File Hu - J

Name	Rank	Certified By
Robert Huggins	Soldier, Minutemen	Elijah Clarke, lt. col., 4 Nov. 1784
Isaac Hughs	Private, Minutemen	Saml. Jack, col. 13 Mar. 1784

[A petition attached to this certificate explains that Isaac Hughs died while serving in Captain David Dickson's company of Minutemen. Isaac Hughs was the son of John Hughs of Camden District, S. C.]

Name	Rank	Certified By
John Hughs	Private, Minutemen	Saml. Jack, col., 13 Mar. 1784
Nicholas Hews	Soldier, Minutemen	Elijah Clarke, lt. col., 3 Apl. 1784
William Hunt	Soldier, Minutemen	Elijah Clarke, lt. col., 5 Nov. [?]
John Hulls [Hutts?]	Soldier, Minutemen	Elijah Clarke, lt. col., Dec. 1784
Peter Inlow	Private, Minutemen	Saml. Jack, col., 26 Apr. 1784
John Jackson	Soldier, 1st Bn. Minutemen	Elijah Clarke, lt. col., 21 June 1784
William Johnson	Soldier, Minutemen	Elijah Clarke, lt. col., 6 Apr. 1784
David Johnston	Soldier, Minutemen	Elijah Clarke, lt. col., 6 Apr. 1784

Name	Rank	Certified By
Daniel Johnston	Sergeant, Minutemen	Elijah Clarke, lt. col., 20 Apr. 1784
James Johnston	Sergeant, Minutemen	Elijah Clarke, lt. col., 5 Apr. 1784
Wm. Johnston	Soldier, Minutemen	Elijah Clarke, lt. col., 3 Apl. 1784
David Jones	Minutemen	Elijah Clarke, lt. col., 22 May 1784
James Jones (heirs of)	Minutemen	Elijah Clarke, lt. col., 28 July 1786
Jesse Jones	Soldier, Minutemen	Elijah Clarke, lt. col., 3 Jan. 1785
Richard Jones	Soldier, Minutemen	Caleb Howell, major 29 Sep. 1784

[The certificate for Richard Jones shows that he served until after the "floridy Expodition."]

File K

Archibald Kell	Soldier, Minutemen	Saml. Jack, col., 21 Sept. 1784
Edward Kelly	Soldier, Minutemen	Elijah Clarke, lt. col., 3 Apl. 1784
John Kelley	Soldier, Minutemen	Elijah Clarke, lt. col., 7 Apl. 1784
Thos. Kelley	Soldier, Minutemen	Elijah Clarke, lt. col., 7 Apl. 1784
Wm. Kelley Sr.	Soldier, Minutemen	Elijah Clarke, lt. col., 7 Apl. 1784
Hugh Kelsey	Sergeant, Minutemen	Samuel Jack, col., 13 Mar. 1784
James Kelly	Private, Minutemen	Samuel Jack, col., 6 Apl. 1784
Thomas Kelsey	Private, Minutemen	Samuel Jack, col. 13 Mar. 1784
John Kilgore	Soldier, Minutemen	Elijah Clarke, lt. col., 6 Apl. 1784
Benjamin Kimbell	Soldier, 1st Bn. Minutemen	Jno. Stewart, col., 27 July 1784
William Kembell	Soldier, Minutemen	Jno. Stewart, col., 27 July 1784
Henry King	Soldier, Minutemen	Elijah Clarke, lt, col., 10 Oct. 1784
John Kitchens	Private, Minutemen	Saml. Jack, col., 5 April 1784
John Kitts	Private, Minutemen	Saml. Jack, col., 22 Apr. 1784

File L

William Lockhart	Soldier, Minutemen	Elijah Clarke, lt. col., 10 Oct. 1784
Samuel Lomacks	Soldier, Minutemen	Jno. Stewart, col., 19 Apr. 1784
Luke Lamar	Soldier, Minutemen	Elijah Clarke, lt. col., 25 Feb. 1784
Moses Leapham	Private, Minutemen	Samuel Jack, col., 26 Apr. 1784
Gilbert Lee	Private, Minutemen	Samuel Jack, col., 22 Apr. 1784
Benjamin Lemar	Soldier, Minutemen	Elijah Clarke, lt. col., 25 Jan. 1785
Richard Levans	Soldier, Minutemen	Elijah Clarke, lt. col., 7 Apr. 1784
James Lewellon	Soldier, Minutemen	Elijah Clarke, lt. col., Apr. 1784

Name	Rank	Certified By
William Lewelon	Soldier, Minutemen	Elijah Clarke, lt. col., 6 Apr. 1784
Andw. Lithgow Senr.	Private, Minutemen	Saml. Jack, col., 27 Mar. 1784
Robert Lithgow	Soldier, Minutemen	Elijah Clarke, col., 8 Apr. 1784
Andrew Lithgrow Jnr.	Private, Minutemen	Saml. Jack, col., 27 Mar. 1784

File M - Z

Name	Rank	Certified By
Mark Littleton	Sergeant, Minutemen	Elijah Clarke, lt. col., 3 Apr. 1784
Benjamin Lockhart	Private, Minutemen	Saml. Jack, col., 7 Apr. 1784
Henry Long	Second Lieutenant (Captain James Pettigrew's Company, Minutemen)	Elijah Clarke, lt. col., 20 May 1784
John Long	Lieutenant, Minutemen	Samuel Jack, col., 17 May 1784
Jesse Love	Soldier, Minutemen	Elijah Clarke, lt. col., 16 Nov. 1784
John Low	Soldier, Minutemen	Elijah Clarke, lt. col., 20 Apr. 1784
Jesse Lunce	Private, Minutemen	Samuel Jack, col., 22 Apr. 1784
Anthony Metcalf	Lieutenant, Minutemen	Samuel Jack, col., 27 July 1778 (dishcarge, Medway Meeting House)
John Stedham	Soldier, Minutemen	Elijah Clarke, lt. col., 2 Feb. 1784
John Steel	Lieutenant, Minutemen	Saml. Jack, col., 8 Apr. 1784
Joseph Robinson	Soldier, Minutemen	

OTHER CERTIFICATES IN THE SAME FILES

Within the files of certificates for the Georgia Revolutionary War Minutemen, are a few bounty certificates and other records. Those for Revolutionary War service are:

"The State of Georgia

     To Lettice Duke   Dr
To four years Provision made by a Law Pass'd at augusta (in favor of Widows who Lost their Husbands in the Lat Contest) in January 1782 £64.20
    I do hereby certify that Henry Duke was Killed in November Eighty and left three children under ten years of age
The above children
are all her living

/s/ Daniel Coleman

       /s/ Jno. Lindsay
           Elijah Clark Col.
           Daniel Coleman, J.P."

[On the reverse: "Order given 26th Novr. 1784."]

John McDuffey, 2nd Battalion Richmond County Militia, certified by Col. G. Lee, 25 February 1784.

John. Perkins, Georgia State Legion, served from fall of Augusta to evacuation of Savannah, certified by Jas. Jackson, lt. col., 6 April 1784.

Petition, 28 January 1791, for appointment of Captain Walker Richardson in the Elbert County militia. Mentions that Richardson entered the army as a private in 1776 and was later a lieutenant in the foot service and captain lieutenant in the artillery. /s/ Frans. Willis; Thos. Martin, lieut. 3rd Bn. of Infantry; Nathl. Durkee, capt.; and Joseph Ryan, major.

The following certificates, also found in these particular files, do not prove Revolutionary War but relate to service against the Indians in the late 1780's:

Name	Unit	Certified By
Zephariah Franklin	Soldier, Col. John Clark's State Troops	Captain Samuel Beckaem, 8 Sep. 1793
Nimrod Bartlett	Capt. James Giles Company State Troops	John Wereat, auditor, 4 Dec. 1793
Tucker Woodard	1st Regmt, State Troops Captain Thomas Cole's Company	J. Meriwether, Deputy Auditor 2 July 1793
Joseph Williams	Captain William Ross' Company State Troops	

4. Records From the Military Records Collection, Georgia Department of Archives and History.

Georgia

Know all Men by their Presents that We George Walton, Benjamin Thompson, and George Bagby of the County of Wilkes Esquires, are held and firmly bound and obliged unto his Honor John Houstoun Esquire Captain General Governor and Commander in Chief of the said State in the full and just Sum of Eight thousand pounds lawful Money of the said State, to be paid to the said John Houstoun his Successors Governor or Commander in Chief for the time being or his or their assigns, For which payment will and truly to be made and done. We bind ourselves our Heirs, Executors, and Administrators and every of them by these presents

Sealed with our Seals and dated the Sixth day of February in the year of our Lord One thousand Seven hundred and Seventy Eight Whereas the Honorabl the Executive Council of this State have appointed the above bounded George Walton Commissary to the two Battalions of Minute Men raised for the defence of this State and gave an Order on the Treasurers for the payment of the Sum of Four thousand pounds current Money of the State aforesaid to him the said George Walton for the purpose of Buying and providing provisions for the said two Battalions.

Now the Condition of the foregoing Obligation is such that if the said George Walton his Heirs, Executors, or Administrators shall and do from time to time and at all times hereafter until the Twelfth--day of March--next provide for and supply the aforesaid two Battalions with good and in wholesome provisions in the like proportion as is ordered for the Continental Troops within this State, at and after the rate of three Shillings per Ration, and repay the aforesaid Sum of Four thousand pounds, or otherwise account for the same when called upon by the Assembly, Executive Council, or others by them authorized for that purpose, then the above obligation to be void, otherwise to be abd remain in full force and virtue.

George Walton

Sealed and Delivered
    In presence of
Saml. Stirks J. P.

            Geo Bagby   Benja Thompson

[Reverse]

    Jan.6h Feby 1778 recd of the Governor an order on the Treasury
of this Date for four thousand pounds, and or· of the Minite Battalions & of their Commissary.

                              George Walton
Bond of

    George Walton
    Benj. Thomson
    Geo. Bagby

State of Georgia

    This is to Certify that Hugh Alexander was Commissioned to Serve
as a Lieutenant in the Battallion of Minute men, raised for the Defence
of this State, by Resolve of General Assembly passed the 3rd June 1777,
and further that he was on the florida Expedition during the Campaign.

    Given under my hand at Augusta this 21st day of April 1784.

                              Saml Jack   JP

            [On Reverse]
    Lieut Hugh Alexander No 237
        Hugh Alexander   5.

State of Georgia

    This is to Certify that William Ammons was enlisted to serve as a
Soldier in the Battallion of Minute men, raised for the defence of this
State by resolve of Assembly, pass the 3d of June 1777 and the said
William Ammons was not at the time of his enlistment an inhabitant of
this State nor had he resided in any part thereof for Six months preceeding his enlistment & further that he was in Service at the time the
said battallion was reduced by a subsequent resolve of March 7th 1778.

By His order   Given under my hand at Augusta this 2d.

Hora[1] Marbury   day of Feby. 1785

                    E. Clarke Lt Colo

    [On Reverse]
William Ammons
    No 313

108

Morning Report of Coll. James Jackson's Infantry, Georgia
State Troops   27 August 1781

	Commd Offers		None Commd Offrs				Rank & file					Total
	Capt.	Lieut.	Ensign	Qr. Master	Sergt. Mr.	Sergants	Drumr.	fit for Duty	Sick Present	Sick on furrlough	on Commd.	Artificers	
	2	1	0	1	1	3	1	25	6	13	1	10	60

John Morrison
Capt of Infantry

[Reverse]

Morning Report

A Report of Arms & Accounterments in Infantry Company Coll.
James Jackson's Legion Georgia State Troops 27 August 1781

20 Muskets
17 Carabines
10 Cartridge Boxes
10 Bayonets with belts

John Morrison Capt
of Infantry

[Reverse]
Report Arms Ammn.
&c

Return of the Legion Horse & Infantry under Marching Orders 30 Sept. 1781

	Commissd Officers Staff			non Commissd			Total
	Capt.	Subd	Q.M.	L. Majr	Serjt	rank & file	
Horse	1	2		1	4	28	36
Infantry	2	1	1	1	2	28	35
Total	3	3	1	2	6	56	71

Sick in Town & on Furlow   15
Artificers left with   13   Certified Jas Jackson Lt. Col.
Lieut. Hamilton   28   Commt G. L. Legion
To March   28
                            56 Privates   [On Reverse]
                                          Legion of Horse   Returns

109

1. Names of Georgia Continentals from the Virginia Gazette, 1776-1779.

[Except where noted, the men named here deserted in Virginia, and in many instances may not have been arrested and made to serve in Georgia. The author would like to express a special thanks to Dr. Edward Cashin of Augusta College for bringing the 12 March 1779 list of deserters to his attention.]

Virginia Gazette, Dixon and Hunter, 13 December 1776 (p. 4, c. 1)
    Officers: Major S. J. Cuthbert, 2nd Georgia Battalion.

Ibid., 24 January 1777 (p. 4, c. 1)
    Officers: Lieutenant Robert Ward, 2nd Georgia Battalion.
    Deserters: Hugh Green; Micajah Defoos; James Stephens; John Wilson; John Caine; Benjamin Delk.

Ibid., 7 March 1777 (p. 2, c. 1)
    Officers: Lieutenant John Clarke, 3rd Company, 2nd Georgia Battalion.
    Deserters (recruited by Lieutenant Winfree in Albemarle County): Robert Tate; Andrew Hardy; Bartlett Anderson.

Ibid., 19 December 1777 (p. 3, c. 2)
    Officers: Captain Thomas Scott, 3rd Georgia Battalion.
    Deserters: Caleb Hunter from Amelia County; Obediah Ferguson; Ambrose Luthas; Isham Dyke; David Womack; John Johnson; William Bartlett; John Moore Clay; William Woodruff; Alexander Bartlett; William Jones; Andrew King.

Virginia Gazette, Purdie, 14 February 1777 (p. 3, c. 3)
    Officers: Captain Benjamin Porter; Lieutenant William D. Strother.

Ibid., 28 February 1777 (p. 2, c. 2)
    Officers: Lieutenant Alex Baugh, Captain Smith's Company, 2nd Georgia Battalion.
    Deserters: William Dorton of Williamsburg; William Strange of Brunswick; John Williams; Robert Wilkins of Henrico; John Lee and John Stith of Bedford; John Vest of Buckingham; Thomas Kelly.

Ibid., 28 February 1777 (supplement, p. 2, c. 1)
    Officers: Ensign Abraham Jones, Captain Francis Moore's Company, 2nd Georgia Battalion.
    Deserters: Nathaniel Hall; Thomas Ellis; Littleton Williamson; Beverly Shelton; John Jordan; William Adams; Elisha Heathcock.

Ibid., 7 March 1777 (supplement, p. 2, c. 2)
    Officers: Captain William Smith, 2nd Georgia Battalion; Lieutenant John Hawkins.
    Deserters: Patrick Duffy; William Hardy; Owen Cawfield; Charles Melton; Charles Phillis (sometimes called John Ferr).

Virginia Gazette, Purdie, 6 December 1776 (p. 3, c. 2)
    Officers: Captain William Smith, 2nd Georgia Battalion.
    Deserters: Patrick Duffy, Emanuel Kelly.

Ibid., 27 December 1776 (p. 3, c. 2)
    Officers: Captain Joseph Pannill's Company enlisted by Moses Hawkins; Lieutenants Ward, Hancock; Ensign Morrison.
    Deserters: James Parker; William McClure; Edward Cantwell; Simon Savage; James Kemp; Elijah Ellis; Daniel Bailey; James Fleming; Joseph Sampson; Cornelius Fitzgerald; William Grant; John Ray; John McConnelly. They were from Augusta, Frederick, and Dunmore counties.

Ibid., 27 December 1776 (p. 4, c. 3)

TEN DOLLARS REWARD

For securing WILLIAM FRAZER, a soldier in my company, enlisted for the defence of the state of Georgia. He is a slender made man, about 19 years of age, has short light coloured hair, and said he lived in Hampton, but was born in Chesterfield, at or near Osborne's warehouse. The said Frazer enlisted with me in Williamsburg the 27th of last August, and at his request I granted him a furlough for 30 days, at the end of which time he was to join my company at Newgate, in Loudown county, but has not as yet appeared. I will give the above reward to any person that secures the said Frazer in any publick jail, and advertises the same in this paper, or TWENTY DOLLARS if delivered to me at the above mentioned place.

WILLIAM LANE. jun. capt.

Ibid., 3 January 1777 (supplement, p. 2, c. 1)
Officers: Captain William Smith, 2nd Georgia Battalion; Lieutenant John Hawkins.

Ibid., 10 January 1777 (p. 4, c. 2)
Officers: Lieutenant Alexander Baugh, 2nd Georgia Battalion. Recruits: John Lee and John Stith of Bedford; John Vest of Buckingham; Robert Watkins of Henrico; John Dorton, John Williams, William Strange, and Anthony Hooper enlisted at Williamsburg.

Ibid., 21 March 1777 (supplement, p. 2, c. 2)
Officers: Lieutenant Daniel Duval; Captain Francis Moore, 2nd Georgia Battalion.

Ibid., 9 May 1777 (p. 4, c. 2)
Officers: Second Lieutenant Elisha Miller, Captain William Lane's Company, 2nd Georgia Battalion.
Deserters: Steph Rice; John Miller; Sylvester Cary. They enlisted in "Loudown" County.

Ibid., 9 May 1777 (supplement, p. 1, c. a)
Officers: (4th Company, 2nd Georgia Battalion); Lieutenant Mosley; Shem Cook.
Deserters: Thomas Sack; John Sack; Robert Yates; James Arnold of Halifax County.

Ibid., 20 June 1777 (supplement, p. 1, c. 1)
Officers: First Lieutenant John Cunningham; Lieutenant Strother; Captain Benjamin Porter's Company, 2nd Georgia Battalion.
Deserters: Gabriel Wilkinson of Frederick County; Timothy Gerard of Winchester in Frederick County; Aaron Dilley; William Jenkins of Berkley County; Randolph Frigate of Culpepper; Nathaniel Berry (alias Smith); Joseph Price; Jeremiah Burley of King William; William Barton, William Hood, John Phillips of Dunmore; Thomas Robertson of Frederick; Benjamin Jones of Spotsylvania.

Ibid., 13 June 1777 (p. 3, c. 3)
"John Webster Joined Capt. Baird of the Georgia Service"
Officers: Isaac Hicks, 3rd Georgia Battalion.
Deserters: Benjamin Seaward; Thomas Williams.

Ibid., 12 September 1777 (p. 1, c. 3)
Officers: Captain John Dooly
Deserters (deserted from the Virginia troops and went to Georgia with Dooly): John Russell, George Russell, and William Harness, from Pittsylvania County.

Ibid., 28 November 1777 (p. 3, c. 1)
Snow Creek, Henry County October 27, 1774.
Deserted from Fort Salter's, in the New Purchase [Wilkes County]

111

of the State of Georgia, the following soldiers, viz. Benjamin
Meggerson, sergeant, from Buckingham. John Webster and David
Jennings, corprals, from Prince Edward. Joel Holland from
Cumberland. John Ramsey, Thomas Church and Jesse Mills from
Amherst. Joseph Lawrence and Ambrose Hutcheson from Henry.
James Navarre from Halifax. Andrew Clark from Loudon. Likewise
James Smith and Wallace Dunston, mulattoes, from Halifax. The
above soldiers chiefly enlisted by Capt. John Baird of the State
of Georgia. . .

· Shem Cook
2nd Georgia Battalion

Ibid., 28 November 1777 (p. 3, c. 2)
Officers: Lieutenant Barnard Paty, 4th Georgia Battalion.
Deserters: James M'Cormick; James M'Farland; John Mitchell;
John Hodges; Conor Sullivan, sergeant.

Ibid., 12 December 1777 (p. 3, c. 2)
Officers: Captain Jesse H. Walton, 2nd Georgia Battalion.
Deserters: James Harrifield from Prince Edward County:
Hawkins Briant of Bedford County; Thomas Moore of Brunswick
County; Charles Brooks of Loudon County; John Cock of
Halifax County; Joseph Ingram of Lunenberg County; Edward
James.

Virginia Gazette, Dixon and Hunter, 12 March 1779 (p. 3, c. 2)
Whereas the following soldiers have deserted from the third
[Georgia] continental regiment [or battalion], stationed in
the state of Georgia, and now lurking in this state, to the
great predjudice [sic] of the common good of America; this is
therefore to acquaint them, that if they will voluntarily
join their regiment by the first of May next, that they shall
be pardoned, and receive their pay and clothing that may be
due them, otherwise if they fail to accept of this indulgence,
I will give forty dollars reward for each deserter which shall
be secured in any of the jails of this commonwealth after the
above date. All soldiers who are on furlough in this state
or otherwise, are ordered to repair to Purgsburg, South
Carolina, immediately.
Given under my hand this 21st day of February, 1779.

RAWLEIGH DOWNMAN, 3d continental regt.

Return of the deserters names, deserted from the 3d continental regiment, since its arrival in the state of Georgia.

FIRST COMPANY

Calep Hunter, Corporal, Isham Dychs, Obediah Ferguson, William Bartley,
Philemon Burks, John McClay, William Wooderoffe, Ambrose Lucas, Roger
Tandy, John Johnson, Alexander Bartley, David Womack, and William Jones.

THIRD COMPANY

Charles Jones, James Randolph, Moses Batley, Francis Gams, Francis
Hopkins, John Wills, James Berry, Patrick Cochran, James Page, and
John Johnson Florry.

FOURTH COMPANY

Anthony Williams, Thomas Jones, John Canterbury, Jun. John Thomas,
James Smith, John Thompson, John Hailey, James Cunningham, William
Price, and William Musteen.

112

FIFTH COMPANY

Henry Donnel, Omes Walker, Benjamin Steward, Thomas Williams, Alexander Rise, William Hopper, James Cook, James Brakeen, Benjamin Edmundson, and James Butler.

SIXTH COMPANY

David Johnson, Munford Wilson, Joseph Burnet, Joseph Stacy, William Atkins, Soward Price, Joseph Smith, William Smith, Henry Lee, John Bates, and Guthridge Garland.

SEVENTH COMPANY

John Vaughn, Daniel Murray, John Sadler, Daniel Toley, Samuel Crawford, William Zidlidge, John Wells, John Carney, and John Culember.

EIGHTH COMPANY

John Philip, Richard Brown, John Nash, Champness Tearry, Joseph Clark, John Soleham, John Oldham, John Bowens, Richard Brim, James Brumfield, John Hewett, William Eastes, Richard Shores, James Burns, William Dearin, John Turley, John Bentley, Jesse Bradley, Peter Jones, Godfrey Burnet, and Benjamin Edmonson.

2.0. National Archives.

The following was compiled by Mrs. June Clark Hartel from the Revolutionary War Pension Statement of Samuel Scott, W 5998, Military Service Records, National Archives. It is used here with Mrs. Hartel's very kind permission.

Georgia, Virginia, Samuel Scott, Ann, W5998.
Captain, Ga., retired, Jan. 18, 1779.
wounded in an engagement with Tories
March 1778, Battle of Savannah.

7 papers containing accounts
an account book
a history of Capt. Samuel Scott's men's time.
(removed from this claim to be sent to the War Department, sent January 16, 1913).
Frame 0899, pension application.

Capt. Samuel Scott's pension application for widow Ann.

Ann Roy Scott married Samuel Scott, _____

Samuel Scott died, 20 June 1822

1776 - Nov 5 to 25 May 1777

State of Georgia to Capt Samuel Scott, Ł 2085.5.3

To:	Lt John Burk		Ł 176.
	Lt Joseph Cook		Ł 176
	Qr Mr		Ł 60.2.6.
		+	Ł 412.2.6

Note: There is a list of proofs forwarded with this application. Some items filed in other files.

List of Soldiers

1. William Cooper, Fincastle County
2. John Childress, Halafax County
3. Charles Wilson, Halafax County
4. Matthew Thomsin, Redford
5. Peter Wilson, Ha(lafax)
6. Thomas Hughs, Pittsylvania
7. Ben Hutson
8. Ben Donathan
9. Thomas Jeferis
10. Hull Hudson
11. Hawkins Donithan
12. Mark Powell
13. Stephen Wilson
14. William McGill
15. Thomas Hardin
16. George McDowling [?]
17. James Nawling
18. Philip Jacob Christy
19. Peater Blackley
20. John Patmore
21. Josiah Puckate
22. James Hendley
23. Francis Northcut
24. John Vaughn
25. William Atwood
26. Thomas Lewis
27. John Crain
28. Joseph Burke
29. Richard Hazelwood
30. Samuel Beasle

This is to certify that I have received the contents of the above of Capt Saml Scott expended for the soldiers given from by hand April 29th, 1777.   William Armstrong

Peter Blackley, enlisted 13 Aug
John Parmer, Sept 5th
Josiah Perchet, Sept 5th
Francis Northcut, Sept 5th
William Alwood, Sept 5th
Thomas Lewis, Sept 5th
John Crain, Sept 5th
Phillip Jacob Chrisby, 1 Aug
James Nowlin, 25 July
Benjamin Hutchson, 4th July
Peter Wilson, 8 July
Thomas Huse, Jun 27th
Stephen Wilson, 8 July
Charles Wilson, July 8
Mark Powell, July 17th

Benjamin Jonathan, July 10th
George Nowlin, Jun 28
Richard Hazlewood, Sept 10th
Thomas Jeffras, July 8th
Raul Hutchson, July 1st
Hawkin Donathan, 20 July
William McGill, July 8th
Thomas Harding, July 9th
William Gibs, Sept 27th
Peter Blackley, Sept. 27th
_____ Huse, Sept. 27th
Thomas Hardin, Sept 27th
John Crain, Sept 27th
_____ Hindly, Sept 27th
Thomas Jeffras, Sept 27th

George Brock, dr to ballance for horse	12.16
Thomas Jones, dr to ballance for horse	3.11
William Craff___, dr to Ballance for horse	36.1
Thomas Watkins, dr to ballance for horse	11.4
William Lake, dr to ballance for horse	30.3
William Butler, dr to ballance for horse	6.16
William Robinson, dr to ballance for horse	18.16
William Shuman [?] dr to ballance for horse	3.11
Sollomon Porter, dr to ballance	0.14
Jonathin Hunt, dr to ballance	9.1
Thomas Butler, dr to ballance	5.7
William Tidler, dr to ballance	9.3
Phillemon Crain, dr to ballance	.14
Thomas Gimbo, dr to ballance	.19
William Warren, dr to ballance	.7
Daniel Wormack, dr to ballance	17.1
Wetham Watkins, dr to ballance	12.8
John Scales, dr to ballance	1.1

                    Ł 181.14.3
                    Ł 338.8.6
                    Ł 520.2

The above accounts are due to Capt Samuel Scott from the soldiers for horses for the use of this state, the whole amount is Ł 520.2.9.

July 7, 1777

kec'd of Captain Samuel Scott wages in full to the 25th of May from
the date enlisted in the Georgia service:

W. Bartlett	Jacob Crist
Isham Ward	Edmond Hart
William H. Fulcher	George Brock
John Draper	Benjamin Lawless
David Holly	Daniel Wormack
Larkin Rogers	Thomas Jones
Malin Mabry	William Butler
R^d Commichael	William Robinson
Moses Wade	Joshua Butler
Thomas Crawley	Thomas Butler
Archelus Silvey	Jonathan Hurst
Benjamin Truner	William Stewart
Richard Carmichael	Vallentine Brock
Benjamin Tellison	Timothy Warren
Elish Gibson	George Ballard

Men Recruited from Prince Edward County, Va. by Lt. Walton and Lt.
Dickerson for Capt. Samuel Scott's Georgia Regiment: [Copied from
Old Book Nr 1 - A List of Capt. Samuel Scott's Men's Time:]

William Fedler, Nov. 16 to May 25, 190 days
Richard Cormick, Nov 16 to May 25, 160 days
Rodnick Cormick, Dec 16 to May 25, 160 days
James Hunt, Dec 19 to May 25, 157 days
John Scotes, Nov 19 to May 25, 187 days
John Boyd, Jan 2 to May 25, 143 days
Thomas Watkins, Dec 19 to May 25, 157 days
John Draper, Jan 5 to May 25, 142 days
Joshua Butler, Jan 3 to May 25, 142 days
Thomas Butler, Jan 3 to May 24, 142 days
Timothy Warren, Nov 16 to May 25, 190 days
Arthur Conner, Dec 19 to May 25, 157 days
John Hatcher, Nov 6 to May 25, 200 days
Larkin Rogers, Nov 16 to May 25, 190 days
Moses Wade, Nov 16 to May 25, 174 days
William Watkins, Nov 6 to May 25, 190 days
Josiah Whitlock, Dec 16 to May 25, 157 days
Daniel Warmuck, Dec 16 to May 25, 157 days
Edmund Bart, Dec 20 to May 25, 153 days
Ishua Ward, Dec 20 to May 25, 153 days
John Claborn, Jan 1 to May 25, 145 days
William Cottreel, Dec 1 to May 25, 176 days
Stephen Collins, Dec 1 to May 25, 176 days
William Collins, Jan 1 to May 25, 145 days
William Warren, Nov 15 to May 25, 191 days
John Pound, Nov 15 to May 25, 191 days
Benjamin Turner, Jan 2 to May 25, 144 days
Philemon Crain, Jan 24 to May 25, 144 days
William Butler, Jan 5 to May 25, 143 days
William Fulcher, Nov 16 to May 25, 190 days
Elish Gibson, Nov 16 to May 25, 190 days
William Bartlett, Nov 19 to May 25, 187 days
Thomas Gimbo, Dec 16 to May 25, 160 days
Valentine Brock, Jan 3 to May 25, 145 days
Solomon Porter, Jan 5 to May 25, 144 days
David Haley, Jan 5 to May 25, 144 days
William Luke, Jan 5 to May 25, 144 days
Jacob Crist, Jan 4 to May 25, 142 days
William Stewart, Jan 6 to May 25, 137 days
Benjamin Lawless, Jan 1 to May 25, 145 days
George Brook, Jan 3 to May 25, 143 days

Archy Selvy, Jan 5 to May 25, 141 days
Benj Tillison, Jan 4 to May 25, 139 days
Williamson Robinson, Jan 7 to May 25, 156 days
Henry Vincent, Jan 8 to May 25, 135 days
George Ballard, Jan 3 to May 25, 143 days
Sgt Elisha Dickenson, Jan 1 to May 25, 145 days
John Brock, Jan 5 to May 25, 141 days
Daniel Besile [?], Jan 4 to May 25, 139 days
Niven [?] Jones, Jan 3 to May 25, 143 days
Thomas Crawley, Jan 5 to May 25, 141 days
Jonathan Hunt, Jan 2 to May 25, 144 days
Charles Holloway, Jan 1 to May 25, 145 days
The Drummer, Nov 5 to May 25, 201 days

Index - Names on Accounts - 1777

[Not all of the men on the following list were Georgia Continentals.]

Jacob Curt
Daniel Bence
Henry Vincent
Elishu Gibson
Josiah Whitlock
Edward Echols
Stephen Heard
Robert Williamson
Capt Thomas Scott
William Wiley
David Boyd
Capt   Fountain
George Walton
Robert Walton
Job Rountree
Negroes: Bullock, his wife
                     and child
          Charles, his wife
Samuel Elbert, Col
William Whitlock
Daniel Womack, dcsd,
  Ga. Light Horse
Elijah Dickenson, Lt.
Francis DeGraffinrisdh [?]
Josiah Whitlock
7 Sept 1779
Lt John Conner, light dragoons
James Lindsey
John Collins
William Collins
William Walton
Thomas Scott
Thomas Crawley

Vallentine Brock
Arthur Conner
Patrick Carmichael
Stephen Holstin
Lt Col Leonard Marbury
John Draper
Moses Wade
David Haley
Thomas Crawley
Larkin Rogers
Noland Mabry
Archelus Silvy
Benjamin Turner
George Ballard
Benjamin Tellison

John Brock
Richard Cormicle
Josiah Whitlock
William Bartlett

Elijah Dickson
Timothy Warren
Stephens Collins
Isham Ward
William Collins
Rodrick Cormicle
William H. Fulcher

2.b. Rosters from "Georgia Continentals," Records Group 93, National
      Archives.

[To avoid repetition, not all of the rosters in this collection are
included here.]

Silver Bluff July 21st 1779

Dear Hendly please pay to Lieut glascock the pay due the under
Mentioned Men as I have given them furloughs to go to Virginia I
promised to get their pay for them I will be accountable to them and
this will indemnify you.
                              your's   Frans. Moore

116

N.B. The men's names are

James Rivers Sarjt.   Willm. Bond
Lewis Hollaway Do   Denis Egan
Christopher Linn   [illegible]
Nicholas Morris   David Handy [Danl. Handy?]
Moses Eieves   Jno Jurdin

[Information on how much was paid on this account is included on the
original manuscript.]

A Pay Roll of the Field Commissiond Staff and Non Commissiond Officers
& Privates belonging to the first Georgia Continental Battalion.
Commanded by Colonel Robert Rae from the 1st Day of July to the 1st
Day of November 1779.

[Amount of money owed, period of time served, and signatures of each
man arc shown on the original manuscript.]

Robert Rae	Colonel	John Pryor	Private
Frans. H. Harris	Lt. Colo.	Samuel Ware	Do
Geo. Handley	Capt.	John King	Do
Shadk. Wright	Do	John Linn	Do
Alexr. Danl. Cuthbert	Do	John Ryan	Do
Thos. Glascock	Lieuts.	William Austin	Do
Jesse Walton	Do	Hugh Bole	Do
Geo. Handley	Paymr.	James Burns	Do
Jesse Walton	QuarMr.	David Peters	Do
James Houstoun	Surgeon	Rubin Windrum	Do
John Le Duc	QuarMr Sergt	George Jones	
John Twedele	Sgt. Major	William Gibbs	Do
John Knight	Sergt	Ziering Ascue	Do
John Evans	Do	Conrad Fergonier	Do
Charles Fields	Do	Josiah Bird	Do
Ethl. Futral*	Corpl.	John Futral	Do
Thos. Jeffrys	Do	Jordan Jackson	Do
Thos. Hill	Do	James Parks	Do
William Love	Drum Majr.	George Williams	Do
Thos. Wilson	Private		

[*His signature on the original manuscript appears as "Ettrelerad
Futrall."]

A Pay Roll of the Field Commissioned Staff & Non Commissioned Officers
& Privates belonging to the 2nd. Continental Georgia Battalion, under
the Command of Colo. Samuel Elbert from the first day May to the first
day July 1779.

[Amounts owed, time served, and signatures of each man are shown on the
original manuscript.]

Frans. Moore	Major	Prest. in Camp
Geo. Hancock	Capt.	abst. with leave
Frans. Tennill	Lieut.	Prest. in Camp
Jno. Morrison	Do	Do
Robert Howe	Do	Do
Frederick Shick	Do	Do
Henry Allison	Do	Do
Robert Howe	QMr.	Do
John Strom	QMS	[This name is crossed out on the original manuscript.]
John Board	Serjt	Present in camp.
James Rivers	Do	[This is crossed out on the original manuscript.]
Joseph Maise	Do	in Genl Hospital

117

Wm Jones	Serjt	pres. in Camp
Meshack Willis	Do	Do
Lewis Holloway	Do	Do
Wm. Palmer	Do	Do
John Brown	Corpl.	Silver Bluff
John Rains	Corpl.	abst. with Leave
Wm. Dorton	Do	prest. in camp
Reuben Pound	Do	Do
Absolam Reynolds	fifer	Chs. Town
Thoms. Webster	Drumr.	prest. in Camp
Thoms. Reed	Corpl.	Silver Bluff
Zachr. Butrey	private	Pres. in Camp
Grant Tylor	Do	Do
Wm. Bond	Do	Do
Thoms. Baker	Do	Do
Jams. Naven	Do	Do
Stephen Terry	Do	Do
Thoms. Salisbury	Do	Do
Hartwell Stokes	Do	Chas. Town
John Bryant	Do	pres. in Camp
Denis Ryon	Do	Do
John Davie	Do	Do
John Jones	Do	Chas. Town
Beverly Chase	Do	Pres. in Camp
Jno. Dugan	Do	in Genl. Hospital
Jas. Wilabey	Do	at Charles Town
Wm. Brice	Do	at Silver Bluff
Jno. Foster	Do	Prest. in Camp
Wm. Linvil	Do	Do
Nicholas Morris	Do	Do
Wm. Tapley	Do	at Chas. Town
Ezecial Wright	Do	Do
Jams. Connelly	Do	Do
Jno. Pitman	Do	at Augusta
Jno. Johnson	Do	Prest. in Camp
Richd. Jones	Do	Do
Jno. Mason	Do	in Gen. Hospital
Josiah Landrum	Do	at Charles Town
John Jordon	Do	at Silver Bluff
Danl. Handee	Do	Prest. in Camp
Wm. Willeby	Do	Do
John Rivers	Do	abst with Leave
Stephen Davenport	Do	prest. in Camp
Joseph Capher	Do	Do
Wm Walker	Do	at Silver Bluff
Wm Peasly	Do	Do
Wm Woodson	Do	Killed Field & Staff
Jarvin Winkfield	Do	Dead

/s/ Col. Saml Elbert

L List of Officers & Men belonging to the Second Geo Contl Battalion whose Pay has been drawn to the 1st January 1779.

[All names below are spelled as they appear on the original roll. No actual signatures were present.]

Danl Roberts	Lieut Colo	Sherwood Wilkerson	Serjiant
Edward Wood	Captain	William Jones	Serjiant
Francis Tennell	Lieutenant	Joseph Marj.	Serjiant
John Morrison	Lieutenant	James Sugar	Serjiant
Robert Howe	Lieutenant QM	Reuben Bound	Corporal
Frederick Chick	Lieutenant	Thomas Read	Corporal
John Strone	QM Serjiant	John Brown	Corporal
Edward Crundon	Serjiant Major	William Porter	Corporal
John Board	Serjiant	John Rains	Corporal
Britten Brantlett	Serjiant	Absolam Reynolds	private

Stephen Davenport	Private	John Jones	Private
Grant Tylor	do	John Johnston	do
Benjamin Webster	do	John Davis	do
William Stith	do	Jno. Dugan	do
William Christian	do	Stephen Weatherford	do
Andrew Lynch	do	Zechr. Butterns	do
Daniel Jostlin	do	Jno. Foster	do
Meredith Davis	do	Jas. Willoughby	do
Samuel Simpson	do	Nicholas Morris	do
William Tapley	do	William Boyer	do
William Walker	do	Stephen Terry	do
William Bond	do	Denis Qyan	do
Thomas Saulsberry	do	James Connelly	do
James Navin	do	Hartwell Stokes	do
Henry Pack	do	Beverly Chase	do
Thomas Baker	do	Thomas Lister	do
Daniel Boatright		Thomas Simmons	do
Charles Dameron	do	Stephen Hancock	do
John Bryant	do	Richard Jones	do
John Pitman	do	John Leveing	do
William Linvill	do	Zekiel Wright	do

A Pay Roll of the Commissioned & Non Commissioned Officers & Privates belonging to the second Continental Georgia Battalion Commanded by Colonel Samuel Elbert from the first day Decemb. 1779 to the first day February 1780.

[Amount paid, period of service, and signature of each man are shown on the original manuscript. Except where indicated, all men were present in camp.]

John Cunningham	Capt.	John Flanigan	Serjt.
Frans. Lieut.		Jesse Parker	Do
John Morrison	Do	Thoms. Webster	Drumr.
corneleus Collins	Do	William Tapley	private
Thos. Payne	Do	Andrew Linch	Do
Robert Howe	Do	Richard Cascoin	Do
Frederick Shick	Do	Stephen Davenport	Do
Henry Allison	Do	John Collins	Do
			Leave of Absence

I do swear that the above Pay Roll is just & true without fraid to the United States of America or any Individual to the best of my knowledge.

attested before me
This 26 Inst 1780
  /s/ Wm. Downs

Examined & approved of
/s/ Jos. Pannill Lieut. Colo

A Pay Roll of the Field Commissiond. & Non Commissioned Officers & Privates belonging to the Third Contl. Georgia Battalion Commanded by Lieut. Colo. John McIntosh from the 1st Day of May to the first Day of July 1779.

[Amount owed, period served, and signature of each man appear on the original manuscript. All men, except where indicated, were apparently in camp.]

Nathl. Pearre	Leiut.	John Connelly	Sergeant
Do.	& Adjuct.	Jesse Brawder	Do
Pascal Sucker	Do	Alex. Roberson	Do Augusta
John Boyd	Do	John Tomleslin	Do
Jams. Barnett	Do	Will. King	Do
Basil Hatton	Do	John Johnson	Do
Will. Rilly	Do Augusta	John Abbott	Do Augusta

Will. Corbens	Corpral	Patrick Cochrand	Do with Col. White
Griffen Dickenson	Do		
Geo. Turner	Do	Patrick Stacks	Do
Henry Deshazers	Do Augusta	Geo. Thomas	Do
Will. Thompson	Do Do.	Will. Osborn	Do
Mansd. Jones	Drum Maj.	John Wedgewood	Do
Josa. Norrington	Drum. Augusta	John Davey	Do Augusta
Obeh. Hendrick	Fife	Moses Reaves	Do
Josa. Cissele	Private	Fredk. Thompson	Do
Jesse Peters	Do	Will. Clabruck	Do
James OBryan	Do		
James Lane	Do		
John House	Do		
Curtis Linn	Do		
Paris Langford	Do		
Terry McHaney	Do with Col. White		
Will. Hicks	Do	Capt. Isaac Hicks Exd.	
Wm. Coleman	Do	" Wm. Scott	
Nathl. Eaves	Do	" Rains Cook Exchanged July	
James Bryan	Do Augusta		
Thos. McClain	Do		
Solo. Draper	Do		

A Pay Roll of the Commissioned non Commissioned Officers and Privates Belonging to the third Georgia Continental Battalion Commanded by Lieut. Colo. John McIntosh from the 1st Day of November 1779 to the 1st Day of February 1780.

[Amounts paid, period served, and signatures of each man are shown on the original manuscript.]

Isaac Hicks	Capt.		
Willm. Scott	Do		
Rains Cook	Capt.		
John Manley	Lieut.		
John Frazer	Do		
Nathl. Pearre	Do		
John Wagnon	Do		
John Connoley	Serjt		
John Boyd	Serjt	Descharged [sic] Jany. 1	
Henry Deshazer	Corpl	Do	
Mansfield Jones	Drumr.	Do	December 1st
James Obryan	Private	Do	Jany 1st
George Wilison	Do		
Obed Fergason	Do		
Obed. Plumbley	Do		
Pattrick Sticks	Do		
John Wedgwod	Do		
David Motley	Do		
John McIntosh	Lt. Colo		

I do swear that the above Pay Roll is just and true without fraud to the United States or any individuals to the Best of my knoledge [sic]

Attested before me
this 25 day Jany. 1780   Examined & approved of
/s/ Wm. Downs J.P.   /s/ Jos. Pannill Lieut. Colo.

A List of the Officers & Men belonging to the third Georgia Continental Battalion whose Pay has been drawn to the 1 Jany. 1779.

John McIntosh	Lieut. Colo.	Heny. Deshazer	do
Gideon Booker	Captain	Obediah Gravett	do
Clement Nash	do	Wm. Thomeson	do

William Scott	Captain	Geoe. Turner	do
Isaac Hicks	do	Wm. Whitmore	do
[illegible]	Paymaster	Mansfield Jones	Drummer
Nathl. Pearre	Lieut. & Adj.	Joshua Northington	do
John Boyd	Serjiant	Hadiah Hendrick	fifer
James Burnett	do	Abbott, Jon	private
Jesse Browden	do	Brooks, Wm.	
Jno. Hoggat	do	Biden, Jas	do
Bazwell Hatten	do	Cockran, Patrick	do
Mark Judkins	sgt. Major	Chapbrook, Wm.	do
Saml. Freeman	Serjt.	Coleman, Wm.	do
William Reilly	do	Draper, Solomon	do
William Sisson	do	[illegible]	do
Paschal Tucker	do	Flaningan, Michl	do
William Corben	Corpral	Ferguson, Shadr.	do
Griffith Dickason	do	Hicks, Wm.	do
House, Jno	do	Mason, Jno	do
Hill, Jno	do	OBrien, Jams	do
[illegible]	do	Peters, Jesse	do
Linn, Curtis	do	Robertson, Alexr.	do
Langford, Paris	do	Smith, Joseph	do
Lane, Jas.	do	Sissell, Joshua	do
Mitchell, Chaney	do	Tomberlin, Jno	do
McHaney, Terry	do	Whitehead, Wm.	do
McClean, Thos	do	Thomas, George	do
		Warren, Benjn	do
		Wobb, Alexr	do

Pay Roll of the Field Commissioned Staff & Non Commissioned Officers
& Privates belonging to the 4th Georgia Battn. of Continental Troops
Commanded by Col. Jno. White from the 1st June to the 1st July
Inclusive 1779.

[Amount paid, period served, and signature of each man appears on the
original manuscript.]

Jno. White	Col.	Absent wt Leave
Joseph Pannelle	Lt. Col.	Do. Do to Georgia
Phillip Lowe	Majr.	Present Prisoner on Parole
Geo Melvin	Capt.	Chas. Town
Brussard	Do	resigned 15 June
Jas. Stedman	Lieut.	
Patrik. Fitzpatrick	Do	
Wm. Jordan	Do	
Jno. Carswell	Do	on Parola [illegible] Town
Arthur Hayes	Do.	Present on Parole
Jas. Stedman	Paymaster	[This line is crossed out on the original manuscript.]
Joseph Delespone	Surgeon	Resigned 30 June
Jas. Stedman	Adjt.	
Jno. Hilliard	Serjt.	wth. Col. White in Camden
Jno. Anderson	Do.	Do Do
Henry Ellis	Do.	Do. Do.
Danl. Dempier	Do.	
Jas. Lett [Sett?]	Do.	on Command at Golphins
Geoe. St. George	Do	
Thos. Johnson	Corpl.	on Command at Golphins
Willard McGennis	Do	Do. Do.
Jno. Hendrix	Drumr.	
David Kovack	Do	wth. Lieut. Caswell
Jno. [?] Smith	Fifer	[illegible]
Geo. Townsend	Do.	wt. Brussard & the Lt Dragoons [This is crossed out on the original manuscript.]
Jeremiah Fleming	Do.	wt. Col. White
Thos. Browne	Privt.	in the Hospital at Golphins
Isaac Coyan	Do.	Prisoner War at Golphins

```
Saml. Wood            Privt.    Prisoner War at George Town
Saml. Rummerfield     Do.       with. Capt. Melvin Chas. Town
Wm. Bishop            Do.
Christopher Shiader    Do        wt. Brussard & the Lt Dragoons
                                [This is crossed out on the original
                                  manuscript.]

Wm. Mitchell          Do
Chas. Clark           Do.       in the Flying Hospital
Smith Carpenter       Do.       wth. Col. White
Joseph Boyce          Do.       on Command at Galphin
Patk. Corbin [?]      Do.          Do.         Do.
Joseph Scepio         Do.       wth. Col. White
Adam [?] Grubb        Do.          Do.         Do.
John Private          Do.       wt. Brussard & the Lt Dragoons
                                [This is crossed out on the original
                                  manuscript.]
Wm. Hanning           Do.       in the Genl. Hospital
```

I do Swear that the above Pay Roll is Just & True without fraud to the
United States or any Individual

sworn to before me the 3d day of July 1779

/s/ John Lindsay JPeace   /s/ Jas. Stedman Lt. Paymaster

                         4 : G : B

A Pay Roll for the Field and Staff Officers of the Geo Battalion, from
Jany 1 to Decr. 31st. 1782 both days Included

[Amount paid to each man is shown on the original manuscript.]

```
John Habersham          Major
Nathaniel Pearre        Lieut. & Adjt.
John Peter Wagnon       Lieut. & QM
James Boyd Sharpe       Surgeon          appointed Dec. 6, 1782
Frederick Long          Sarj. major      appointed July 19, 1782
John Chrostopher Buntz  QM. sarj.        appointed June 20th: 1782
```

                         /s/ John Habersham
                              Major Commt. Geo: Battn:

A Pay Roll for the Extra Officers of the Geo Regiment from January 1st.
to Decr. 31st. 1782 both days Included. . .

[Amount paid and time served for each man is shown on the original
manuscript.]

```
Saml. Elbert       Colo.       11. Littlebury Mosby    ditto
John McIntosh      Lt. Col.    12. Rains Cook          ditto
 1. Joseph Lane    Maj.        13.    Brozard          ditto
 2. Phillip Low    ditto        1. Lachlan McIntosh    Lieut.
 3. Isaac Hicks    ditto        2. John Morroson       Lieut.
 4. A. Danl. Cuthbert ditto     3. Cornilius Collins   ditto
 5. William Scott  ditto        4. John Meanly         ditto
 6. Gideon Booker  ditto        5. John Mitchell       ditto
 7. George Henley  ditto        6. Henry Allison       ditto
 8. John Milton    ditto        7. Josiah Maxwell      ditto
 9. P.E.D'L. Playne ditto       8. John Frazer         ditto
10. Elisha Miller  ditto        9. William Jordan      ditto
                               10. Chrisn. Hillary     ditto
```

/s/ John Habersham

Major & senior officer in actual Service of the Georgia Line

Pay Roll of the First Company of the Georgia Battalion

[This is a composite roll made from the roll of January 1 to December
31, 1782, under the command of Captain Lachlan McIntosh; and the roll
of June 9, 1782, to November 3, 1783, under the command of Captain John
Lucas. The original manuscripts include the amount paid and the time
served by each man. Names in brackets appear only on the earlier roll.]

[Lachlan McIntosh   Capt.
1. John Ducoin   Lieut.
2. Thomas Payne   Do.]

                                          enlisted

1.   Frederick Long   Serj. Maj.   July 19th 1782
2.   Samuel Ihly   Sergt.   June 25   Do.
3.   George Armstrong   Do   Decr. 27   Do.
4.   Simon Leaveam   Corp.   July 24   Do.
5.   Lewis Acord   Do   June 19   Do.
6.   Francis Scott   Dr. Majr.   August 9   Do.
7.   John Gamble   Drumr.   Do   19   Do. deserted since
                                                         January 1783

8.   Matthew Weidman   Fifer   June 19   Do.
     [John Weidman   Fifer   June 19   Do.]
9.   Richard Dowdy   Private   Sept 4   Do. [June, 1782]
10. Samuel Snider   Ditto   ditto 25   Do. [June, 1782]
11. William Overstreet   Ditto   August 19 Do.
12. Richard Bennet   Ditto   Ditto 19   Do.
13. David Andrews   Ditto   Nov. 21   Do.
14. John Woods   Ditto   June 19   Do.
15. John Gilstrap   Ditto   July 10   Do.
16. Peter Sipro   Ditto   June 25   Do.
17. James Burns   Ditto   Ditto 25   Do. [for war]
18. Fredrick Plaskoy   Ditto   Augst. 7   Do. deserted since
     [Plaskor?]   January 1783
19. Daniel Chizler   Ditto   June 25   Do.
20. Benjamin Cooke   Ditto   Augst. 19 Do.
21. Robert Fair   Ditto   July 23   Do. deserted since
                                                         January 1783

22. Jonathan Snyder   Ditto   June 25   Do.
23. Michael Mick [Meek?] Ditto   Ditto 19   Do.
24. Peter Dowell   Ditto   Augst. 20 Do.
25. William Harris   Ditto   Ditto 18   Do. deserted since
                                                         January 1783
26. Thomas Phadkin   Ditto   Augst. 5   Do. deserted since
                                                         January 1783

27. John Walnock
     [Walnick?]   Ditto   Ditto 16   Do.
28. Solomon Gnann   Ditto   June 19   Do.
29. William Pickring   Ditto   July 24   Do.
30. William Bishop   Ditto   Jany. 1   Do. Enlisted for
                                                          War

31. Jesse Barber   Ditto   Augst. 17 Do.
33. William Tirplet   Ditto   Ditto 19   Do.
[33. James Pierce   Ditto   Augst. 10 Do.]
34. Daniel Touchstone   Ditto   Ditto 15   Do
35. Matw. Weincoiff   Ditto   June 25   Do.
36. Jacob Ihly   Ditto   Ditto   Do.
37. Patrick Fitzpatric   Ditto   August 26 Do.
38. Whitmal Odam   Ditto   Sept. 29   Do.
39. Jacob Metzgar   Ditto   June 10   Do.
40. Ezekiel Atway   Ditto   Ditto
41. Joseph Daughtry   Ditto   Augst. 10 Do. Deserted since
                                                         January 1783

42. William White   Ditto   Ditto
43. Peter Tidwell   Ditto   June 30   Do. Deserted since
                                                         January 1783

44. James Brackenridge   Ditto   Ditto 10   Do. Ditto
45. Samuel Boyd   Ditto   Ditto   Ditto
46. John Carson   Ditto   Ditto   Ditto

47.	William Cooker (Crooker?]	Private	Augst. 9 1782	
48.	Francis Dunlaw	Ditto	Do. 3 Do	
49.	Arthur Roberts	Ditto	Ditto 19 Do	discharged for inability

Pay Roll of the Second Company of the Georgia Battalion.

[This is a composite roll made from the roll of January 1 to December 31, 1782, Captain John Lucas commanding; and June 9, 1782, to November 4, 1783, Captain William McIntosh commanding. Amount paid and time served by each soldier is shown on the original manuscript. Information in brackets is found only on the earlier roll.]

[1.   Jno. Lucas   Capt.
  2.   Francis Tennell   Lt.
  3.   Frederick Sheick   Lt.]

1.	Chritr. Buntz	Qt. Master Serjiant	enlisted June 25, 1782	
2.	Matthew Rahn	Serjt.	Do. 25 Do.	
3.	William Parton [Paxton]	Serjt.	Nov. 28 Do.	
4.	Jonathan Rheim	Corpl.	June 19	
5.	Lewis Frazer	Ditto	July 21	
6.	Thomas Webster	Drumr.	June 19	
7.	William Richardson	Private	Augst. 19	
8.	John Potts	Do.	Do.	Deserted since January 1783
9.	Thos. Forrest	Do.	June 26	Do
10.	Hardy Richardson	Do.	Augst. 19	
11.	Wm Shirly	Do.	Do.	
12.	Isaac Wood	Do.	June 21	
13.	Charles Fresh	Do.	July 30	
14.	Jonathan Gnann	Do.	June 21	
15.	Robert Boyd	Do.	Ditto	
16.	Willm Poter [Porter]	Do.	Augst. 28	Deserted since June 1783
17.	George Thrasher	Do.	June 24	
18.	Jno Rutledge	Do.	Do. 21	
19.	Saml. Gordon	Do.	Do. 19	Deserted Since Jany. 1783
20.	Laurance Leonard [Lenchan]	Do.	August. 17	Do.
21.	Samuel Gibson	Do.	June 20	Do.
22.	Jno. Sims	Do.	Augst. 19	
23.	Joseph Emanuel	Do.	Jany. 1, 1783	
24.	Nathaniel Oatt	Do.	June 20, 1782	
25.	George Peot [Peoling]	Do.	July 24	Deserted Since June 1783
26.	Andrew Mitchell	Do.	Augst 8	
27.	George Bassell [Bassett]	Do.	Augst 28	Deserted Since June 1783
28.	William Crawford [Grafford]	Do.	July 5	Do
29.	Paris Sims	Do.	Augst 19	Deserted Since June 1783
30.	John Bonnell	Do.	Do.	Do.
31.	Thomas Wood	Do.	June 22	
[31.	Thos. Stuman	Do.]		
32.	Samuel Smith	Do.	Ditto	Deserted Since Jany. 1783
33.	John Crawford (Grafford]	Do.	Ditto	
34.	John Penrose	Do.	Augst 16	

```
35.   Simon Hindox [Kender]   Private   Augst 14
36.   Alexander Webb          Do.       Ditto
37.   Mat Motts               Do.       June 24
38.   John Moss               Do.       Sepr. 17
39.   Richd. Eastman
         [Eastined]           Do.       Do  5
40.   Saml. Montgomery        Do.       June 21
41.   Daniel Johnson          Do.       August. 19   Deserted Since
                                                      Jany. 1783
42.   Ephraim Ihly            Do.       June 25
43.   Aquila Jones            Do.       Do.
44.   James Rousham
         [Rausind]            Do.       Novr. 30
45.   John Harvey             Do.       Do.  21
46.   Willm. Dailly           Do.       Decr. 27
47.   Jeremiah Brantley       Do.       June 21
48.   William Mooze           Do.       Do.  25
49.   Martin Bogget           Do.       Feby 18, 1783
50.   James Brown             Do.       Jany 13   Do.
51.   Archd Woods             Do.       June 20, 1782
52.   Richard Wade            Do.       Jany 7, 1783
```

Pay Roll of the Third Company of the Georgia Battalion

[This is a composite roll made from the roll of January 1 to December
31, 1782, Captain William McIntosh commander; and the roll of June 9,
1783, to November 4, 1783. The original manuscript contains the time
served and the amount paid each man. Information in brackets is found
on the later roll only.]

```
1.    Wm. McIntosh             Capt.
2.    Edward Cowen             Leut.
3.    Arthur Hayes             Leut.     [enlisted:]
4.    George Hardwick          Sergt.    [Sepr. 4, 1782]
5.    William White            Do.       [June 19]
6.    Henry Beningar           Corpl.    [Do.]
7.    Benjamin Lenier          Do.       [Augst. 26]
8.    John McLee               Fifer     [Do.]
9.    David Monday             Drumr.    [Jany. 5, 1783]
10.   Thomas Allman            Private   [Decr. 16, 1782]
11.   David Bondy              Do.       [Augst. 20  Do.]
12.   Gideon Bishop            Do.       [June 19]
13.   John Sheirly
         [Shirley]             Do.       [Ditto]
14.   John Clapperd            Do.       [Dec. 24] Deserted 5 March
15.   Enal Higgenbricker       Do.       [Do.  23] Deserted 5 March
16.   Wm. Cook                 Do.       [Augst. 25]  Deserted 26 March
17.   Henry Cook               Do.       [Do. 19]
18.   Jessey Brown             Do.       [Septr. 19]
19.   Isaac Clayatt [Clyat]    Do.       [Do.  10]
20.   Joseph Nichols           Do.       [Do.]
21.   John Martin              Do.       [Augst. 19]
22.   Michal Burkhalter        Do.       [Do.  18]
23.   Joseph Allen             Do.
24.   Charles Griffith         Do.       [Sepr. 4]
25.   Hugh Alexander           Do.       [June 19  Deserted Since
                                                   January 1783]
26.   James White              Do.       [Sepr. 15]
27.   Jacob Hail               Do.       [Do.  4]
28.   James Attaway            Do.       [June 19]
29.   Jos. Attaway             Do.       [Do.]
30.   Fredk. Rester            Do.       [Sept. 4, 1782]
31.   Alex. Caswell            Do.       [Do. 15]
32.   Jos. Harigate            Do.       [Do.]
33.   Christoh. Bailie         Do.       [June 21  Deserted Since
                                                   Jany. 1783]
```

34.	John Cambell	Private	[Augst. 27]	
35.	George Beckley [Beakly]	Do.	[June 21]	
36.	James Hayes	Do.		
37.	Durrum Hancock	Do.	[Augst. 16	Deserted Since Jany. 1783]
38.	John Stuart	Do.	[Oct. 1]	Deserted 4 March
39.	Peter Purveyor	Do.	[July 1]	Deserted 5 March
[39.	Archibald Miller	Do.	Augst. 19]	
40.	Philip Minsey [Miney]	Do.	[Augst. 19]	
41.	David Wall	Do.	[Sepr. 15]	
42.	Joseph Conner	Do.	[June 19]	
43.	Geo. Miller	Do.	[Ditto]	
44.	Ricker Mills	Do.		
45.	Thoms. McBride	Do.	[June 19]	
46.	Jas. Ryon	Do.		
47.	Wm. Tidwell	Do.	[June 30	Deserted never joined]
48.	John Crosher	Do.	[Do 13	Deserted Since Jany. 1783]
49.	Benj. Bulloch	Do.	[Do. 19	Never joined]
50.	John Gibson	Do.	[Do.	Deserted Since Jany. 1783]
51.	Matt. Micke	Do.	[Do. 25]	
52.	Saml. Mitzker [Metygar]	Do.	[Do. 19]	

A Return of Officers of the Georgia Line of the American Army...
Names - Rank - Date of Commissions - Time of Service & other occurences [sic]

1. *Samuel Elbert Col 2d Regmt 5th July 1776 Deschanged in Octo: '82 22d
2. *John McIntosh Lt Col Commt 3d April 1778 ditto 22d Oct: 1782
3. Joseph Pannel of 3rd Regt. Lt. Col. Nov. 1778 ditto by resolve of Octob. 1780
4. *John Habersham Major 1 April 1778 In Service during the war
5. Joseph Lane Major 2d April 1778 descharged by resolve of Oct. '80
6. *Phillip Lom Major 18 June 1778   do   do   do
7. Isaac Hicks Captain July 1776 Returned to Virginia in 1779
8. George Handley Captain 19 October 1776 Returned in July 1782 15
9. John Bard Captain Novr 1776 Returned to N. York 1779 while prisoner
10. John Lucas Captain 1st March 1777 In Service during the War
11. George Melvin Captain 1 March 1777 descharged 12 July 1782
12. *Emanuel Peter Delaplain Captain 26 May 1776 in France during the war
13. *Daniel Cuthbert Captain 12 June 1777 In Service during the war
14. *Monsr. Ropard [Celerine Brossard] Captain 26 June 1777 Returned to France in 1782
15. *John Milton Captain 15 Septr 1777 Returned 15 July 1782
16. *Wm McIntosh Captain 17 Septr 1777 In Service During the War
17. Joseph Day Captain 20 Septr 1777 In Service during the War
18. Gideon Booker Captain 28 Jany 1778 descharged 22d Octob. 1782
19. *___ Mosby 1st Lieutenant 23 July 1776 Returned to Virginia 1780
20. *Lachn McIntosh   do   1777 In Service during the War
21. *Francis Fannell do   20 June 1777 In Service during the War
22. Thos Glascock   do   1 July 1777 In Service during the War
23. *John Duforn (DuFaupeyret) do 22 July 1777 In Service during the War
24. *Edward Cowan   do   1st Sept 1777 In Service during the War
25. *John Meanly   do   4 Feby 1777 In Service during the War
26. John Morrison   do   5 Feby 1777 descharged 22nd Octob: 1782
27. *Corns. Collins   do   15 March 1777 descharged 22d Octob. 1782
28. John Fraser   do   4 April 1778 Returned to Virginia about 1779
29. John Mitchell   do   5 April 1778 Returned in Octobr: 1782
30. *Nathl. Perry [Pearre] do 29 April 1778 In Service during the War

```
31. *Arthur Hays 2d Lieutenent 1 October 1777 In Service during the War
32.  Thos. Payne        do    1 Dec. 1777 In Service during the War
33. *Wm Jordan          do    Jany 1778 In Service during the War
34.  Joseph Maxwell     do    April 1778 In Service during the War
35. *Fredk. Shick       do    26 April 1778 In Service during the War
36.  Henry Allison      do    27 April 1778 descharged 22d Octob: 1782
37. *Jno. Peter Wagnon do     1st July 1778 In Service during the War
38.  Christopher Hilliary  do 1st August 1778 In Service during the War
```

The members marked thus * on the above List I think are entitled to
promotion by the resolve of 30 Septr. 1783. Lachn McIntosh M.G.

3. Composite Roster of the Georgia Continental Regiment of Horse from
    A. McC. Duncan, Roll of Officers and Members of the Georgia Hussars
    and of the Cavalry. . . (Savannah, 1907).

     Mr. Gordon B. Smith of Savannah, who provides the information in
the brackets that accompanies this roster, warns that this roster cannot
be completely confirmed by existing sources and should be used with
caution.

              Battalion of Georgia Light Horse -- Continental
July 2, 1776. Lieutenant Colonel William McIntosh; Resigns.
Oct. 13, 1776. Major Leonard Marbury; Resigns.
               Adjutant Anthony Norway.
April, 1777. Lieutenant Colonel John Baker; Resigns Oct. 15, 1777.
              Major Wm. Baker; Resigns.
October, 1777. Lieutenant Colonel Leonard Marbury.
               Major Samuel Scott
               Adjutant Patrick Walsh.
               Quartermaster Robert Thompson.
               Surgeon John Cater. [From S.C., died 1782]
               Sergeant Major Geo. Bledsoe.

                          Captains.

L. Marbury, Promoted Major Regiment Light Dragoons.
Wm. McIntosh, promoted Lieutenant Colonel Light Dragoons.
Benjamin Few, promoted Lieutenant Colonel Minute Men. [This should be
   "militia."]
James [This should be "Thomas."] Hovenden, promoted Lieutenant Colonel
   Fourth Georgia Continental Regiment. [Died 16 April 1778.]
James McFarland, retired.
[Drury] Cade, retired.
Samuel Scott, promoted Lieutenant Colonel [Major?] Regiment Light
   Dragoons.
John Salter.
William Hill.
Joseph Faulks. [Also Faulkner, Fowlkes, etc.]
James Bryant.
Leoncenatus [Lehancius] Dekeyser, promoted Lieutenant Colonel [Major?]
   Regiment Light Dragoons. [Lived in Fayetteville, N.C. after the war.]
John Dooley [Dooly], promoted Colonel Wilkes County Militia.
Charles Middleton, resigns.
Hatton Middleton.
Ignatus Few.
Wm. Williams, resigns.
John Stewart.
Benjamin Walker.
John Morel.
John Bilbo, illed. [Died in captivity on 8 May 1780 of wounds.]
Wm. Bugg.

Lieutenants.

James [?] Hovendon, promoted Captain.
Hatton Middleton, promoted Captain.
Ignatus Few, promoted Captain.
John Stewart, promoted Captain.
William Williams, promoted Captain.
John Hill.
[James] Pugh. [Decommissioned in 1776; not a Continental.]
Wm. Bugg, promoted Captain.
Anthony Norway, Adjutant.
John Morel, promoted Captain.
John Bilbo, promoted Captain.
____ Fraser, killed. [1777]
____ McGowen (or McGown), killed. [18 May 1777]
____ Robinson (or Robison).
Nicholas Bryson (or Braxton). [Also Braston.]
Peter [Pierre] Colomb.
Henry Cannon.
____ Anderson, killed. [1777]
Wm. Gilmour (or Gilmore). [Also Gilman.]
John Connor.
Wm. McDaniel (or McDonald). [Actually two different men!]
[John] Pope.
[John] Cooper.
Samuel West.
Geo. Randal, Pay Master. [or Randolph]
____ Aspey, Second Lieutenant.
James Bradley. [Formerly a captain in the 3rd N. C. Regiment.]

Quartermaster Sergeants.

Thos. Claiborn (or Clayton).
Parmenas Dawes.
Elijah Dickinson.

Sergeants.

Jos. Culpeper (or Culpher).
Benjamin Evans.
Hardy Jenkins.
____ Moore.
John Twedell.
John Pace.
Henry Dinkins

Privates.

Alford, Wm.
Asby, John
Asby, Wm.
Banks, John
Banks, Thos.
Billings, Joseph
Billings, Chesper
Bryant, John (or James)
Bullman, Geo.
Butler, Joseph
Burton, Wm.
Bizzel, David (or Birrel)
Barber, James

Clarke, ____
Carter, Thos.
Coal, Geo
Cole, Jesse
Cooper, John
Curtis, Jonathan
Donaldson, James
Darby, Arthur
Dean, Samuel
Dickinson, Henry
Dwelle, Arthur (or Durnley)
Dunniho, Daniel
Finlay, Thos.

Foreman, James
Gamillorn, Chris
Green, ____
Hart, Edmund
Hicks, Edward
Hilburn, Henry
Hunt, Jonathan
Hutchinson, John
Hutchinson, Wm.
Hays, Anderson
Horton, Nathaniel
Jackson, Jacob
Jackson, Nathan
Jones, James
Jones, John
Joyner, Benjamin
Lidell, Geo
Lilly, ____
Lowrey, John
Madd [?], Stephen
Malone, James
Middlebrook, Isaac
Miles, Jeremiah
Morain, Pat
Mosley, Wm.
Mosely, Wm. Hatt.
Murray, R. D.
Moorfield, Wm.

Moorfield, James
Nipway, Hardy
Ogdon, Joseph
Ogdell, James
Ogdell, Josiah
Oneal, James
Porter, Solomon
Rice, John
Sarcedo, Abram (or Sarzedas)
Slade, Fredk.
Smith, Wm.
Sneed, Alex
Strother, Wm.
Thompson, Jasper
Tillurson, Benjamin
Turner, Edward
Twilley, ____
Trevor, ____
Wade, Hezekiah
Wade, Moses
Ward, Wm.
Webster, Henry
Wood, Wm.
Wyatt, Wm.

4. Copies of rosters found in a box marked "DeRenne," Special Collections, University of Georgia Libraries.

There were copied in pencil on the back of late-19th-Century steamship broadsides. There is no information presently available as to what sources were used to cmpile this information. Comparisons with other rosters proves the credibility, with the exception of minor spelling differences, of these rosters, and proves that the sources used were earlier than 1779.

Artillery Battallion
Major Roman de lesie
Surgeon John Waudin
Qr Mast. Andrew McFarran & Lieut Laban Johnson
Sgt Majr John Mason
Waggon Mast. James Chesy

1st Company	2nd Company	3rd Company
Captain George Young	Capt. Morris	Capt Defau
Captain-Lieut		
Jas Alexander		Captain-Lieut Wm Johnston
Lieut Laban Johnson		Lieut Thos Sutte
Sergt George Spang		
Robt Caddy		Phillip Dexton
Robt Cleg	Capt Less	John White
John Long		Thos Horn
Hugh Lynis		Thos Corn
	Jno Sevadeu Sgt	
	[This is just	
	barely legible.]	
Thos Night		xFelix Bonche
Richd Watkins		xJoseph Hookner
Elijah Wilson		xMichail Grossey
Anthony Gorgetty		xJohn Sattes
xJoseph Duchene		xJames Mazyek
xJosephe Salquemon		xGeorge Eastmeat
xThos Sade		xAbrm Childers

1st Company	2nd Company	3rd Company
xJohn LaFarge		xWm Fitzgemes
xJacque Philipe		xChristope Edling
xAbraham Stenzo		
XBenjamin Strighnis		

3rd Ga Continental Regmt

Colonel James Seriven resigned [date illegible]
Colonel Mar 21 / 78 John Stirk
Lt Col Robert Rae promoted Col [rest of sentence illegible]
" Apr 78 John McIntosh - promoted Lt Col - [date illegible]
Major Daniel Roberts - promoted Lt Col
" April [?] 1778 Joseph Lane
adjutant Wm Lowe
Qr Master Jno Peter Wagnon
___ Sergeants John Coller
              Wm [illegible]
              Thos Claiborne
Surgeon Thoas Davinport
" Mate Ebenezer Callander
Sergt Major Jno P. Wagnon
             Geo Bevill Promoted Ensign
A. C. Issue John Oneil [not clear that he was of the Regmt]
Waggon Master James McCallim

Captains

Joseph Lane - 3rd Co Promoted Major 3rd Regmt April 2 78
Clement Nash - 2nd Co. [cannot be read from the Xerox]
Andrew Jefer - 5th Co.
Burrel Smith - 8th Co.
Gideon Booker - 6th Co.
Thos. Scott
R Downman - 4th Co.
Isaac Hicks - 5th Co.
Wm Scott - 7th Co.
Thos Theadgrie - 1st Co.
Raniss Cook - 3 "
Wm Wall

Lieutenants

Chas Clark Lt 4th Co.
Thos Threadgree - Lt 5th Co. - Promoted Capt 1st Col
Randalph Smith - Lt 8th Co
John Phillips - Lt 3rd Co
Thos D Etes - Lt 2nd Co
John Walter
Raines Cook - 1 Lt 1st Compy Promoted capt 3rd Co.
John McKinney Lt 5th Co
John Mcanty Lt 3 Co - Promoted 1 Lt 7th Co
John Fraser Lt 1st Co
Joseph Maxwell
Nathaniel Pearre Lt 3rd Co
John Dumouchel Lt 3rd Co
   Wylly

Ensigns

John Mitchell Ens Capt Scotts Co
Josiah Hatten Ens 5th Co
Nathaniel Pearre Ens 3rd Co. Promoted Lt 3rd Co
John Dumouchel   Promoted Lt
George Devill

Sergeants

John Chamberlin Capt Hisks Company
Stephen Sissel (Cecil) - 3rd Company
John Wm Conally - Capt Downmans Company
Sampson Cordel - 7th Company
Tyre Harris - 1st Company
John Hoggatt - 2nd Company
James Hayn - 3rd Company
Bassil Hatten - 7th Company
Joshua McKinny -5th Company
Robt Poythress - 1st Company
Wm Price - 6th Company
Wm Reily - Capt Downmans Company
Daniel Raine - 8th Company
Wm Sisson - 7th Company
Benj Wall
Thos Weden - 8th Compy
Daniel Wilson - Capt. Hicks Co.
George Berkley
Ralph Cobbs
    Frazer
Samuel Freeman
Joseph Stuart
John Rains

Corporals

John Boyd   Corp 7th Compy
Richard Sparks Corp 8th Compy
Patrick Sullivan Corp 7th Compy
Abraham Watson   Corp 7th Compy
William Wilson   Corp 8th Compy
George Lumas   Corp 5th Compy

Privates

Abbot John
Acree John
Aiken John
Allen
Bartrah John 1
Barnett Samuel
Bond Nicholas
Bradley
Bradley Francis
Bryant Daniel
Burnet Chas
Burnet Richard
Bush John
Callicoat John
Cecil John
Cissel Joshua
Chnster John
Clark John
Cockburn Michael
Cooper Thos
Corwin Wm
Dasher Benjn
David James
Derhazer Thos
Despasin Henry [?]
Diepman Griffith
Dobbs Morman
Eastman Geo
Earnes Nathaniel

Elliot Thos
Flanagen Michael
Fraiser Alexr
Gilmon James
Grim Burrell
Griffith Rawleigh
Gunter Chas
Harness Wm
Hatchel Lewis
Harris Wm
Hightower Stephen
Hill John
Hindman Robt
Bind Thos
Homes Geo
House John
Howell Chas
Humphrey John
Johnson
Johnston David
Jones Peter
[Jones]
Jones Mansfield
Jones Mansan
Jones Solomon
Juakins Mark
Junior John
Kelly
Lane James

Privates, Continued

Lawless Henry
Lively
Lepar Wm
Lenin Curtin
Lenin John
Luck Asa
Luck John
Mabry Riels
McStay Henry
McLain Thos
Moore James
Morgan John
Morris Moses
Moystyn Wm
Mumkin John
Mumkin Richard
Musteen Wm
Mullen Harris
Northington Joshua
(drummer 8th co.)
Obrien James
Obrien James
(drummer 1st Co.)
Permax John
Peruze John
Peters Jesse
Phillips John
Pratt Henry
Puckett Benjn
Reilly Thos
Robinson Alex
Romers Francis
Rouse Wm (7th Co)
Russell George
Russell John
Ryan Wm
Sanders Jonathan
Shelly Thos
Smith Elisha
Smith Jesse
Smith John
Smith Joseph
Spencer John
Stapleton Geo
Torny Thos
Thompson Wm

Tomblin John
Tucker David
Tucker Paschal
Tucker William
Turtle Thos
(Drummer 6th Co.)
Rines Harbart
War Wm
Wash Wm
Wells Alex
Whitman Wm
White Joseph
Whitmill Henry Job
Whitman John
Whitman Richard
William Isham
Wilkman Wm
Wilmon Joshua
Winn Joshua
Wood James
York Richard

2nd Bat. Ga. Continentals

Col. Samuel Elbert
Lieut Col. John Stirk
   do   Daniel Roberts
Major Pannell
Major Benjn Porter
Major Francis Morris
Adjutant Matthew Roche
Surgeon David Brydie
 Do mate Adam Alexander
 Do Do Ralph Edward Cramden
 Do do Andrew Smith
QrMaster William Matthews -
   Promoted Qm
   do   Saml Camp
   do   Lt Robert Howe
Qm. Sergt. J. Strong

Qm. Sergt. Wm. G. Dell
Depy do   Wm Damant
Pay Master Lieut John Waudin
Depy Pay master Capt [Corp?]
   Littleberry Mosby (probably
   Brigade)
Judge advocate Samuel Stirk
Hospital Steward Richard Gascoyne
Fife Major   Kinan
Sergt Major
Conductor [?] of waggen Robt
   Harrison
Captain Benjn Porter promoted maj
Captain Francis Moore 1st Co -
   promoted maj Oct 1778

132

Captain William Lane (Lain)
Captain Jacob Wimpey
Captain John Barrel 4th Co
Captain Smyth (Smith
Captain Shem Cook
Captain Edward Wood 2nd Co

Captain Littleberry Mosby 6th Co
Captain John Cunningham 7th Co.
Captain Elisha Miller 8th Co.
Captain Geo Hancock 5th Co.
Captain John Clarke 1st Co.

Lieutenants:

Elisha Miller - Capt Mar 78
John Cunningham Capt Ap 78
John Clarke - Capt Ap 78
George Hancock - Capt July 78
Littleberry Mosby - Capt

1st Lt Dec 77:

Baugh Alex C
Henry Allison
Robert Mosby
Thos Davenport   Grenadier
John Willson
Thos Porter
Wm Turner
Wm D Strother
Thos Pain
Matthew Roche - adjutant
John Rae
Abraham Jones
Joseph Bayly
Cornelius Collins
Robert Howe - Ensign to Mar 1778 & Lieut.
Fredk Shick
John Morrison
Ben Lloyd
Jas Hill
Jno Waulden
Ensign - Apr 78 Daniel Goffer
(ward Robt Killed May 18, 1777)

Sergeants:

Adams Arch
Boatongh
Baker Wm
Campbell
Childress Thos
Camp Samuel
Cornett John - 7th Co
Damant Wm
Halsy Thos - 7th Co
Leslie Chas - 1st Co
Oakley Erasmus
Palmer Wm
Rniss James
Hardwick Geo

Privates:

Adamson Chas
Allen Ebenezer - Lains Co. - also 8th Co.
Arnold Wm
Blakery John
Bourke Alex

133

Blethem Wm
Berge John
Brannon Wilson
Bryan Hawkins
Barker Wm
Brown John - 1st Co
Bryan John 2nd Co
Berns John - 7th Co
Campbell Angus
Clifton - 1st Co
Cannon Joseph - 2nd Co.
Cyells James - 1st Co.
Dugan James
Deveseaux Michael - 7th Co.
Davenport Stephen
Daven Thos
Dawson William
Earn John
Edlay Christian [?]
Ethridge Thos
Fagan Hugh
Forest Thos
Foster John - 5th Co
Flannagan John
Fraser Wm
Garton Uriah
Gunn Wm - 1st Co
Howard Ben - Millers Co
Hutson Jas
Hutson Benj
Hint Martin
Hambleton John
Hiley Cornelis
Handee Daniel
Hughes Thos
Holt Beverly
Jack John - Porter's Co
Jones Samuel
Jones William
Jones John - 7th Co
Joshing Daniel
King Cornelious
Lane Wm
Loving John - Millers Co
Lindsay Benj - 5th Co
McBride John - Capt. Lane's Co.
Mint Wm
Morrison Ezra
Mastin Thos - Clarke's Co.
Mustin Wm
Mulbourning Michael
Mastin Wm
Meyers James
Matthews Pane
Newman John
Nmen King
Pca Elias
Rains John
Roberts John
Robert John
Summerin Thos
Savage Richard
Soday Thos
Stokes Hartwell
Stony Elias
Spradling Jas
Smith Thos
Smith Benjn - 7th Co

Taylor John - Smythe's Co.
Trent Wm - 1st Co
Upham Abraham
Willowbe Wm - Wimpey's Co.
Wilkinson Sherwood
White John
Wall Benj
Wilimer Thos
Wooley Arch
Wright Ezezial
Watts John
Waten Andrew

2nd Battalion - Georgia Continentals

July 5, 1776 Colonel Samuel Elbert
    Lt Col John Stirk Promoted Colo 3rd Bat Mar 21 1778
Apr 1st 1778 Lt Col Daniel Roberts
    Major Seth John Cuthbert
    Major Joseph Pannell
    Major Benjn Porter
    Major Francis Moore
    Captain Joseph Pannell 1
    Captain Benj Porter 2
    Captain Francis Moore 3
    Captain John Bard 4
    Captain Wm Lane 8
    Captain Smythe 5
    Captain Isham Cook 7
    Captain Lenior 4
    Captain John Mosby 1
    Captain Thos Scott 4
    Captain Jesse Winfree 2
    Captain Thomas Dooley
    Captain Random Smith 3
    Captain E Miller 4
    Captain Jno Morrison
    Captain Ed Wood 1

    Jno Cunningham 5
    John Clarke 6
    Geo Hancok 7
    Herd died sep 1778

    [On a separate piece of paper it mentions that Herd. died
     Feb. 14, 1778.]

5. Rosters from the "Revolutionary War" file, Keith Read Collection,
    Special Collections, University of Georgia Libraries.

    A Provision Return for the Sick in the Hospital of the
    Third Georgia Battalion 21st. April 1778

    Very Sick

    1   Burwell Green
    2   Rich. Burnett
    3   Joshua Winsor

    s/s Curtis Linn. orderlyman

    Recovering

    1. Charles Burnett   14. Charles Turner
    2. Charles Gunter   15. John Arken
    3. Jesse Peters   16. John Pinnex
    4. Thos McLain   17. John Linn
    5. John Russel   18. Joseph White
    6. John Abbott   19. Henry Pratt
    7. George Russel   20. Joseph Stewart
    8. William Harnis   21. Thos Killey
    9. John Munkus   22. Daniel Bryant
    10. Richd Munkus   23. Alexr. Robinson
    11. John Persize   24. Robt. Hindman
    12. William Moystyn   25. John Spencer
    13. Moses Morris

Sir

I am of Opinion that the four Very Sick Draw half Rations and That the twenty five Recovering and the orderly man Draw their Rations as Usual.

Phillip Box Esqr.   /s/ Thos. Davenport Surgn.
Commissary of Hospitals

A [illegible] return of men Doing duty on board of the Bulloch galley from Aug 18th 1778 to august 21st

Names	Stations
Matthew Macomber	Lieut.
James Baird [?]	Boat [illegible]
Wlm. Toeloderel	guner [sic]
Joseph Nobly	[illegible]
Absom Franklin	Armer
Wlm Trenjon [?]	Seaman
John Legnofth	Do.
Jonath Egle	Do.
Wlm. Drimgter [?]	Moreaos [?]
Path Stanton	Do.
John Lain	Do.
Francis Howard	Do.
Wlm. Crup	Negro
March	Do.
Black Sam	Do.
Yellow Sam	Do.
Bookery [?]	Do.
Black John	Do.
Barrick	Do.
Jack	Do.
Paddy Coy	Do.
Moukco	Do.
Nick Miers	
John Ozbon	

6. Petition from "Elbert, Samuel," Miscellaneous Letters, Papers of the Continetal Congress, Records Group 360, National Archives, Washington, D.C.

To Samuel Elbert Esq. Colo Commandant of the Georgia Brigade

Sir

From the readiness you have ever shewn to conduce [sic] to the ease and happiness of the troops under your command we have no room left for a doubt but your ears are still open, and that nothing on your part will be wanting to redress every well grounded complaint from those who have the honor to be commanded by you.

We the officers of the second Battalion of Continental Troops for the state of Georgia met for the purpose of representing to you the many intolerable grievances under which we have too long laboured, do most earnestly request you will interfere in our behalf, and without whose interposition we have not the most distant hope of redress.

You cannot but retain in mind the instructions given us when ordered on the recruiting service in Virginia we mean those of promising the men whom we recruited upon the faith of the United States, that they should receive their wages in money current thro: the continent, this the soldiers insisted on for many reasons, one of which is and without assigning any other is sufficiently cogent, that their necessitous families had no other dependance [sic] than their wages for support and Existence. That they might frequently have opportunities of remitting money to, and by those means in some measure alleviate the distress of their constituents.

But, Sir, the good intentions they might have had are entirely frustrated they have received their wages in the currency of Georgia alone, depreciated at the lowest computation One hundred pr. cent below the value of Continental Currency, in which we ought to have been paid, and to which we have have [sic] an undoubted right. On one moments retrospective reflection upon the amazing depreciation of the Continental, and currency of each particular State thro: the Continent, The surprising spirit of Jewish Extortion which like Electricity has taken place throughout the same Vast Continent and the moderate price every necessary article of life bore at the time of raising the Second regiment our pay, will at once be sunk into annihilation, Were we paid in the currency of the Concinent our situation would not be so deplorable, An Instance no longer since, than the late expedition to the Southward, will sufficiently prove the glaring imposition, when being on service with the Troops of South Carolina We to our great Mortification saw the soldiers of that state go to a sutler and with Continental Currency purchased rum for fifty Shillings, while the Troops of Georgia with their money, if it deserves the name, could not purchase of the same person and of the same quality for less than Six pounds per Gallon

What must our feelings have been on this Occasion, knowing that we were all continental troops engaged in the same glorious cause, But however much our passions were moved at this circumstance they were still more so on our return from the Expedition, when many of the Soldiers who by your permission have obtained leave to go and visit their friends in Virginia were wandering about Town and had it not in their power to travel even across Savannah River for want of Continental money to bear their Expenses and others who have served faithfully the time for which they enlisted obleiged [sic] to put themselves upon the charity of the Inhabitants while travelling five or Six hundred miles to their respective places of residence--Justice to Individuals forbides [sic] it nor can the good of the service or you any longer suffer it.

In setting forth this our grievance we have not studied the embellishment or decoration of sentences but have given you the plain honest dictates of hearts susceptible of wrongs and must end with the resignation of the commission we have the honor to hold in the army

The thinness of the Battallions of this state makes it again necessary for officers to enter on the recruiting service, in order to fill them up, But Sir we cannot ask a man to enter into the service of the State while its Soldiers are thus treated

In fine [?], the only reason that the minds of the people are thus sourd [sic] and averse [sic] to the service is that the troops have not been treated as they ought to have been with respect to their pay. To the same reasons we attribute the frequent desertions that have happened in the regiment Since its arrival in this state.

We would not be thought desirous of prescribing but must add that if some person were dispatched immediately from among the officers to Congress with a proper draught for the money, and a representation of matters of fact by you, Congress would not hesitate to send the money necessary for us, this step we recommend as the more necessary in consideration that there is now due for the greatest part of the Second Battalion Eight or Nine months pay for which they are become clamorous, and its to be supposed that no person would be more Alert than an Officer who is interested in the matter and in whom trust could be reposed.

We are with respect and Esteem
Savannah Georgia, 31st August 1778
Sir Yr Very Humble Servts.

[All of the names below were copied from signatures.]

Frans. Tenrill Lieut
Robert Mosby Lieut
James Hill Lieut.
Thos. Davenport Lt.
Jno. Morrison Lieut
Abm Jones Lieut
William Turner Lieut.
Henry Allison Lieut
Robert Howe Lt.
Matt: Roche Adjt.
Thos. Payne Lt.
Cornelius Collins
Jos. Bayley Lt.

Jno Wauldin Lt
D Roberts Lt Colo
B Porter Major
Fran. Moore Captn
John Bard Capt.
Edwd Wood Capt.
Jno. Cunningham Capt.
Elisha Miller Capt.
Geo. Hancock Capt.
Litby. Mosby Capt.
John J. Clarke Capt.
William D. Strother Lt.

[The following names appear on a similar, undated petition of the Third Georgia Continental Battalion that accompanied the previous petition.]

Sir

    Having seen and highly approved an address from the officers of the second Regiment to you. . .

John McIntosh Lt. Colo.
Jos. Lane Senr. Major
Isaac Hicks Capn.
Clement Nash Capn.
Raleigh Downman Capn.
William Scott Capt.
Gedion Booker Capt.
Thos. Theadgill Capt.
Rains Cook Capt.

John Meanly Lieut.
John Frazer Let.
John Mitchell Lt.
Nathanl. Perry Lt.
John Dumouchell Lt.
Josiah Maxwell Lt.
Jno. Phillips Capt. Lieut.
Josiah Hatton Lt.
J. C. Clarke Lieut.

7. From the Benjamin Lincoln Papers, reproduced courtesy of the Massachusetts Historical Society.

    The roster of Captain Robert Campbell's Company and the list of men who received gunpowder belonging to the State of Georgia probably contains the names of some South Carolinians, as well as Georgians.

    Return of Men taken Prisoner in the Washington and Bulloch Galleys 13th January 1779 viz:

John Edwards
Joseph Jenevely [?]
Jonathan Eagle
Benjn. Brown   Privates
Nachell. [?] Parret
James Allen
A Boy Called Nicholas

138

A Return of the Names of the Georgia Continental Troops under my
Command taken by the Sloop Mermaid a Tender to his Brittanick Majesty's
Ship Vigilante   January 13th 1779.

Battn.	Names on Parole	Joined the Enemy	Prisoners on Board
2d.			Phillip Dumford
do.			Michael Cain
do.			Joseph Cannon
3d.			Rolly Griffith
			Jonathan Whitmen
			David Johnston
		John Baretrap	
4th.		Serjt. Jas. Kingham	
		William Walsh	
		Richard Powers [?]	
		Danl. Powell (drummer)	
	Isaac Cogan		
	William McCormick		
	Samuel Wood		
	John Smith		John Sharp
	On Parole 4	Joined the Enemy 5	Prisoners on Board 7
	Total 16		

/s/   A Hayes Lt.
4th G. Battn.

A list of Officers Taken in Savannah Decr. 29th 78

first for Exchange

John Habersham	Majr.	1st G.C. Batt:	No. 1
Phillip Lowe	Do.	4 Do.	No. 2
John Bard	Capt.	2d. Do.	3
Shadrack Wright	Capt.	1st Do.	4
John Lucas	Do.	4 Do.	5
Joseph Day	Do.	4 Do.	6
William Hornsley	Do.	4 Do.	7
William McIntosh	Do.	1st Do.	8
John Cunningham	Do.	2 Do.	9
Littlebury Mosby	Do.	2 Do.	10
John Hennington	Lt.	3d. S.C. Do.	1
Thomas Davenport	Lt.	2 G Do.	2
Robert Mosby	Lt.	2 Do. Do.	3
John Fraser	Lt.	3 Do.	4
John Mitchell	Lt.	3 Do.	5
Benjamin Newsom	Lt.	3 S.C. Do.	6
John Goodelin	Lt.	3 S.C. Do.	7
Thomas Payne	Lt.	2 G Do.	8
John Campbell	Lt.	Georgia Artillery	9

David Bradie Surgeon 2nd G.B. to be exchanged next
Thomas Davenport Surgeon 3d G.B.
Adam Alexander Surgeon Mate. . .

A List of Officers Taken in Sunbury Jany. 79

Joseph Lane	Majr.	3d. G.C.B.	No. 1
Thomas Morris	Capt.	Artillery	2
Rains Cook	Capt.	3 G.B.	3
John Dollar	Lt.	Artillery	1

Cornelius Collins	Lt.	2d. G.B.		No. 2
John Meanley	Lt.	3 G.B.		3
Walter Dickson	Lt.	4th Do		4
Josiah Maxwell	Lt.	3 Do		5
John P. Wagnon	Lt.	3 Do		6
Richard Hillery	Ensign 4th Do.			7
John Cowen	Lt.	4th G.B. Taken at Mr. Bryants Plantation Briar Creek 3d March 79		8

Samuel Elbert	Colo. 2d Georgia Battn			No. 1
John McIntosh	Lt. Colo. 3d. Do. Do.			2
Isaac Hicks	Capt. 3		Do. Do.	3
Clemt. Nash	Do.		Do. Do.	4
Alexr. D. Cuthbert	Do.	1st	Do. Do.	5
William Scott	Do.	3	Do. Do.	6
Andrew Templeton	Do.	4th	Do. Do.	7
Gideon Booker	Do.	3d	Do. Do.	8
Edward Wood	Do.	2d	Do. Do. Resd. before Savannah was Taken	

David Douglass A.D. Camp to Genl. Elbert
Solomon Hawling   Surgeon
Ralph Edward Crundell Surgeons Mate 2d Battn.
Robert Arish Lt. Dragoons Taken in So. Carolina
John Frazer Lt. So. Carolina Taken in the Galley
William Lowe Lt. 1st. Georgia Battn. Taken at Briar Creek
John Francis Dejoung S. Mate So. Car. Service
Lieut. Morell

Return of the Men belonging to Captain Robert Campbells Company of
Independents Seamen raised for the Defence of the United States of
America - Purrysburgh March 22nd. 1779

Names	Present	Killed or absent
Captain Robert Campbell		killed
1st Lieut. Wm. Moore	present	
2nd Lieut. Wm. Jones	ditto	
George Warren		absent
Wm. Crabtree		do.
John Richards		
Thomas Sivorn [?]		
Sylvester Holmes	present	
Luke Hunt	do.	
John Cooper	do.	
John Morgan		killed
John Yates	present	
James Ward		absent
John Bowman	present	
James Stevenson	do.	
John Adams	do.	
John Green	do.	
John Bucher		
John Hewatt	present	
James Atherly	do.	
Mont: Cope Austen	do.	
John Cherry [Chevry?]	do.	
Samuel Horton	do.	
William James	do.	
John Bates	do.	
James Henderson	do.	
Richard Martin	do.	

Names	Present	Killed or absent
Corns. Sullivan	present	
John Davis	do.	
Nicholas Lawson	do.	
Anthony Silver	do.	
Christian Arant	do.	
Cornelius Holton	do.	
George Hooker	do.	
George Drudge	do.	
Thomas Hall	do.	
John Robinson	do.	
James Thompson	do.	
James Atkinson	do.	
Chambers		absent

Powder belonging to the State of Georgia delivered out of the Magazine at Purysburgh 6th. Jany. 1779 by Major Bourquine.

To David Weeks - Waggoner
   10 Keggs   100 Each C:P   1000

To Thomas Hills
   10 Keggs   100 Each C:P   1000

To James Harper
   18 Keggs   50 Each
   1 Ditto   100   M:P   1000

To Danl. Campbell
   3 Keggs   100 Each
   1 Ditto   50   M:P
   3 Ditto   100 Each
   5 Ditto   50 Each C:P   900

To John McFarling
   3 Keggs   50 Each M:P
   4 Ditto   50 Each
   7 Ditto   100 Each
   1 Ditto   25   C:P   1025

To Wm. Rankins
   10 Keggs   100 Each M:P   1000

To Alexr. Haffey
   10 Keggs   100 Each C:P   1000

To Wm. Duffey
   7 Keggs   100 Each C:P   700
   1 Ditto   50   50
   5 Ditto   100 Each M:P   <u>500</u>

                                            8175

8. Enclosure from Major Thomas Lane to Major General Benjamin Lincoln, 22 February 1779, Thomas Addis Emmet Collection, used courtesy of the New York Public Library.

    The following also include, as indicated, a return of the Sunbury, Georgia, militia company, and a unit of the Third South Carolina Continental Battalion.

A Return of the Garrison in Fort Morris commanded by Major Joseph Lane, January 9th, 79, made prisoners by B. Genl. Prevost.

Second Company of Georgia Artillery

Thomas Morris	Captain
John Dollar Captain Lieut	Subaltern
Philo Henley 1st Lieut	Subaltern
John Walmore Qr Mr Serjt	Quarter Master
John Ponchier	Sergeant
Samuel Boyd	"
Samuel Peck	"
Daniel Hovey Corporl	"
John Burch	"
Henry Read	"
Thomas Bond	Drummer
William Curtis	Fifer
John Webb	Private
Robert Kenny	"
Dominic Gerold	"
John Newman	"
William Taylor	"
Thomas Davis	"
Luke Paul	"
William Thomas	"
John Campbell	"
George Davis	"
John Wright	"
Saml. Harrison	"
William Tanner	"
John Finley	"

Return of the Third Georgia Battalion

Joseph Lane	Major
Rains Cook	Captain
John Meanly First Lieut.t	Subaltern
Josiah Maxwell Second Lt	Subaltern
John Peter Wagnon Third Lt	Subaltern
David Rees	Subaltern
Ebenezer Calender	Surgeon's Mate
Davis Austin Commissary of Issues	
David Fleming	Qr. Master
Jonathan Holden	Sergeant
Nathan Northington Qr. Mr. Serjt.	
James Hays Serjt.	Sergeant
Benjamin Wall	Sergeant
David Wilson	Sergeant
Nicholas Bond Corporal	Private
John Petillo	"
Michael Cogbourn	"
Camp Burnell	"
Henry Pigg	"
John Masters	"
William Harnass	"
Swan Saunders	"
James Mills	"
William Perdue	"
William Allgood	"
David Motley	"
Herbert Vines	"
William Tucker	"
John Bush	"
Joseph Pearson	"
Velentine Perry	"
Wiott Hunley	"
James Davis	"

```
Jesse Hall                    Private
Thomas Hinds                     "
Peter Stuart                     "
Burgess Moor                     "
Richard York                     "
Peter Jones                      "
Henry Smith                      "
Obadiah Plumley                  "
Solomon Jones                    "
Harris Mullen                    "
John Rickmon                     "
Richard Biorton                  "
Zachariah Reed                   "
```

/s/ Jos. Lane Majr. 3 B.

Fourth Georgia Battalion

```
Walter Dixon                  Subaltern
Christopher Hillary           Subaltern
James Brown                   Subaltern
Charles Millen [Miller?]      Sergeant
John Burnett                  Private
Daniel McGinnis                  "
John Private                     "
Joseph Read                      "
James McDannell                  "
Thomas Dixon                     "
Richard Savage                   "
Lucrick Handgarter               "
Henry Fisher                     "
John Campbell                    "
Joseph Webster                   "
James Combs                      "
```

Third South Carolina Battalion

James Robinson 2d Lt.	Benjamin Davis	Thomas Gready
John McMahon	William Sprowle	Thomas Condon
Hartwell Husky	Thomas Burns	Carter Donahoe
John Edmundson	John McLean	Hezekiah Davis
William Williamson	Michael Davis	James Hilton
Mark Hodges	Curtis Winfield	Benja. Campbell
George Hightown	Philip Miller	Peter Watson
Isaac Scott	Absalom Dean	Benjamin Harrison
Thomas Harper	William Hunter	

Francis Coddington C.P.
  Anhobus C.P.   I certify the above List to be exact
                              & agreable [sic] to inspection
Sunbury 12th Jany. 1799   J. M. Prevost Lt. Col. 60th Regt.

Sunbury Militia Company made prisoners by B. G. Prevost 9th Jany. 79.

```
Officers  (John Kell    Captain
          (William Watson  2d Lieut.
          (George Cabbage  1st Lieut of a Company in Chatham County

          James Hamilton)  Serjt.
          John Simpson  )  Serjt.

Privates  Matthias Lapina        x John Graves
          Jeremiah Dickinson       Jacob Christopher
```

William Davis
Wm. Bennet Senr.
x Wm. Peacock Senr.
Samuel Davis
x Thos. Dickinson
John Cabbage
Adam Confey
David Mott
x Stafford Somersall
x William Wallace
Samuel Main
John Gilchrist
Willm. Sallat
Wm. Maconchy
John Duker
x Wm. Peacock Junr.
Adam Gray
Jean Piriart
Antonio Arlas
Julian Duchatcaif

Joseph Still
Roger Lawson
Alexr. Stuart
Stephen Jenkins
Jacob Vernon
John Glazier
Jeremiah Plumer
Edward Mahorn Senr.
Richard Stevens
x James Lancaster
Vincent Gray
x John Howell
x Francis Blackrole
Henry Waggoner
James Flemming [crossed out]
William Patterson [crossed out]
Henry Manly [crossed out]
Jean Chanier
Antonio Vouffy

I certify the above number
of forty five to be exact.

Jos Lane

Majr. 3 G.B.

J. M. Prevost
Lt. Colo. 60th Regt.
Sunbury 12 Jany. 1799

9. Copies of Rosters from the Joseph V. Bevan Papers, Peter Force
Collection, Library of Congress.

[The editor would like to thank Mrs. June Clark Hartel for providing
copies of these documents.]

A Muster Role [sic] of the 1st Georgia Battalion of Continental Troops
Colonl. Robert Rae. Augusta August the 2nd 1779

Robert Rae Coll 1st April 1778   sick
Francis H. Harris Lieut Colo   absent with leave
Major John Habersham   Prisoner of war with the enemy
George Handley Capt. 19 October 1776   Present
Lachlan McIntosh Capt. 30 October 1776   Do.
Shadrack Wright Capt.   Prisoner of War on parole
Alexr D Buthbert Capt.   Prisoner of War with the enemy
John Wilton Capt.   Do.
Wm McIntosh Capt.   Do.
Thomas Glascock Lieut 1st July 1777   Present
Jesse Walton Lieut   Do.
William Low Lieut   Prisoner of war with the enemy
James Houston Surgeon   Present
John Leduck Qr Mr Sergt   During the war Commd.
John Twedele Sergt Maj   Do.   present
Charles Fields Sergt   Do.   present
John Evens Sergt   Do.   present
John Wright do.   Do.   Deserted
Thomas Jeffrys Corporal   Do.   present
Ethral Fatrul   Do.   Do.   Do.
Thos. Hart   Do.   Do.
Daniel Mathews   Do.   Do.   Deserted
William Love   Drum Major   Do.   present

Privates   Remarks

1. Thomas Wilson   During war Genl Hosp. Augusta
2. John Priar   Do   Present

144

3.	Samuel Ware	During war Genl Hosp August	Furlough
4.	John King	on commd up River	
5.	John Linn	Do.	Genl Hosp Augusta
6.	John Rain	Do.	on Furlough
7.	William Austen	Do.	Present
8.	Hugh Bell	Do.	Genl Hospital Ch Town
9.	James Burns	Do.	Present
10.	David Tellers	Do.	Absent wounded
11.	Rubin Waudrum	Do.	Present
12.	George Jones	Do.	Do.
13.	William Coucksie	Do.	Deserted
14.	Andrew Foster	Do.	Do.
15.	William Gibbs	Do.	Furlough
16.	Searing Askew	Do.	Prisoner of war Paroled
17.	Conrad Frigonier	Do.	Do.
18.	Josiah Bird	Do.	Do.
19.	John Futrel	Do.	Do.
20.	Jordan Jackson	Do.	Do.
21.	James Parks	Do.	Do.
22.	Andrew Shields	Do.	Waggonner at Shelson

Augusta 1st August 1779 Then mustered the 1st Geo Continental
Regiment as specified in the above muster roll

Lachl McIntosh Junr
Capt. 1st Geoa Regt

I do swear that the within muster Roll is just & true & that the same
is without fraud to these United States or any Individual thereof to
the best of my knowledge
Geo Handley Capt.

Sworn to before me
the 3rd of August 1779

A Muster Roll of the Third Continetal Georgia Battalion commanded by
John McIntosh Augusta 2d 1779

John McIntosh Lt Colo	Prisoner of war with the enemy
Joseph Lane Major	Prisoner of war with the enemy
Isaac Hicks Capt.	Do Do.
Clement Nash Do	Prisoner on parole
William Scott Do.	Prisoner with the enemy
Gideon Booker Do	Do Do.
Rains Cook Do	Do Do
John Manly Lt	Do Do
John Frazer Lieut	Do Do
John Mitchell Do	Prisoner on parole
Nathan Pearre Lt & Adjt	Present
Josiah Maxwell Lt	Prisoner with the enemy
John Wagnon Lt	Do Do
Thomas Davenport Surgeon	Do Do

		when Enlisted	term of service	Remarks
John Hoggett Sergt.			three years	Discharged
Jesse Bowder Do			Do	sick in hosp
Paskel Tucker Do			Do	present
John Boyd Do		Jany 7, 1777	Do	Do
Samuel Barnet Do			Do	left sick at genl hospital Stone
Basill Hatton Do		Feby 20 77	Do	present
John Connoley Do			Do	left sick on road

	when Enlisted	term of service	Remarks
William Riley Sergt		three years	Absent
William Corbin Corpl		Do	Waggoner Present
Griffith Dickinson Do		Do	present
George Turner Do		Do	Discharged
Henry Deshazer Do		Do	Discharged
Willm Thompson Do		Do	Absent
Mansfield Jones Drum		Do	Present
Joshua Nortington		Do	Descharged
Obed Hendrick Do		Do	on furlow

Privates

1. Joshua Cissle   Present
2. Jesse Peters   Do
3. James Bryan   Discharged
4. James Lane   Left at Genl Hospital Stone
5. John House   Present
6. Curtis Linn   Absent with leave
7. Parish Lankford   Deserted
8. Terry McTaney   absent Col White
9. Wm Slicks   Present
10. John Tombolin   Deserted
11. Wm King   Deserted
12. John Johnston   Sick at hospital Augusta
13. John Abbot   Deserted
14. Wm Clabruck   waggoner present
15. Moses Reaves   absent Town
16. John Davy   Sick at Hospital Augusta
17. Frederick Thompson   Deserted
18. Wm Coleman   Present
19. Nathl Eves   Do
20. James Obrien   at Hospital Augusta
21. Thomas McClain   Discharged
22. Solomon Draper   Do
23. Alexander Roberson   Absent Town
24. Pat Cockrow   Present
25. Pat Slacks   waggoner present
26. George Thomas   waggoner present
27. Will Osband   Deserted
28. John Wedgewood   waggoner present

Augusta 2d August 1779. Then mustered the third Georgia Continental
Regiment of Infantry as specified in the above muster Role [sic]

Lachn McIntosh Junr.

Capt 1st Geo Regiment

I do swear that the within muster Roll [sic] is just and true and the
same is without fraud to the United States or any individual thereof
according to the best of my knowledge Sworn before me this 3d day of
August 1779.

S. W. Cuthbert JP

Nathnel Pearre Lt 3 G R

A Muster Roll [sic] of the 4 Georgia Continental Georgia Battalion
Commanded by Colonel John White Augusta August 2nd 1779

John White Col   Absent   Camden

```
Joseph Pannel Lieut Col        Absent
Philip Lowe Major              Present on Parole
George Melvin Capt             In Qr Mr Department
John Lucas  Capt               present with the enemy
William Hornby  Do                Do
Joseph Day       Do               Do
Andrew Templeton               Prisoner on Parole
James Stedman        Lieut. Present fit for duty
Patrick Fits Patrick  Do          Do
Edward Cowen          Do       Prisoner with the Enemy
William Jordan        Do       Present
Walter Dixon          Do       Present with the Enemy
John Carswell         Do       On Parole
Arthur Hays           Do          Do
Christopher Hilery    Do       Prisoner with the Enemy
Robert Simpson        Do       Absent with leave
James Lett          Sergt.  Sick About Beach Island
Daniel Dampier        Do       Present
George St George      Do       on the Commisarys department
John Anderson         Do       Col White   Camden
Henry Ellis           Do          Do
John Willard          Do          Do
George Kune           Do          Do
Thomas Johnston    Corporal  Present
John Hendrix        Drummer     Do
Charles Grand         Do          Do
Samuel Runnerfield    Do       Charlestown with Col [illegible]
David Kovack        fifer    with Lieut Carswell Greyham
John Smith            Do       Present
Jeremiah Levering     Do       Camden Col White


Privates

 1.   William Bishop         Present
 2.   George Townsend        Do
 3.   William Harson         Chas Town sick in general Hospt
 4.   Joseph Boys            Discharged by Maj Moor & enlisted during
                               the war
 5.   John Private           Absent without Leave
 6.   Cristopher Tryther     Do
 7.   Charles Clark          Charlestown at the gen Hosp.
 8.   Patrick Couden         Do at Head Quarter without
 9.   Thomas Nichols         Taken by the enemy
10.   William McCormack      In Charles Town
11.   John Furrel            In Hosp at Augusta
12.   John Harris            with Col White Camden
13.   Smith Carpenter        Do
14.   Adam Grub              Do
15.   Joseph Sipeo           Do
16.   William Bull           Deserted
17.   George Hamilton        Do
18.   Stephen Kindal         Do
19.   Thomas Brown           Do
20.   Isaac Cogan            Do
21.   Edward McGennis        Do
22.   Samuel Wood            In George Town Prisoner of War
23.   Wm Mitchell            Butcher
```

Augusta 2 August 1779 Then mustered the Fourth Georgia Continental
Regt of Infantry as within the above Muster Roll [sic]
Lachn McIntosh Cap 1st Geo Regt

To His Excellency Lauchlin McIntosh Esqr Brigadier General of the
Forces in the State of Georgia &c

   Your Petitioners Humbly Sheweth That Whereas we the subscribers

Ingaged [sic] in the 3d Company of Light Horse under the Command of
Capt. John Baker now our Honourable Collo Inlisted [sic] by Lieutnt
John Hill who promised us pay once a month during the time of our
Inlistment, and that we should be stationed on the western frontiers of
this State and to march unto any part of said State upon any occasion
of emergency when ordered which we was always willing to do. We
Inbodied [sic] upon the line at the upper Trading path at Fort Bullock
waiting for orders but being in a continual State of alarm was always
in scouting duty. One half of us was ordered to the Cherokees which we
performed and at our return near three months in the service and being
devoted to the use of this State without the help of the militia at
that time; and making no crops for the support of our families, depending on our money according to promise when Inlisted it being impossible
we could live upon the air We tryed our credit to the utmosts. Now all
fails no money, no credit, unavoidably our familys must Perish which we
cannot bare. We had better [to] fall into the hands of our Enemys than
starve for we are ruined to all Intents and purposes Except our Discharge or pay. But if paid our arrears according to agreement with
Lieutent Hill we are still willing to remain in any capacity that we
can subsist under during the Term of our Inlistment (as we are
determined to serve our Country at the Risque of all thats near and
dear unto us). We are now on the frontiers in the service of our
Country and has been on duty since Inlisted. We leave our case to
your wise consideration hoping you will either procure us our money or
discharge by which means we would be enabled to provide for ourselves
and familys and your petitioners sheele ever pray

[All names below are from copies of signatures.]

signed   John Flinn

his
Solomon + Barefield
mark

John Tennesson	Robir [?] Telman	Abraham Hill
George Barnherd	William Lamar	Wells Simmons
John Kelly	Robert Jenkins	John Sawyer
Jas Jones	James Cox	Joshua Hill
Cellier [?] Powell	William Curenton	Samuel Lamar
Harris Telman	Thomas Miller	John McDaniel

10. List of Georgia and South Carolina Continentals Captured at
     Fort McIntosh, Georgia, 18 February 1777, Colonial Office
     Papers, 5/557, British Public Record Office.

     Georgia's chief defenses against British East Florida during the
American Revolution were Forts McIntosh and [Robert] Howe, formerly
Fort Barrington. Both of these outposts fell to British, Loyalist,
and Indian troops even before the main British invasion of Georgia in
December of 1778.

     The following documents deal with the fall of Fort McIntosh to
Indians and Loyalists in 1777. The account of the capture of the fort
by Thomas Brown is from a transcript prepared by Heard Robertson of
Augusta and Ken Thomas of the Georgia Department of Natural Resources.
Brown's letter and the list of men captured at Fort McIntosh are in
the Colonial Office Papers, British Public Record Office. Facsimilies
of Crown Copyright documents are used with the kind permission of the
Keeper, H. M. Stationary Office.

[Copy] Lieutenant Colonel Brown's of the East Florida Rangers, Letter,
to Governor Tonyn dated at Murrays Lines, Santilla River the 20th
February 1777.

Sir,

It affords me not a little satisfaction to inform your Excellency, that Fort McIntosh situated on Santilla River has fallen into the hands of his Majestys Troops.

On Sunday the 16th the regulars being camped at the Old Fort, situated upon Santilla River 20 miles from Fort McIntosh, I set off with two Indians to reconnoitre the Rebels encampment, or fort--an Indian looking for track returned and acquainted me that he had seen a number of the Rebels Horses he imagined One hundred and Sixty, upon receipt of this intelligence I dispatched an Express to acquaint Colonel Fuser of the Indians report--I immediately took an interpreter with me to the place where he had observed the Rebels horses, in order to form some idea of the number of the rebels, after a march of about a Mile at Six o'Clock in the Evening I (   ) about forty horses grazing by the Fort, the moon shining very clear I laid in ambush with the Indian interpreter in expectation of surprising one of the Sentrys, being disappointed in this from the negligence of the rebels in not keeping any. I proceeded to observe the ground, and where the fort might be accessible, on creeping up to the Fort I perceived it was built of split puncheons [p. 346] after the usual method in erecting Stockade forts, the earth thrown up about four feet, and secured by small pines from the ditch upwards--the ditch was only begun upon--the flanks and curtain extended about Sixty paces--a sketch of the Fort I have enclosed--the ground to the South and East commanded the Fort--a Creek passed the Fort within forty paces to which leads a small branch (between the heights) well covered with small Trees and Bush from the Rebels neglecting to remove, it effectually prevented them from annbying us with their rifles, having no Swivels for that purpose--on examining the Creek I found from it they received their Water, this, a few Indians, and white men in ambush could easily command as well as a swamp behind the Fort about two hundred paces from the river--after observing the above I returned to Camp, and gave directions to the Indians, (consisting of fifty men) and a part of Captain Moores men to secure every pass to the fort whilst I made a lodgment in the Creek under the Fort with twelve Men--the Cowkeeper and his gang with five rangers laid in Ambush across the Altamaha road - Hycot and his party in the Swamp towards the river. Philoutougi with him men betwixt the Branch and Creek. As it was my intention to secure one of the Garrison to acquaint us with the state of the Fort I desired every one to use his endeavour for that purpose, and not to fire if there was a possiblity to taking one alive. The Cowkeeper on observing three men quit the fort to cut wood - set up the War-hoop thro' impatience whilst the men were near the Fort by which means they made their escape.

On this the Indians and rangers began a warm fire from every quarter, which toninued near seven hours without intermission - I then from my location called upon the people in the Fort to Surrender, and that the Indians should be prevented from doing them the least injury, they told me they would return an answer in an hour, after expiration of the limited time they sent a (   ) enclosed Card.

(   ) panic with which they were struck by the hooping of the Indians they imagined they would receive no quarter from them, as it is difficult to restrain Indians particularly if they lose any men from the commission of Outrages.

Upon this I dispatched an Express to Colonel Fuser, and acquainted him how matters were circumstanced, and requested him to march with some of the regulars, the Greens, and remainder of the rangers as I had only twenty in the Attack - the Colonel ordered the Troops to march immediately, and by Eleven O'Clock made their appearance on the heights - having informed the Colonel he might reconnoitre with safety and conduct his men down the branch (aforementioned) after making the necessary observations (   ) his men under cover in the branch - determined not to fire against the Fort - beat a parley - hoisted a white flag - Captain Moore took the flag I followed in a Red-Coat, and called upon the Commander to send an Officer to speak with the Colonel -

an officer was immediately Ordered - the Colonel having drawn up his men in one line I ordered the Indians not to fire upon any person who quitted the Fort - to this they immediately consented.

The Colonel having shown the Officers the regulars, and/acquainted them with the vast number of rangers and Indians he sent in the inclosed Articles of Capitulation, and desired a conference with the Commander - the Commander readily agreed on condition I would restrain the Indians from injuring them to which I as readily consented - Poor fellows they generally associate the ideas of Indians with fire and faggot.

The Indians took all the rebels horses - The Fort being delivered up in the customary form - we took possession, and the day following reduced it to Ashes.

To Doctor McKay the bearer I must refer your Excellency who can inform you of the particulars of our Expedition.

The Indians - Cowkeeper, but particularly Perryman and Philotougi behaved like men, and like boys have they been treated by the Colonel - he has affronted them - the rangers and Greens to such a degree not one will go near him.

He has told them repeatedly in an imperious tone to go about their business - not an Indian has been asked to his Table - the rangers insulted with the Epithet of plunderers, thought to do them justice scarce one has received any thing in this Campaign.

The Indians are so discontented with the treatment they have experienced, that on their return unless your Excellency can mollify matters I dread the worst of Consequences - at so critical time when 'tis uncertain what turn affairs in the nation may take - surely 'tis policy to accomodate oneself to their humours, or rather customs, and manners - on my having the honour to wait upon your Excellency I can inform you at large.

I have prevailed with difficulty upon some of the Rangers to hunt Cattle - the Colonel's haughtiness or rather insolence has almost ruined the plan for supplying the Garrisons.

I shall wait the return of the (   ) set off for St. Augustine,
I am
                    Sir, with just respect and esteem
                        Your Excellencys most Obedient
                            humble Servant
                            (Signed) Thos. Brown

Endorsed   East Florida
                  Lieut. Col. Brown
                        To
                  Governor Tonyn

                  No. 15
                  with 2 other papers of the same number

                  In Gov. Tonyn's (No. 35)
                  of 2 April 1777.

"Copy. List of the Garrison of Fort McIntosh on St. Tilla River sur-rendered Prisoners of War this 18th February 1777.

                    South Carolina Rangers

Captain of the Troops and Commander of the Fort   Richard Winn

Lieutenants

1. William Caldwell
2. Oliver Fowels

Serjeant

John Holles

Privates

1. Timothy McKinney
2. William Jones
3. John Montgomery
4. William Brewers
5. James McClear
6. John Steel
7. Philip Anderson
8. Ansel Pruet
9. Alexr Chappel
10. Richard Holly
11. James Adams
12. Thomas Winningham
        absent at Savannah
13. John Wooley
14. Thomas Pain
15. Thomas Gose (wounded)
16. John Watts
17. Richard Duggings (absent)
18. William Ham [Harn?]
19. John Winn
20. Thomas Gore [Gose?]
21. William Rottenberry
22. Francis Kirkland
23. Samuel McKinney
24. Cator West (absent)
25. Richard Wooley
26. James Ham [Harn?]
27. William Duggens (absent)
28. George Watts
29. Christopher Mulkester (absent)
30. George Corks (absent)
31. William Duff
32. William Webster (wounded)
33. Daniel Duff
34. Mark Love
35. Thomas Hullin
36. William Harbinson
37. Peter McMaham
38. Ruben Rigedale
39. Joshua Sphivies
40. John Silcock
41. William Silcock
42. John Millwin
43. Lewis Sanders
44. James Tebor
45. Cornelius Jetor
46. Randall McDonald
47. Samuel Wood
48. Thomas Alexander

Detachment of the first Georgia Battalion

Lieutenant Milton

1. Sergeant Smith
2. Corporal Owens (absent)
3. Corporal Baker
4. George Proctor Private
5. Geordeon Proctor
6. Geordon
7. Armstrong
8. Stevens
9. Lee
10. Reid
11. Moore
12. Mcfie
13. Sikes
14. Turner
15. Rickamus
16. Cook
17. Heaven
18. Armstead
19. Scott
20. Rolles
21. John Turner
22. Jones

11. <u>Records</u> <u>of</u> <u>Captain</u> <u>John</u> <u>Mosby's</u> <u>Company</u>, <u>Nash</u> <u>Family</u> <u>Papers</u>,
<u>Virginia</u> <u>Historical</u> <u>Society</u>.

Records reproduced in this section are copied with the kind permission of the Virginia Historical Society, Richmond, Virginia.

"A pay Roll of Capt: John Mosby Company from the 22 Augt to the 1st
April 1777

Names	When enlisted	Names	When enlisted
Jno. Mosby Capt.	Aug 22d:	John Evins	
Lieut: Wimpey	Do.	Stephen Weatherford	Nov: 4
Lieut: Clarke	Do.	Jos: Terry	Do
Ensign Mosby	Do.	Stephen Terry	Do
Sergt Jones	Oct. 1	Jno. Terry	Do
Sergt Wilkinson	Oct. 22	Jno. Martin	Do 11
Sergt Woodson	Nov. 14	Norman Kidd	Do 13
Sergt Novill	Nov. 14	Andrew Hardy	Do 14
Sergt Parker	Feby 11	Thos. White	Do 17
Thos. Mayter	Oct. 26	Rice Price	Do
Thos. Turtle	Feby 1	Robt: T. White	
Wm Palmore	Octo: 12	Barnabus Williams	Do 20
Robert Tunstill	Decr: 2	Geo. Osborne	Dec. 2
Geo: Hardwick	Octo. 19:th	Jno. Harris	Do 4
Patrick Howell	Do 1	James Cooper	Do 5
Jesse Parker	Do 11	Thos. Mann	Do 7
Edward Metcalf	Do 5	Peter [?] Walker	
Hez:h Robinson	Do 11	Danl. Boatwright	Do 18
Thos. Philips	Do 14	Geo. Saunders	Do 2
Jno. Newman	Do	Jacob Scott	
Andrew Anfing	Do	Richd. Eastern	Jany. 14
Matthew Cartright	Do 16	Wm. Bond	Do 8
Edwin Hazelwood	Do	Jno. Adams	Feby. 2
David Hazelwood	Do	Ben Wetherford	Do 2
Thos. Baker	Do 25	Danl. Wetherford	Feby 2
Jno. Bolling	Do	Phil Dunford	Do 2
Jas. Willoughby	Do	Grant Tyler	Do 11
Wm. Willoughby	Do	Thos. Hodge	Do 21
Jno. Crawford	Do 23	Edward McBride	Sept. 16
Wm. Benton	Do 19	Benj. Megginson	Do
Isaac Benton		Jno. Binns	Do ·
Bartlett Anderson		Charles Morton	Do ⸱
Jno. Beard			
Abram Goff	Do 13		
Wm Castake		Sworn to before me this 31 March	
Wm Peasley	Do 28	1777	
Thades La Desma	Do 21		
Jno. Hancock	Do 20	/s/ Wm. O'Bryon	
Jno. Smith			
Nick Wilkerson	Sept 3	/s/ John Mosby	
Phil Davinson	Do 9		
Jno: Snort	Do 9:th	Received the above	
Jacob Wright	Do 13		
		/s/ Jno. Mosby"	

```
"Capt moore f for Dell                                    2..6
Wm. Roe                                                   2..6
Tho. Hodge                                                1...
Paid at Dorchester
Continent so pd. at Dorchester for
    three Blanketts                                   Ł5
Tho Turtle Pr Stockings                                  13
Edwd Medcalf                                             3.6
Ed. Magbride  Hatt                                       1.8
Tho. Hodge  Hatt & 2 pt. Rum                             1.
Sherd. Wilkerson                                         3.6
Thos. Moyler                                             3.6
Wm. Dell                                                 3.6
Drury Stokes                                             3.6
Rob. Mosby                                             1.2.6
Ed. Medcalf W. Rey                                       1.6
Tho Moyler                                               2
Thos Turtle                                              3.6
Wm. Woodson                                              1.6
Hez Robinson                                             1.6
Wm. Dell                                                 3.6
Ed Medcalf                                               1.6
George Hardwick                                          1.7
Part. Howell                                             3.6
Continent so paid George Raikerly for
    mending waggon at Derihester                      Ł18
Tho Turtle Cash p.p.                                     2.6
Wm. Jones so pd. Blacksmith for
    services done                                        1.7
Continent so pd. Black smith for
    services done to horses                              3.
Wm. Woodson                                              1.
Capt moore for Hayse
Rob Trensill                                             1.
Capt moore to supper at Bryers                           1.6
Mr. Gilmore do                                           1.6
to grog                                                  2.6
to horse gelding                                         2.6
Capt. Moore to grey geldg                                3
Rob Mosby do                                             5
Wm Jones do for supper                                   1.6
Capt Moore pd Rivers Sup                                 1.6
Continent so pd John Hueghes for
    1/2 Bush Salt                                        6
Capt Moore to pd. ye expenses                            5
Mr. gilmore do                                           5
Jacob Winfrey                                            2
Rob Mosby                                                2
Capt Pannell so pd so pd the expense
    of your per[?]                                    Ł5.12..6
Capt Moore to Cash f Rum                                 3
Capt Burke for nails
Sherwood Wilkerson                                       10
Tho Turtle Shues                                         12
Continent so expense for ferriage
    to Savannah
Capt moore so cash lent at Union 45 dollars Ł13.10
Dan Boatwright                                           6
Capt. Moore so the expense ferrage                       3
Sher Wilkerson                                           6
Wm Palmore                                               6
Edwd. medcalf cash                                       6
Patrick Hwell                           3s12
Jno. Hancock                            633
Edwd Medcalf                            6s3
Sherwd Wilkerson                        6s3
Hezh Robinson                           6s3
Jno. Smith                              6s3
```

153

```
Jno. Evins              6s3
Grant Tyler             6s3
Jos. Terry              3s12
Edwd. McBride           6s3
Jesse Parker            6s3
Wm. Peasley             6s3
Tho Hodge               6s3
Jno Harris              6s3
Jno. Snart              6s3
Jacob Scott             6s3
George Saunders         6s3
Rice Price              9s4p
Edwin Hazlewd.          6s3
Tho White               6s3
Wm Willoughby           6s3
Jas. Willoughby         6s3
Will: Jones             6s3
Will Gaslake            12s6
Will: Jones             3.2.6
James Cooper            12
Rob Trenstill           6
Tha Ladesma             6
John Newman             6
Tho Moyler              6
Pet. Walker             6
John Board              6
```

Memorandum

All accounts in this book before this are settled Those which stand
after are not.

[All of the below are crossed out.]

Savannah Georgea March 28

```
Jacob Winfrey Cash              4.10
Edw medcalf do.                 4.10
Tho Phillips Cash               1.3
Wm. D. Strother to Cash
lent 13 Dollars
Thos. Porter to do 14 Dollars
Capt moore so pd fifteen dollars Bill
Tho Hodge                       4.4
To do pd G. Hancocke            2.2
Tho Porter Cash 3 dollars
Wm. Caslake to Cash paid
Robert mosby                    Ŀ2.10
John Evins do                   4
Rice Price do                   4
Lieut. Gedion Booker to Cash
lent & thirteen dollars bill Ŀ19.10
Wm. Jones to Cash lent
forty six dollars               Ŀ13.16
```

April 7th 1777
Received of John Mosby Eleven shillings balance due me from Wm. Jones

                        /s/ Wm. Gilmoure
Continent to J. Mosby   Dr

154

To Cash at Wenoree for Musket   Ŀ8
To do at do for do

Continent   Dr
To Cash pd for Muskett   Ŀ10
To do for do   Ŀ7.15
To do for accountements   1.5
To do pd. John Adams Blank   1.5
Dan Boatwright to Cash 26 Dollars 7.16
Left in the Care of Mr. Putney a Chest with my Cloths & some money
in it also a granidier muskett & one gug

[Below is not crossed out.]
Left in care of Mr. Susliff pay master to 2d. Battn Three thousand
Four hundred & forty dollars to be returned when demanded

[Below is crossed out.]
Left with the Taylor near Coll. Habersham's corded dimnity for 4 pair
breeches & do jackets also a Sattin gackett to turn

Left with shoemaker leather for pr shoes near Honl. Walton's tenament

[Below is not crossed out.]
Sunbury April 14th 1777
John Hancocke to Cash   Ŀ3
Thos. White Cash   3
Thadeo Ladesma Cash   2.2

[Below is crossed out.]
Edwd. Magbride to Cash to pay rum for Ben Weatherford   6
Mr. Putney to over pay in last settlement   Ŀ1
Rob Mosby to paid your expenses at Putneys   Ŀ2
Robert Ward to Cash lent at Sunburry 30 Dollars   Ŀ9

[Below is not crossed out.]
Tha. Ladesma   6
To do 2 dollars   12

[Below is crossed out.]
Continent to Cash paid for horns 6
Tho. White Cash   12
Lieut. Strother Cash   12
Tho Moyler Cash   18
Tho Hodge Cash   Ŀ3.6
Thad Ladesma Cash   12
James Cooper Cash of Rob. Mosby   6
Coll. T. Stirk to Cash 50 Continental dollars   Ŀ15
Sherwood Wilkerson to Cash at Sunbury   Ŀ1.10
Rob Tunstill do   1.1
Grant Tyler to pd your expence at J. P. T & Terry   7

[Below is not crossed out.]
Tho. Hodge Cash   Ŀ3.18

[Below is crossed out.]
Little Mosby to Cash pd Milly   Ŀ1.10

Continent to Cash pd George Hardweek for Blankett   1.10
To do pd Ben Mosby for do   1.10
Continent to J. Mosby Dr
To Forriage for two Horses bought of H. Shipwish for publick from
12 January till 25th April at 1.6 pr day Cash 106 days   Ŀ17.8
To 1 do. of L. Mosby 2d Novr.   175 days   13.2.6
To 1 do. F. Williams 25th Decr. 121 days   9.6
To 2 do Wm Cannon 10 Octr 197 days   29.11
To 1 do. C. Robinson 24th Decemr. 122 days   9.3
To 1 do. Wm. Scruggs 16 Decr. 114 days   8.11
To do for 4 pack horses on our march from 1st February till
   25th April 84 days   25.4

155

To Cash pd Doctor A. Harvie at Sunbury for tending John Adams   1.4
To Expense for ferriage of Wagons & Horses from Purisburg
Major S. J. Cuthbert to Dr to Cash as pd   ₺100
Jacob Winfrey to the expr of Horse at Putneys   18
Edwin Hazlewood   6
Andrew Harvey   12
Sunbury April 29th 1777
Memorandum that this day Capt. Moore & Mosby present settled all
    accounts due the said Mosby from Moore from the beginning till
    this day Ballance due   ₺129.6.8
Capt Moore to John Mosby Dr. for Cash Expense in marching & every
    thing whatever now amounting in Virginian Currency to ₺129.6.8
Dan Goff   1.4
Jacob Winfrey   12
Andrew Hardy   12
Left in the care of Mr. Antrobus Three thousand dollars to be
    returned when required
The mess on board Dolphin
To Cash for Sugar 11 Doll   2.15
to do. for do.   ₺14.11.9
Cr. by cash of Lesardes for Sugar 8 doll   16
Savannah in Georgia
John Mosby   J.T. John
memorandum that the pay from the Country is to me & my company from
    the first dya of April with rations for Officers
Jesse Parker to Sugar   ₺1.17.6
John Newman   do   1.10
Tho Weatherford o   1.2.6
John Martin do   17.6
Tho White do   16.3
Wm Walker do   1.11.3
Tho. Phillips do   13.9
George Hardwick do   1
John Evins to cash   12
Jacob Winfrey cash   ₺1.4
To: do. at Frederica   .18
Dan Goff Cash   6
Ens. Sessades to ballance
    due for sugar   6
Saint Mary's 27th May 1777
John Harris Cash   1.6
Lieut. Daniel Duvall Dr
To Cash Left at Savannah at sundry times   ₺550

Thou art woman a true copy of the first in whome the Race of all man
    kind was cursed your sex by beauty I I I I promise to pay to
    Benjamin Netherland on or before the twenty E E Eight Savannah
    June 20th 1777
Tho. Hodge Cash over your pay   ₺3.3.2
Cr. Tho Phillips By Cash   ₺1.13
Bat. Anderson to over pay in your wages   .3
Cr. Wm. Caslake by Cash to be paid D. Copeland 4.7.9
Cr by your service 1 month   1.15
Rob Tunstill to ever pay in three months pay   18
N. Wilkerson to over pay in three months pay   18
Sher Wilkerson to over pay   1.16
in three months pay   12
Tho Hodge over pay   1.3.2
Cr. Benjn. Mosby by Cash   ₺8

[The below is not crossed out.]
Memorandum received of Benj. Mosby Eight pounds to be paid him in
    Virginia Currency
Major S. J. Cuthbert Dr. to Cash   ₺100
Lieut John Clarke Dr
To ballas. due on settle   ₺182.12.10
Lieut. Dan Duval Dr
To Cash Lent   ₺584.10

156

To do pd Claringdon   80.10
To do Won   50
To do paid in exchange for Continental money   12.10
Cr. By Cash on settlement   23.10
Benj. Netherland Dr
To Cash   Ь37.10

January 25th. 1778
Paid Mr. Davd. Coupland for his two men servants time till 1st August
1777

[Below is crossed out.]
Creed Haskings   Dr
To Cash won   Ь1.10
Sam Hannay   Dr
To 1 Sword   Ь7

[Below is not crossed out.]
Delivered to Mr. Whitfield at Suffolk an order on Henry Brown of
Smithfield for Ь4
Memorandum of Mem Lodged with me to be laid out in France [?]
John Royal   Ь2.6
Fanny Curd   1.10
Wm. Harriss   3.12
A. K. Chamber   11.10
T. P. Posey   30"

"Mr. Jacob Winfrey to Jno Mosby   Dr.
1776 to Cash Delivered by George Walton   64.46
To Cash purchase Blanketts Arms potts &c   117.
To Cash at Charlottesville   6.6
To Cash at Cumberland Courthouse   30.3
To Cash lent   .18
Jany. 27 To Cash lent   10.
To Expences in marching from Virginia   21.11.9
April 3d to Cash in full for your pay abd rations from your entering
   the service to the first of April   6.1.3
To Cash to pay expenses of Waggon Horses   7.10
To Cash lent 91 dollars   27.18
June 28 To Cash in Settlement   19.18.3
                                             311.19.3
                                             289.1
August 1st 1777   Ballance due   22.18.3"

"The State of Georgia.
To John Mosby   Dr   Ь   S   D
1777 to Rations for 7 Men from 1st April
   till 24th May   23   12   6
To Rations for 1 Cadet from 9th January
   to August 1st   12   1   0
To Cash paid at Sunbury for Flour for
   Soldrs.   7   6   8
To Do. paid at Sunbury for Beef   26   16   4
To an Allowance of 1/2 pint of Rum for
   57 Men from the Time of Enlistment to
   March 23rd 1777 at Eps. 1/2 pint   195 10   6
To my recruiting Expences from 22nd
   August 76 till March 28th 77 at
   10 s pr Day   106 10   0
To Do. for Lieut. Winfrey   106 10   0
To Do. for Lieut. Clarke   106 10   0
To Do. for Ensign Mosby   106 10   0
               Savannah Georgia"

E. FRONTIER FORTS OF WILKES COUNTY, 1774 - 1783

The following information on Revolutionary War forts of original Wilkes County (today Wilkes and surrounding counties) is included to provide researchers with background information on locations mentioned in individual Revolutionary War pension claims. As this information is chiefly gleaned from Revolutionary War pension statements and other sources of similar reliability (or lack of), this information should be used with caution. All locations shown are only approximate. What are referred to as roads on the map [see the following page] are wagon tracks at best and trails at worst, based upon maps immediately preceding the Revolution or immediately following it. No maps of the area during the war are presently known to exist. All locations, except where indicated, are in Georgia.

The complexity of these forts and stations varied considerably. Many were probably no more than a fortified house or a blockhouse surrounded by a stockade wall. Some were far more impressive, however, and appear to have been closer to a "Boonsborough" type of settlement with blockhouses at each corner and small cabins and a parade ground in the interior. Whatever their size or sophistication, these forts and stations were of major importance to the people of this frontier area as their defense against the Indian raids that they had to contend with almost yearly from 1774 to 1783.

Every valuable house in Augusta is surrounded by a strong wooden fortification, formed of three inch plank, in deep grooves of upright posts, not less than ten or twelve feet high. These forts are differently constructed; some have large strong pentagonal flankers [bastions] at each corner in which twenty to forty men may flight. The flankers have two stories, and on the upper floor are mounted a number of three pounders. Others have demi-flankers projecting from the middle of each side to answer the same purpose. The buildings serve, in times of peace, for chair houses and other offices, but, in war, render the inhabitants secure in the midst of savages.

--- William Tennent's description of forts in Augusta, 1775, in R. W. Gibbes (ed.), Documentary History of the American Revolution . . . 3 vols. (Charleston, 1853-1857), I, 237.

The Enemies fort was a Strong Stockade with a square Log House built in the middle of it, two Storeys high with Port Holes in the Upper Story that commanded the ground around the Stockade. . .

--- Andrew Williamson's description of a Burke County fort in Williamson to Benjamin Lincoln, 28 April 1779, Lincoln Papers, Massachusetts Historical Society.

The reduction of most of these was not, however, a work of great difficulty, as they consisted only of stockade forts, calculated for defence against the Indians.

--- Wilkes County forts of 1779 described in Charles Stedman, The History of the Origin, Progress, and Termination of the American War, 2 vols. (London, 1794), II, 119.

By their own voluntary labor the people of each neighborhood, when numerous enough, built what was dignified as a fort, a strong wooden stockade or block-house, entrenched, loop-holed, and surmounted with look-outs at the angles. Within this rude extemporized fortress ground was enclosed to allow room for huts or tents for the surrounding families when they take refuge therein -- a thing which continually occurred; and, indeed, it was often the case, that the Fort became a permanent home for the women and children, while the men spent their days in scouring the country, and tilling with their slaves, lands within convenient reach; at night betaking themselves to the stronghold

158

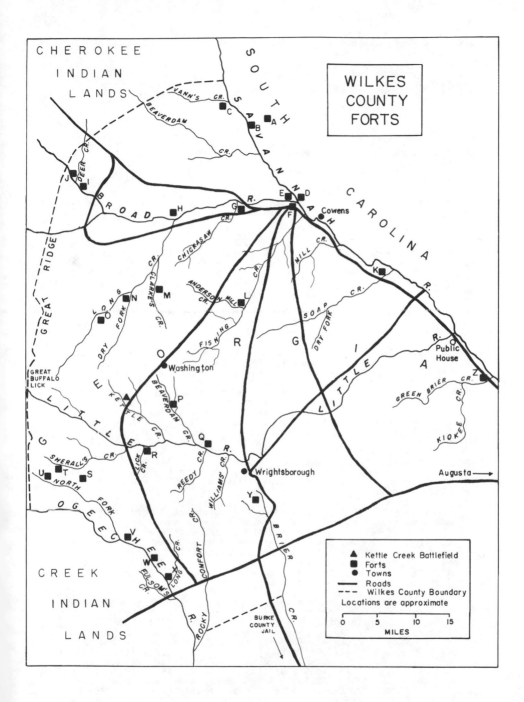

CHEROKEE INDIAN LANDS

SOUTH CAROLINA

WILKES COUNTY FORTS

VANN'S CR.
C
A
B
V
BEAVERDAM
CR.

DEER CR.
J
I

BROAD
H
G
R.
E
D
CR.
F
Cowens

GREAT RIDGE

CHICKASAW CR.
MILL CR.
K
CR.
R.

LONG FORK
N
M
CLARKE'S CR.
ANDERSON MILL CR.
L
SOAP CR.
CR.
DRY FORK
GREAT BUFFALO LICK

DRY FORK
FISHING CR.
R
G
I
A
Public House
R.
Z

O
Washington
KETTLE CR.
BEAVERDAM CR.
P
LITTLE
GREEN BRIER CR.
KIOKEE CR.

LITTLE
O
G
E
E
LICK CR.
R
Q
REEDY CR.
WILLIAMS' CR.
R.
Wrightsborough

SHERALL'S CR.
U T S
NORTH FORK
BRIER CR.
Augusta →

O
G
E
E
CHEE
V
W
H
E
E
LONG CR.
FULSOM'S CR.
COMFORT CR.
Y

CREEK INDIAN LANDS

ROCKY R.
BURKE COUNTY JAIL
CR.

▲ Kettle Creek Battlefield
■ Forts
● Towns
— Roads
--- Wilkes County Boundary
Locations are approximate

0   5   10   15
MILES

159

for the society and protection of their families, as well as for their own safety.

--- Absalom Chappel's description of Georgia frontier forts he had seen in Caroline C. Hunt, "Oconee: Temporary Boundary," University of Georgia Laboratory of Archealogy Series, Report No. 10 (Athens, 1973), 17-18.

A. FORT INDEPENDENCE, S. C. -- A regiment of Loyalists (Tories) under a Colonel Boyd passed above this fort enroute to Cherokee Ford in February of 1779. They were attempting to reach a British army then at Augusta. See South Carolina and American General Gazette, Charleston, 25 February 1779. This fort is shown on the map of Abbeville County in Robert Mills, Atlas of the State of South Carolina: A New Facsimilie Edition of the Original Published in 1825 (Columbia, 1938), Lucy Hampton Bostwick and F. H. Thornby (eds), n.p.

B. MC GOWIN'S BLOCKHOUSE AT CHEROKEE FORD, S. C. -- Cherokee Ford was an important crossing point on the Savannah River between the Georgia and South Carolina frontiers. A high ridge that reaches the river here allowed travelers to avoid the low swampy river bottoms while the thousands of huge rocks in this shallow area formed a natural and partially man made bridge across the river.

Mc Gowin's Blockhouse was in existence on the South Carolina side of the ford as early as 1778. It stood atop a high steep hill that blocked passage to the ford.

In early February of 1779, a Colonel Boyd leading some six hundred Loyalists attempted to use Cherokee Ford to cross the Savannah River into Georgia. The Loyalists were stopped by seven South Carolina militiamen under a lieutenant (variously identified as Lieutenant Shanklin, Ramsey, and Calhoun) who defended the blockhouse with two swivels (small cannons mounted on stumps or posts rather than carriages). Georgia's "Guardian at the Gate," as the lieutenant has been referred to, held the Loyalists back with only bluff until forty Georgia militiamen under Captain James Little reinforced the blockhouse from the Georgia side of the ford. Perfering not to attack the blockhouse, Boyd led his men five miles further up the river to the next place where the high ground cut through the dense cane swamps to the river, opposite the mouth of Georgia's Vann's Creek in present-day Elbert County. There, they began crossing the river on rafts while swimming their horses across.

Sixty South Carolina militiamen under Captains Robert Anderson, William Baskins, John Miller, and Joseph Pickens reached the blockhouse at Cherokee Ford and, after being joined by the militiamen there, set out to stop the Loyalists crossing at Vann's Creek. After being defeated by the Loyalists at Vann's Creek, the militiamen used McGowin's Blockhouse at Cherokee Ford as a rallying point. In the later years of the war, this blockhouse was used as a refuge by Captain Little's family.

Cherokee Ford is shown on the map cited in A. FORT INDEPENDENCE, S. C. For sources see Robert G. Little to Rev. James H. Saye, 26 April 1840 and Revolutionary War Pension statement of John Harris, 23 VV 221 and 11 VV 394 ff, respectively, Lyman'C. Draper Collection, State Historical Society of Wisconsin (cited hereinafter as Draper Collection); Hugh McCall, The History of Georgia. . . (Atlanta, 1969 reprint), 394; Revolutionary War Accounts Audited of Burrel Morris (5349), John Cunningham (1690), William Pickens (5936), Pierre Gibert (2781), and Jacob Holland (3689), South Carolina Department of Archives and History; Revolutionary War Pension Statements of John Verner (S. C. S 7793), John Harris (S. C. S 21808), Francis Carlisle (S. C. W 10576), Patrick Cain (S. C. S 1185), and Thomas Hamilton (S. S. S 30470), Military Service Records (NNCC), National Archives

160

(GSA), Washington, D. C. (cited hereinafter as Revolutionary War Pension Statement of. . .). Revolutionary War Pension statements and the Draper Collection are available on microfilm at the South Carolina Department of Archives and History.

C. CAPTAIN JAMES LITTLE'S STATION -- A native of Virginia, James Little settled near the mouth of Vann's Creek just prior to the American Revolution. Little served as a captain in the Wilkes County militia during the Revolution and he is said to have fought in twenty-two battles including Kettle Creek (where he was seriously wounded), the Siege of Savannah, and Musgrove's Mill (in South Carolina). Captain, later Colonel, Little died in Franklin County, Georgia, in 1807.

On February 11, 1779, a regiment of six hundred Loyalists under a Colonel Boyd attempted to cross the Savannah River into Georgia near Little's home. They attacked on the Georgia side of the river by one hundred Georgia and South Carolina militiamen under Captain Little of Georgia and Captains Anderson, Baskins, Miller, and Pickens of South Carolina. The militiamen were badly defeated in the battle that followed and forced to flee, leaving at least thirteen of their men, including Captains Baskins and Miller, prisoners. Boyd and his Loyalists continued their march towards Augusta but were defeated enroute on February 14 by 340 Georgia and South Carolina militiamen under Colonels Andrew Pickens and John Dooly at the Battle of Kettle Creek.

For sources see those cited in B. MC GOWIN'S BLOCKHOUSE AT CHERO-KEE FORD, S. C. and the Loyalist Claim of Zachariahs Gibbes, Vol. LII, p. 239, American Loyalist Transcripts, New York Public Library.

D. FORT CHARLOTTE, S. C. - Loyalist leader Thomas Brown described this fort as second only to the stone castle at St. Augustine, Florida, in being the most formidable fortification in the south. He wrote that it had a garrison of sixty men. See Edward J. Cashin and Heard Robertson Augusta and the American Revolution Events in the Backcountry (Darien, Ga., 1975), 12-13 (cited hereinafter as Cashin and Robertson, Augusta and the American Revolution). Fort Charlotte is shown on Philip Yonge's "A Map of the Lands Ceded to His Majesty by the Creeks and Cherokees. . ." (1773). Copies of this map are available from the Georgia Surveyor General Office. Also see Nora Marshall Davis, Fort Charlotte on the Savannah River and Its Significance to the American Revolution (Greenwood, 1949).

E. FORT JAMES -- A colonial and Revolutionary War stockade on the north side of the Broad River, some four miles from Fort Charlotte, Fort James was described by William Bartram after a visit there in 1773 as "a four square stockade, with salient bastions at each angle, mounting with a block-house, where are some swivel guns, one story higher than the curtains, which are pierced with loop-holes, breast high, and defended by small arms." The small colonial town of Dartmouth stood near the fort and after the war the important town of Petersburg grew up on this same ground. Neither town exists today.

Early in the American Revolution, the company of Colonial Rangers assigned to Fort James joined the First Georgia Continental Battalion. A Patriot garrison that later occupied the fort were beseiged there by Indians in 1776.

For sources see Robert S. Davis, Jr., "Captain Edward Barnard and the Ceded Lands Rangers," Georgia Pioneers Genealogical Magazine, Vol. XV (February, 1978), 20-22; Revolutionary War Pension Statements of Charles Lane (Ga./N.C. R 6118), Shadrack Nolen (Ga./S.C. S 4622), and Evans Haines (Ga. W 8897); Pay Roll of the First Georgia Continental Battalion, 1 July to 1 November, 1779, M246, Records

Group 93, National Archives (included elsewhere in this book); Francis Harper (ed.), The Travels of William Bartram Naturalist Edition (New Haven, 1958), 383.

F.   FORT NEAR THE LATER SITE OF LISBON, GA. -- Near this fort, a wagon train led by then Captain Elijah Clarke of the Wilkes County militia was attacked by Indians in 1776. Clarke and two of his men were wounded and three others were killed. Both the militia and the Indians withdrew, the Indians' casaulties being almost the same. This wagon train had been transporting supplies from "Jacob Patterson's & Richard Moore's" to Fort James, to protect the supplies from the Indians. Captain William Pulliam set out to pursue these Indians and had a skirmish with them north of the Broad River. See the Revolutionary War Pension Statements of David H. Thurmond (Ga. S 32010) and Charles Gent (Ga. S 1903). Thurmond claimed that the militiamen wounded in Clarke's battle with the Indians were Job Hinton and James Smith and those killed were Giles Talbot, Jacob Patterson, and Peter Davis. Also see McCall, The History of Georgia, 317.

G.   HINTON'S FORT -- This fort was near the mouth of Chickasaw Creek near the later town of Norman, Ga., in Wilkes County. For sources see "Hinton's Fort," John H. Goff Collection, Georgia Surveyor General Department (cited hereinafter as Goff Collection); Revolutionary War Pension Statement of David H. Thurmond (Ga. S 32010); and Ezekiel Cloud's pension statement in David W. Morgan, Captain George Barber of Georgia (1975), 3.

H.   KERR'S FORT OR THE FORT NEAR THE MOUTH OF LONG CREEK - This fort has often been confused with Robert Carr's fort with regard to the events leading to the Battle of Kettle Creek (see P. ROBERT CARR'S FORT). It was located fourteen miles from the mouth of the Broad River and almost as far east of Nail's Fort on the Broad River. Information on this fort is found in "Kerr's Fort," Goff Collection; and the Revolutionary War Pension Statement of John Bynum (Ga. S 3111).

I.   STEWART'S FORT - Supposedly, this fort was on the Broad River, two miles east of Nail's Fort. It is mentioned in the Revolutionary War Pension Statement of Alexander Smith (Ga. S 16530).

J.   JOSEPH NAIL'S FORT - A native of Virginia, Joseph Nail erected his fort on the north side of the Broad River at Deep [Deer?] Creek, some twenty-six miles from the river's mouth. Some Revolutionary War pensioners claimed that this fort was at the head of the Broad River, although they probably meant at the fork.

Nail's Fort was attacked by Creek Indians in August of 1778 and by Cherokees in November of that same year. It was destroyed by Indians and rebuilt at least once.

In early February of 1779, Captain Joseph Nail marched his company from this fort to Fort Charlotte in South Carolina. There, they joined the militia regiments of Colonel John Dooly and Andrew Pickens. During the campaign that followed, terminating in the Patriot victory at Kettle Creek, Nail's men provided Cooly and Pickens with valuable guides while they were above the Broad River. They were participants at the Battle of Kettle Creek and at the brief seige of Robert Carr's Fort.

When Colonel Dooly surrendered most of the Wilkes County militia to the British in 1780, Nail was among those who accepted a British parole and protection. He later rejoined the Patriot cause and was killed in the fighting near the end of the war.

For sources see Grace G. Davidson (comp.), Early Records of
Georgia Wilkes County, 2 vols. (Macon, 1932), I, 26 (cited hereinafter
as Davidson, Wilkes County); Hugh McCall, The History of Georgia,
395; "Nail's Fort," Goff Collection; Revolutionary War Pension State-
ments of Ezekiel Cloud (Ga. W 6920), William Black (Ga. W 9730),
Mathew Neal or Nail (Ga./S.C./ N.C. S 14004) and John Webb (Ga. S 31055)
Audited Account of William Pickens (AA 5936), South Carolina Department
of Archives and History; Voucher of Thomas Johnston, 28 January 1780,
Telamon Cuyler Collection, Special Collections, University of Georgia
Libraries.

     K. JOHN DOOLY'S FORT -- According to a biographical sketch
that may have been written by his son, John Dooly was born in present-
day Wilkes County, N.C., between 1735 and 1740. He brought his family
to Georgia from Ninety Six District, S.C., in 1773. Dooly had been a
trader, land speculator, planter, and minor civil official in South
Carolina and continued these occupations in Georgia. During the
Revolution, he served as a captain in the Georgia Continental Regiment
of Horse, a colonel in the Wilkes County militia, commandant of the
Georgia militia, member of the Supreme Executive Council, and attorney
for the state. Under his command, the Wilkes County militia served in
several campaigns, among them being the Battle of Kettle Creek and the
Siege of Savannah. Dooly was murdered by Loyalists while a British
prisoner of war on parole in 1780.

     John Dooly's home was known as "Lee's Old Place" and is believed
to be one of the Savannah River settlements shown on Thomas Yonge, "A
Map of the Lands Ceded to His Majesty by the Creeks and Cherokees. . ."
(1773). On the site, Cooly maintained a plantation, a fort, and possibly a ferry. It was here that in 1780 Dooly and a majority of his men
decided to surrender when Charleston fell to the British. Today,
Dooly's land is a part of Elijah Clark State Park in present-day
Lincoln County.

     See the Revolutionary War Pension Statements of John Collins
(Ga. R 2179), David H. Thurmond (Ga. S 32010), Moses Perkins (Ga.
S 3677), and John Smith (Ga./S.C. R 9769); Adiel Sherwood, A Gazetteer
of the State of Georgia (Philadelphia, 1829), 198; Robert S. Davis,
Jr., and Kenneth H. Thomas, Jr., Kettle Creek: The Battle of the
Cane Brakes (Atlanta, 1975), 73-76; Alex M. Hitz, "The Earliest
Settlements in Wilkes County," Georgia Historical Quarterly, XL (1956),
265; Carroll Proctor Scruggs, Georgia Historical Markers (Valdosta,
1973), 333-34; William Bonner, Map of Georgia (1847);and the map of
Abbeville County, S. C., cited in A. FORT INDEPENDENCE, S. C.

     L. HEARD'S FORT - This fort was built at the mouth of Anderson's
Mill Creek, a tributary of Fishing Creek, near the beginning of the
American Revolution. A party of Loyalists occupied this fort briefly
in 1779 and, in 1780, it was Georgia's temporary state capital. For
sources see William Bonner, Map of Georgia (1847); Willis C. Lindsay,
"A History of Washington, Wilkes County, Georgia" (typed manuscript,
Mary Willis Library, Washington, Ga., 1921), 7, 23, 26; Revolutionary
War Pension Statements of John G. Heard (Ga. R 4822) and Evans Haines
(Ga. W 8897); Allen D. Candler (ed.), The Revolutionary Records of the
State of Georgia, 3 vols. (Atlanta, 1908), II, 212, cited herein-
after as RRG; Walter Scott to Alexander Cameron, March 27, 1779,
Colonial Office Papers, 5/80, British Public Records Office.

     M. ELIJAH CLARKE'S STATION - The home Georgia Revolutionary
War hero Elijah Clarke (born in Edgecombe County, N. C., in 1736,
died in Richmond County in 1799), this fort stood on what was later
Clarke's Creek. Clarke served with distinction in several battles
in Georgia, Florida, and South Carolina during the war and in efforts
to settle the Georgia frontiers in the post-war era. See Revolutionary
War Pension Statements of Charles Gent (Ga. S 1903) and Moses Perkins

(Ga. S 3677); and Louise Frederick Hays, Hero of Hornet's Nest (New York, 1946), 295-96.

N. FORT AT THE FORK OF LONG CREEK - Mentioned in the Revolutionary War Pension Statement of James Swords (Ga. S 32002), this fort may be the one where Captain Thomas Dooly's detachment of Continental troops were stationed prior to being ambushed by Creek Indians in 1777 (Revolutionary War Pension Statements of David Haley, Va. R 4451). Swords' statement also mentions "Awl's old place" near the mouth of Long Creek and Dennis' Mill on Little River (also see SALTER'S FORT at the end of this section).

O. JOHN HILL'S FORT - This fort is mentioned in the Revolutionary War Pension Statement of Micajah Brooks (Ga. W 27694).

P. ROBERT CARR'S FORT - Robert Carr, a settler from North Carolina, built his fort at the fork of Beaverdam Creek of the Little River. Colonel Samuel Elbert visited this fort in 1777 and there were battles with the Creek Indians here in 1778 and the spring of 1779. During the latter incident, Captain Carr was robbed and killed.

In February of 1779, Carr's Fort was occupied by eighty Loyalists under Captains Dugald Campbell and John Hamilton. Georgia and South Carolina militiamen under Colonels Andrew Pickens and John Dooly besieged the Loyalists until they were forced to retreat in order to attack an approaching regiment of Loyalists under a Colonel Boyd. Pickens later remembered that Carr's Fort was "an old Stockade fort, full of little old cabbins [sic] & very dry." The Battle of Kettle Creek was fought near there on February 14, 1779.

Sources for Carr's Fort include Andrew Pickens to Henry Lee, August 28, 1811, 1 VV 107-107[7], Draper Collection; Revolutionary War Pension Statements of Asa Morgan (Ga. S 31870) and Benjamin Thompson (Ga. S 32016); Deposition of Samuel Beckaem, 1 June 1812, vii-E, 3, Peter Force Papers, Library of Congress; "Robert Carr's Fort,' John H. Goff Collection; South Carolina and American General Gazette, 25 February 1779; Archibald Campbell, "Journal of an Expedition Against the Rebels of Georgia. . ." (typed manuscript, State Library of Georgia), 102; Davidson, Wilkes County, I, 11, 24, 37.

Q. JOEL PHILLIPS' FORT - Colonel Samuel Elbert visited the fort in 1777 which was built by Joel Phillips, formerly of North Carolina. It probably stood near Reedy Creek on the north side of the Little River. See Davidson, Wilkes County, I, 11; "Order Book of Samuel Elbert. . .," Collections of the Georgia Historical Society (Savannah, 1902), V, pt. II, 55 (cited hereinafter as Elbert, "Order Book").

R. ZACHARIAH PHILLIPS' FORT - This is the "Capt. Phillips Fort" that Elbert visited following the Indian troubles of 1777. It probably stood at the mouth of Lick Creek on the south side of the Little River and was built by Zachariah Phillips, formerly of North Carolina. Indians destroyed this fort in 1777. For sources see Davidson, Wilkes County, I, 17; Elbert, "Order Book," V, pt. II, 55; Carolina C. Hunt, "Oconee: Temporary Boundary," University of Georgia Laboratory of Archeology Series, No. 10, 18; Hays, "Georgia Military Affairs," I, 33.

S. POWELL'S OR CHILDER'S FORT - This fort stood on a creek that flowed into the Ogeechee River, although near the headwaters of the Little River. The name of the fort was changed to Childer's Fort when its commander was replaced. See "Powell's Fort," Goff Collection; the Revolutionary War Pension Statement of Alexander Smith (Ga. S 16530).

164

T. WILLIAM SHERRALL'S FORT - Attacked by Indians on January 14, 1774, this fort stood four miles from the head of the Ogeechee River but on a creek that flowed into the Little River. William Sherrall, four white settlers, and two black slaves were killed. For sources see Allen D. Candler (ed.), "The Colonial Records of the State of Georgia" (unpublished typescripts, Georgia Department of Archives and History, 1937), XXXVIII, pt. 1, 163; Cashin and Robertson, Augusta and the American Revolution, 3-5; and Davidson, Wilkes County, I, 18, 21, 22.

U. WILLIAM WHITE'S HOUSE - On Christmas Day, 1773, William White, his wife, and their four children were killed by Creek Indians at their home at the head of the Ogeechee River. This incident was the beginning of a series of raids by a Creek War party that temporarily halted the settlement of the ceded lands. See the sources cited in T. William Sherrall's Fort and Davidson, Wilkes County, I, 19.

V. WELL'S FORT - Very little is known about this fort beyond the fact that it was on the Ogeechee River in Wilkes County. It was visited by Samuel Elbert in 1777 and destroyed by Indians in 1779. Well's Fort and Drury Roger's Fort (see below) may be the same place. See "Well's Fort," Goff Collection; and the Revolutionary War Pension Statements of Mordecai Chandler (Ga./S.C. R 1848) and Samuel Jordan (Ga. W 8224).

W. DRURY ROGER'S FORT - Drury Rogers built his fort on Poplar (or Camp) Creek of the Ogeechee River. Indians led by David Taitt destroyed this fort in the spring of 1779 after its garrison had fled. See David H. Corkran, The Creek Indian Frontier (University of Oklahoma, 1967), 318; Revolutionary War Pension Statement of James Swords (Ga. S 32002); and Davidson, Wilkes County, I, 13.

X. BENJAMIN FULSAM'S FORT - Colonel Samuel Elbert visited this fort in 1777, which was built by Benjamin Fulsam of North Carolina. Captain Fulsam and his company were ambushed by Indians near this fort in 1778. This fight occurred on present-day Fulsam's Creek with Fulsam and seven of his men being killed. Taitt's Indians destroyed this fort in March of 1779 as they did Well's and Roger's Forts. The Indians used the ruins of this fort as a camp until they learned of the approach of a large party of Georgia and South Carolina militia under Colonels Andrew Pickens and John Dooly forced them to withdraw. For sources see Davidson, Wilkes County, I, 19; Revolutionary War Pension Statement of James Wood (Ga. W 4405); South Carolina and American General Gazette, 9 April 1779; and "Fulsom's Fort," Goff Collection.

Y. SOLOMON NEWSOME'S FORT - On the south side of Briar Creek, in present-day Warren County, stood the fort built by Captain Newsome. He escaped from Taitt's Indians in March of 1779 and reached his fort in time to warn the garrison of the Indians' approach. That same night, the Indians attacked, but were repulsed. See "Newsome's Fort," Goff Collection.

Z. KIOKEE FORT - The building of this fort is mentioned in the Revolutionary War Pension statement of Alexander Smith (Ga. S 16530).

Other Forts:

FORT CHATHAM - Mentioned in the voucher of Thomas Johnston, 28 January 1780, Telamon Cuyler Collection, Special Collections, University of Georgia Libraries, as having been built as early as 1778. It may have been another name for Fort James (See E. FORT JAMES).

JOHN COLEMAN'S FORT - Probably built on the Borad River, this fort was owned by John Coleman, formerly of Virginia. He was an early member of the Georgia Patriot Executive Council, colonel of the state horse troops, and colonel of the Wilkes County militia. Coleman died of an illness in 1778 and was replaced by Colonel John Dooly as commander of the Wilkes County Patriot militia. See Davidson, Wilkes County, I, 12, 34-35; RRG, I, 115, 306; and Revolutionary War Pension Statements of Charles Gent (Ga. S 1903), Asa Morgan (Ga. S 31870), and John Bynum (Ga. S 3111).

DENNIS' FORT - This fort is mentioned in RRG, II, 115, with JOHN COLEMAN'S FORT and HEARD'S FORT. It was probably on the Little River.

FREEMAN'S FORT - This fort was built on the north side of the Broad River in present-day Elbert County where supposedly there had been a colonial settlement of indentured servants belonging to Lord George Gordon. For sources see William Bacon Stevens, A History of Georgia. . . 2 vols. (reprinted Savannah, 1972), II, 245; George R. Gilmer, Sketches of Some of the First Settlers of Upper Georgia. . . (reprinted Baltimore, 1970), 185; and Elijah Clark to John Dooly, 15 August 1779, item no. 184 in George D. Smith, American Autographs Historical and Literary (New York, n.d.).

DANIEL GUNNELLS' FORT - Built supposedly on Sandy Creek, this was the place where Colonels Dooly and Pickens parted after their Georgia and South Carolina militia defeated David Taitt's Indians in 1779. Daniel Gunnells came to Georgia from South Carolina in 1773 and settled first on the north side of the Little River. A captain in the Wilkes County militia, he served at the Battle of Kettle Creek. See Davidson, Wilkes County, I, 12; and the Revolutionary War Pension Statements of Micajah Brooks (Ga. W 27694) and David H. Thurmond (Ga. S 32016).

HARRIS' OR MARBURY'S FORT - This fort stood on the north fork of the Ogeechee River, according to a deposition in Louise Frederick Hays (ed.), "Indian Depredations, 1787-1825, Original Claims in the Department of Archives and History of Georgia (typed manuscript, Georgia Department of Archives and History, 1939), II, pt. 2, 398.

FORT LOGGY OR SOGGY - This fort (?) is mentioned in the Revolutionary War Pension Statement of Charles Gent (Ga. S 1903).

POTTS, BOTTS, KNOX, AND GEORGE'S FORTS - These forts were erected along Long Creek and Clarke's Creek, according to the Revolutionary War Pension Statement of John Smith (Ga. R 31967). Fort Knox is also mentioned in the Revolutionary War Pension Statement of Isham Burke (Ga. S 1903).

WILLIAM PULLIUM'S FORT - Built on the north side of the Broad River in present-day Elbert County, this may have been another name for Coleman's Fort (see JOHN COLEMAN'S FORT). For information, see the Revolutionary War Pension Statement of Alexander Smith (Ga. S 16530).

SALTER'S FORT - A reference to this fort is found in the Virginia Gazette, 27 October 1777, p. 3, c. 1. It may be the same as the fort at the fork of Long Creek (see the sources cited in N. FORT

AT THE FORK OF LONG CREEK).

TILLET'S STATION - Possibly this fort was built on Tillet's Creek near Borad River by Samuel Tillet, an Indian trader. It is mentioned in the Revolutionary War Pension Statements of Britton Wells (Ga. S 1270) and Isham Burke (Ga. S 3093). Also see Louise Frederick Hays, Hero of Hornet's Nest (New York, 1946), 307.

MICAJAH WILLIAMSON'S FORT - This was apparently a fort belonging to Patriot militia Captain (later Colonel) Micajah Williamson. Williamson was born in Bedford County, Va., around 1768 and died in 1796, from damage to his health caused by the war. According to one family tradition, he lost a finger at the Battle of Kettle Creek, while according to another, he was one of three men who shot the Loyalist leader Colonel Boyd. Williamson also served at the Seige of Savannah, the Battle of Guilford Courthouse, and the Second Seige of Augusta. See W. J. Campbell to Colonel Thomas, 26 February 1872, I V 14ff and 34, Draper Collection; and the Revolutionary War Pension Statements of Richard Heard (Ga. W 4229) and Asa Morgan (Ga. S 31870).

[Anyone with additional information on these or other forts in the Wilkes County area are encouraged to write: Robert S. David, Jr., c/o Mrs. Garland Holbert, Route 2, Jasper, Georgia 30143.]

F. CAPTAIN SAMUEL BECKAEM'S

STATEMENT ON THE WAR IN GEORGIA, 1778 - 1781

For the last document of part two, it is appropriate to include a deposition of someone who witnessed much of what went on in Georgia during the Revolution. Samuel Beckaem's statement is particularly suited for this, as he began with the capture of Savannah by British troops under Lieutenant Colonel Archibald Campbell on December 29, 1778, the period that the war most affected Georgia and the 200th anniversary of which will be in coming months.

The history of this document is interesting in itself. Hugh McCall, Georgia's first historian, published a notice in Volume I of his The History of Georgia. . . (Savannah, 1811) requesting information on the American Revolution in Georgia. Beckaem's statement was apparently in answer to that request, and was probably used as a source in Volume II of McCall's work (Savannah, 1816). McCall died in 1824. Six months later, Joseph Vallence Bevan was appointed by the Georgia legislature as Georgia's first official historian. Among the material that he gathered for the history of Georgia that he never wrote were the papers of McCall, including the Beckaem statement. Bevan died in 1830, but his papers later became the subject of much interest by such early manuscript collectors as Israel K. Tafft, Jared Sparks, Peter Force, and Matthew St. Clair Clarke. Force and Clarke arranged to have the most important documents in the McCall-Bevan Collection copied for a massive publication project that they hoped would be financed by Congress. These documents were used by William Bacon Stevens in his two-volume A History of Georgia. . . (New York, 1847; Philadelphia, 1859), but they were never published. Today the McCall-Bevan Collection is scattered among many libraries and private collections. The transcripts of this collection made by Force and Clarke, however, are now in the Library of Congress, and from the copy of the Beckaem statement in that collection the following was copied. The original of the Beckaem statement is now among the Bevan Papers in the Georgia Historical Society Library in Savannah. For more information on the history of these papers, see E. Merton Coulter, Joseph Vallence Bevan: Georgia's First Official Historian (Athens, 1964).

In the latter part of the year 1778 Colo Campbell took possession of Savannah. Shortly afterwards Colns Benjn and William Few Collected the Richmond County militia and proceeded to Burk Jail now where Wainsborough now stands where they were joined by Major John Twiggs when they had encamped but a few days before they were completely surprised by Colo Brown and the notorious McGirth. The greater part of Coln. Fews command fled in the commencement of the action but the officers with those who stood their ground behaved with uncommon bravery, contending with about three to one and kept the field. The Reverend Silas Mercer contributed greatly to the success of this action by animating and exciting the troops to keep their post: with great fortitude and presence of mind, he quoted Scripture phrases ensuring them that the battle was the Lords and their magnanimus conduct would be crowned with the success due to the justice of their cause. In the early part of 79 Coln Campbell with about 3000 troops arrived at Augusta. Soon after his arrival he sent out Lieut Aquilla Hall with 28 Dragoons who were all made prisoners by Col Marbury. Mr. Hall had come from the upper part of South Carolina where he had betrayed a post to the Cherokee Indians he was consequently taken to ninety six where he was tried and found Guilty and Executed in April 79. Coln Hamilton the present British Consul at Norfolk was then Detached with a large party to pay Wilkes County a visit. But Colons Pickens, Dooly & Clark were soon in pursuit of him their veteran militia Coln H. thought is most Expedient to take shelter in Stock aid [stockade] fort on the frontiers of Wilks called Carrs fort; here he was so closely pressed that the rear men was shot down as he entered the Fort gate supposing him to be one of the enemy. In the course of the night Colns Pickens Dooly and Clark received an express that Col. Boyd from Yadkin N Carolina with 700 Tories were crossing Savannah River at Cherokee ford which compelled them to leave Coln H. in his fort to his great joy. The next morning the Coln left his cage for Agusta reaching Rightsborough that night where he cooled himself in a stock aid fort again. There he remained that night & fortunately for him he arrived in Agusta the next day. The second day after Coln Pickens Dooly and Clark took their leave of Coln H they saluted Coln Boyd at Kettle Creek in Wilks County, killing Boyd and a number of his party & totally defeating the ballance of them. Immediately on Coln Hamilton's joining Coln Campbell at Augusta they made a recipetate march towards Savannah, ahlted at Hudsons Ferry some time; during their stay there General Ashe of N. Carolina came on with the militia of that State and joined Genl Elbert with the remnant of the Georgia Continentals at Augusta. They then pursued Coln Campbell as far as Brier Creek about 15 miles from Campbells encampment where they had remained but a few days before they were Surprised at noon day. Genl Ashe and his militia fled without making any opposition not one was ether killed or taken unless he was taken for want of bottom or speed. Genl Elbert bravely contended with his few Continentals against the whole British force untill compel'd to surrender being overpowered by numbers. In Spring of the year 1780 after the Surrender of Charleston, Coln Clark of Wilks Col Few of Richmond and Col Twiggs of Burke all fled to N Carolina with those of their friends who were determined to share in their fate. Shortly after Coln Clark left Wilks a certain notorious vilian Call'd Capt William Corker & his party inhumanely murdered Col Dooly in his own house. Col Clark of Wilks & Major McCall of Carolina came to Augusta in August of the same year with a command of Georgian and Carolinians and beseiged Augusta five days, and was compel'd to raise the siege in consequence of Col Crugur coming from Ninety Six to the assistance of the enemy. Brown then hung nine brave men without any charge, only their being friends to the cause of their Country viz John Burgany Scott Randen, William Willey, Richard Willey Jordan Ricketson Darling the names of the other three not recollected Then Brown Crugur and all the Tories that Georgia could parade went in a body to subjugate Wilks County which they did completely, compelling them at the same time to surrender up 21 of their most respectable citizens as hostages for neutrality of the said

County of Wilks who were kept in close confinement in the fort in
Augusta from October 20[?] untill June 21 [?] at which time Browns
Fort surrendered to the American arms but from the hardships they
Experienced through enclemency of the Winter and the small pox few
were now living.

In March 1781 the Georgians once more determined on retaking the
State of Georgia. The party who made the first appearance was Col
Micajah Williamson, Col Clark having not yet recovered his wounds
recd at Long Cane. Col Williamson's arrangement was to divide his
small band of vetrans into three parties taking the comand of the party
intended to chastize a few obnoxious Tories in Wilkes County. Capts
Carr, Dunn and Walker were assigned to Richmond County Crossing
Savannah River three miles above the mouth of Little River at a ferry
call'd Pace's Ferry. Carr and Dunn immediately crossed little River
at Paine's ford, into Richmond having but twenty-three men; at night
when they made their Calculation of the Transactions of the day, they
had killed 26 of the greatest Rascals that Georgia held. The day
following they attacked [.] Capts Dunn & Carr took a Tory station in
Rightsborough; killing Capt Wilder and the greater part of his men.
That night was appointed for Rendezvous of the three parties at
Dennises Mill on little River which was punctually done. Col Williamson and his officers now thought it expedient to cool Col Brown once
more in Augusta but being weak kept a flying camp untill joined in a
few days by Col Baker, Capt McKay and Capt Stephen Johnson. They
still kept on the alert untill Col Clark arrived when they closely
invested Augusta. In April of the same year Major Pinkey Eaton of
North Carolina arrived with a command of Eighteen months men Major
Eaton marched with his command in front of Col. Clark's parrellell and
commanced entrenching between Brown & Grierson's forts. The British
and Tories both Sallied out on Majr Eaton an action insued in which
he was wounded in the thigh. His men ran and Tories inhumanely
murdered him. In the course of this mont two other skirmishes took
place Capts Carr & Shelvey commanded in both instances Major Dill
collected all the Tories he could and was marching to the assistance
of Brown. Col. Clark got intellegence of Dill & dispatched Carr &
Shelvey with the command of Georgeans and over mountains and they met
at Walkers bridge on brier Creek where they routed Dill completely,
killing a number of his adherents with a very inconsiderable loss;
Carr and Shelvey returned to Col Clark with their laurels. A circumstance soon occured that rnedered their services necessary. Col Clark
having fixed his horses on an Island six miles below Augusta under a
guard, Brown got news of this & sent a party down the margin of the
River through the plantations consisting of British Tories & Indians.
Canoes were sent down in silence to convey them across to the Island.
Their pilot was one Wetherford an old inhabitant of that neighbourhood.
Col Clark got information by a note sent by a servant of Col Middletons
who was their prisoner by the dawn of the day. They reached the
Island when a general massacre took place, the whole guard being
entirely cut to pieces. Capts Carr and Shelvey with their comrades
were tinariously [?] dispatched to give them a meeting which they did
in the plantation of a Mr. Edmund Bugg a respectable citizen of
Georgia who was then prisoner in Charlestown whose sons were then with
Col Clark. They slaughtered them indescriminately without any killd
or wounded on our side. Mrs Bugg and her family had suffered so
extremely by them that she would not suffer them to be inter'd on her
plantation they had therefore to take them in Canoes and convey them
to the Carolina shore for internment. Several Indians were kill'd
which got a more expeditious internment. In the fore part of May 81
Col Lee arrived with his Legion. Then it was tho't advisable to take
Grierson Fort which was fill'd with Tories when they saw us advancing
through the open field they fled to a man to Browns Fort, without
making any opposition except a few scattering shot in their flight,
only wounding two of Lees Infantry & Capt Dunn slightly across the
knee. Major Howard of the Tories was killed and the old Field was
strwed from one fort to the other. Colns Lee and Clark now tho't it
advisable to get Col Brown out of his strong hold as no time was to
be lost hearing of Lord Rawden being on his march from Charleston to

Ninety Six to relieve Col Crugur which he did, but before this time Brown was Compel'd to Surrender to Col Lee. Col Grierson who commanded the Tories of Richmond & Major Williams of Wilks with all the Tories in the fort were surrendered to Col Clark and were conducted back to Griersons own Fort. Grierson and Williams had some more indulgence than the common Tories. They were in Grierson's own darling house and the Tories in the cellar. A Mr. James Alexander whose family had suffered in the extreme having an aged Father confined, being one of the hostages before mentioned his houses being all burnt, his property borne off, an aged mother, sisters & brothers left to starve, under these agrevating circumstances Mr. Alexander Called Col Grierson to the door as though he wanted to speak to him. On his approaching the door Mr. Alexander saluted him with a rifle ball. Thus ended the Cols career. A Mr. Andrew Shulus took the same step with Major Williams but only wounded him. When Williams desired to be put in close confinement for his safety.

From pages Number 1 to 6 inclusive the contents is correct to my own experemental knowledge and the best information that I can collect from old Revolutionarous characters.

Saml. Beckaem

June 1st 1812

In the Course of the Summer 1780 Col Clark with a number of Refugees from the different Counties in Georgia determined on leaving the State and retreat Northward untill they could meet their friends that would support them. Col Clark left Capts Stephen Johnson & John Hampton at Major Taylors in South Carolina in order to keep up a confidential correspondence, and on Col Clarks coming to Augusta in August as before stated Capts Johnson & Hampton joined him and proceeded on to attack Brown when warm action ensued which is also before mentioned where we had Capts Charles Jordan, William Martin killed, Capt Espey mortally wounded, and a number of brave men killed & wounded on our part. We killed a great number of British Tories & Indians. Col Clark and his unfortunate friends were once more compell'd to Retreat from Georgia through the mountains into North Carolina on the ball mountain Col Clark and his friends met the present Genl W. Hampton who informed Col Clark that Cols Campbell, Shelvey, Cleavland, Levere, and Williams were in persuit of Ferguson. On this information Col Clark in his fatigued and starved situation thot it expedient to proceed to Holeychuchey in order to recruit his men but Col Chandler and Capt Stephen Johnson observed that they had come to fight & immediately pursued on and overtook the army between Gilbert Town and Kings Mountain with about 25 or 30 of their followers where they had the gratification of seeing and assisting in the total defeat of Col Furguson and his party. Elated with the success on Kings Mountain the Georgians once more thot of retaking their beloved Country under the command of Col Benjn Few and Col Clark at the same time sending forward Capt Stephen Johnson Samue Hammond James Cone & Michael Jones for to appraise their friends in Georgia & Carolina that they were coming to there relief. And in order to draw Brown and his principal strength from Augusta Captain Johnson in concert with Qapt McKoy captured all the public assending the river Laden with supplies to the amount of Ł 20,000 Sterling consisting of Indian goods Arms ammunition &c. This so agrevated Col. Brown that he moved off after Capts Johnson & Mc Koy offering a reward of 300 guineas for Capt Johnson as being the principle propogator of this business. Brown then went in pursuit of Mc Koy and Johnson with his Regulars Tories & Indians until he reached Wiggin's hill. Mc Koy and Johnson were there joined Col Harden of Carolina it was then deemed expedent to try Col Browns strength and valor which was done a little before day. Retreated and renewed the action after day but owing to Brown's superior force was obliged to quit the ground leaving seven men dead and eleven wounded which were convey'd away, among the latter Number was Capt Johnson The place fixed on for their hospital was an Island in Cousawhatchie swamp which place was call'd bear hill when they remained nearly three months untill the whole number had recovered their wounds being supplied during this time by William Rawls, Cotton Rawl's and Mr. Leonard Tanner, who was taken prisoner & suffered death rather than betry his suffering friends. Brown laid waste to the whole possession of all those within his reach who were friendly to their country. Cols Clark and Few getting defeated at Long Cane disconcerted the expeditions of the Georgians having to retreat back to thickly. Col Clark in this action got severely wounded and remained there from January untill Spring who so soon as he recovered moved off to Augusta where his presence was greatly needed he there joined his vetrans once more. Capt Stephen Johnson was now appointed coln with a separate and district comand and posted on Ogeechee River guarding an extensive frontier against British Floridins and Indians. During this period Col Johnson and his party kill'd a certain Capt Benjn Brantly of the tories who was the murderer of Myrick Davis, the then Lieut. Governor of Georgia, killing and taking Brantlys whole party a number of those taken prisoners were tried by a court martial found guilty and executed.

The contents of the three last pages viz 7, 8 & 9 inclusive were delivered to the subscriber by Coln Johnsons own mouth

Saml. Beckaem

Junc lot 1812

171

PART III: GEORGIA LOYALIST SOLDIERS

"The Rebels they murder,--Revenge is the word,
Let each lad return with with blood on his sword;
See Grierson's pale ghost point afresh to his wound,
We'll conquer, my boys, or fall dead on the ground.
        "Then brandish your swords, and constantly sing,
        Success to our Troop, our Country and King."

                        From "The Volunteers of Augusta"
                        Royal Georgia Gazette
                        October 4, 1781

Dedicated to June Clark Hartel for her help and hospitality.

A. INTRODUCTION

Tens of thousands of Americans not only remained loyal to the King
during the American Revolution but actively took up arms for the
British cause. All too often, writers have treated these various
Loyalist military units as if they were all the same. The reality was
that the King's men. like their Patriot counterparts, had very different
kinds of troops.

In the South, the least respected of the Loyalist military units
were those that could be calssed as irregulars. Many of these men,
such as the Schopolites of South Carolina and Daniel McGirth's "Gang,"
were bandits and criminals who claimed loyalty to the King as a means
of receiving British protection from punishment by Patriot civil
authorities. Loyalist irregulars sometimes worked with the British
army, usually as foragers or scouts, but while serving as irregulars
these men were not known to have worn uniforms, received regular pay,
or to have kept records of their activities. For the British cause
in the South, the Loyalist irregulars greatest contribution was probably rustling cattle from Georgia to keep the British colony of East
Florida supplied with meat. When all of Georgia and most of South
Carolina fell to the British in 1780, however, these irregulars became
a liability for the British cause as they then turned to stealing
from Loyalist, Neutrals, and former Patriots alike. Daniel McGirth
and other irregular leaders often used their former positions and
service with the British to protect them from prosectuion for their
new crimes.

The next highest level of Loyalist military unit in the South was
the royal militia. In areas occupied by the British army, local
residents and Loaylist refugees were formed into armed militia units,
sometimes on a temporary basis and in response to a military emergency. Georgia was the only one of the thirteen revolting colonies to
be completely restored to British rule and here the old colonial
militia was recreated. Georgia Loyalist militiamen were organized,
received arms and supplies, and were to be paid for their time and
supplies. Like the former Georgia Patriot militia, the restored
colonial militia was responsible for protecting the settlers from
Indians and bandits and maintaining patrols and outposts. Also like
the Patriot militia, the Loyalists often found the supplies and pay
promised them was often in arrears. Among the more famous of the
Georgia Loyalist militia leaders were Colonels Thomas Waters of the
Ceded Lands, James Grierson of St. Paul Parish, and John Thomas of
St. George Parish.

Finally, Loyalist provincial units were formed to supplement the
British army. These regular troops were issued uniforms, given equip-
ment and training, and payed by the British government. Although
Georgians served in several such units in the South, only one provincial
unit is known to have been composed primarily of Georgians--the
Georgia Loyalists led by Major James Wright Jr., son of Royal Georgia
Governor Sir James Wright.* Created in May of 1779, this unit was
merged in 1782 with Lieutenant Colonel Thomas Brown's King's Carolina
Rangers.

A great deal of confusion has existed among researchers as to how various Loyalist units should be calssified. Part of this misunderstanding has come from the fact that some Loaylist leaders in Georgia, notably John Moore and Daniel McGirth, did not always command the same type of units. Moore, for instance, appears to have commanded irregulars, Georgia colonial militia, and provincials at different times. Also, how some Loyalist units were regarded was often subject to opinion, even during the Revolution. The Loyalists who fought at the Battle of Kettle Creek, for example, were seen by the Patriots as bandits (irregulars) but to the British they were members of a hastily created new provincial unit known as the Royal Volunteers of North and South Carolina. Many writers have persisted, however, in refering to these Loyalists as "militia."

The following documents contain the names of some of the Georgians who fought for the British cause. Each of the categories mentioned above are represented.

---

* Several other Loyalist units have been credited, incorrectly, as being Georgia provincials. Thomas Brown's King's Carolina Rangers, one such unit, did have Georgians among the officers and enlisted men but the majority of this unit were North and South Carolinians with experience in dealing with the Indians. The Georgia Light Dragoons were Georgian in name only, being made up of volunteers from the British army and provincial units from the northern colonies that invaded Georgia in 1778. James Ingram's Volunteers of Augusta appears to have been a Loyalist militia unit.

B. LOYALIST IRREGULARS

The following petition, enclosing a list of the followers of Loyalist Colonel Daniel McGirth, is from the Sr James Wright Papers, Telamon Cuyler Collection, Special Collections, University of Georgia, and is used with the kind permission of the Special Collections.

McGirth's followers were not the only Loyalist irregulars (bandits who worked as guides, foragers, and cattle rustlers for the British), other included the men under the infamous Captain Sam Moore of Burke County. Perhaps the names of most of these "vile murderers," as Patriots, and even some Loyalists, refered to them will never be known.

Many individuals in the Patriot forces in Georgia were also seen as bandits and murderers, notably Patrick Carr, George Dooly, Josiah Dunn, and Samuel Alexander. Patriot Lieutenant Colonel Henry Lee once wrote of the Georgia Patriots, "They exceed the Foths & Vandals in further[ing] schemes of plunder, murder & iniquty [sic].

The American Revolution did neither side any honors for humanity or decencey.

Memorial of Colonels Munro & Kelsall Relative to Mc Girt & his People recd. 6th Sepr. 81

To His Excellency Sir James Wright Bart. Governor &c of His Majesties Privince of Georgia.

The Memorial of Simon Munro & Roger Kelsall for themselves & others the Inhabitants of the Parishes of St. Philip, St. John & St. Andrew.

Shewth [sic] that for more than two years past a Number of
Persons, under the Denominations of McGirths men & under the direction
& command of Daniel Mc Girth have [illegible word] themselves in the
Parishes of St. John and St. Andrew & made a Practice of going up
the Country where it is well known they have Committed, indiscriminately,
an infinite number of Robberies, as well as other Enormities; thereby
the Memorialists are well convinced an addition to the Number of our
Enemies have been Created.

That a Great Number of Cattle &c. have been stolen by them & sold
in East Florida within these Two Years to the Great damage of Individuals as well as the Publick.

That they have made a Practice of alarming falsly [sic] the
Country when their Plunder is Collected when (People attentive to their
own safety only) they take those opportunities of getting off their
Plunder & thereby Elude the Vigilance of the Majestrate & Militia
Officer the latter, with Considerable detachments having, Several times,
but in Vain, gone after them, as from Experience, it has been found
that by reason of those falso alarms impracticable to assemble the
Militia till too late.

That they have been always infamous, but infinitely more Pro-
fligate, Daring & abandoned since Mc Girths Lisence [sic] to go (as
he Pretendid [sic]) against the Enemy.

That they set the Civil authority at defiance threatening both
Majestrates & Constables with Death, and unless both are supported
& Protected, they must for their own Preservation decline acting.

That they now go about disguised in the night time, breaking into
Houses, beating, abusing, shooting at the Inhabitants, & Plundering
them in many Cases of their all. annex'd is a List of the Houses
that have actually been broke into, and it is difficult to name a
single Inhabitant, in all that district, who have not been Robbd &
Plunder'd by them of their Horses Cattle, & other stock.

That there is Every reason to suspect, suppose, & believe that
Daniel McGirth himself is Privy to, & Principal in all the Enormities
that have been Committed.

That the Inhabitants in General of those Parishes that have
hither-to Escaped, are under continual & well founded apprehensions,
Each night, of sharing the fate of his Neighbor the night before
Plunder'd & abused.

That several, Especially in the Parish of St. John are preparing
to remove with their Families & Effects, many prevented from coming
into it, and such is the situation of People in General, that they
could not be more Exposed, nor in Greater Danger were they in the
Heart of an Enemies Country; and the Memorialists are Convinc'd that
few or none of those lately Drafted will march, least [sic] in their
absence they be strip'd of the little they have left.

That the whole of these People (a list of the most notorious is
annex'd) refuse to muster or appear under arms, and on all occasions
have refused to do, either Militia or Patroll [sic] Duty; and the
Memorialsts represent that the Militia Officers, on the day the
Militia was Drafted by orders from your Excellency, were obstructed
in their Duty by a Party (Especially, W. Collins Senr. Irvine, Morris
& others) collected the memorialists think on Purpose and with Great
difficulty & danger, That Duty was Effected. Several attempts being
made by them to ride over the men in the Ranks--others were severely
beat in the Presence of both Militia Officers & the Civil Majistrate
[sic], whose authority was set at defiance.

That Daniel Mc Girth not Content with Employing his Gange in the
sole business of Robbery, had, & now has a Great number of Negroes

arm'd the memorialists believe for similar Purposes, which arms the
Memorialists are well assured he got from the Kings or Superintendants
stores, for very different Purposes.

That Daniel McGirth having Industriously & Generall reported that
He is Employed by Commission from your Excellency, and that he is
Countenased [sic] & Protected by those in authoirty, it is next to
impossible to fix those many Enormities upon him, (Guilty as the
Memorialists believe him) as the Principal mover, owing to an appre-
hension which the People in General entertain that their complaints &
informations will not be Properly attended to and that they would in
Consequince [sic] fall Victims to His, & their malice and revenge.

That it is well known that Daniel Mc Girth has Declared that he
has within his reach, so many to swear any thing, against any man,
as well as him, & each other off, by which means the Laws in many
cases are Prevented, always eluded, men are intimidated and their
safety Purchs'd only by their Silence.

That in the Course of Mc Girths late inclursion, they indescriminately [sic] destroyed Fields of corn & from the Back Country
drove off upwards of Three Hundred Cattle &c. many of which are own'd,
the memorialists are informed, & believe, by Loyal Subjects, driven
from their homes, by the Rebels, & now within the lines, who are
afraid even of claiming their own, least [sic] by false accusations
should be made & sworn to by some of that Gang; Instances of which
the memorialists believe are not wanting.

That unless speedy steps are taken to Prevent the further
Depredations of this Lawless & most Excrable Banditti [sic], The
Militia Officers & majestrates will be under an necessity of
resigning, the whole district reduc'd to anarchy & confusion & the
Honest & well disposed in General, must either quit that Part of the
Country or be strip'd of the little which they have hitherto found
means to Preserved.

                                    [s] Simon Munro

        Savannah 5 Sepr. 1781   [s] R. Kelsall

[Following is a list of Daniel McGirth's "gang."]

Colo. Daniel McGirth   Geo. Aaron
Capn. James McGirth   Joel Hoover
Capn. Welch   Jacob Hoover
Capn. Irvine   John Mills
Capn. Morris   Robert Andrews
Ths. Timms   Archd. Robertson
Martin Johnston   John Rogers
John Anderson   Richd. Gregory
John Dunn   Richd. Eastmead
Cornelious Dunn   Will. Collins Senr
Jno. Hamilton   W. Collins Junr.
Benjamin Rawlins   Morris Easton
        Rawlins   James Mote

List of Homes Broke [sic] into:

Mrs. Elliotts, Mr. Powells, Mr. Ben Baker's.

These very lately: Mr. Jos Law's three times, Mr. Low's, Mr. Young's,
Mr. Stacey twice, Mr. Robertson's, and Mr. Caters.

C. LOYALIST MILITIA

The following accounts of the Georgia Loyalist militia are reproduced from volume thirty eight, part two, pages 605-32, of the unpublished volumes of The Colonial Records of the State of Georgia, at the Georgia Department of Archives and History. Permission for this copying was kindly provided by the Georgia Archives and the British Public Record Office. Facsimilies of Crown copyright documents are reproduced with the kind permission of the Keeper, H. M. Stationary Office.

Savanah in Georgia the 27th. March 1782.

No. 64

My Lord

I have the Honor to Inclose your Lordship a Copy of my Account of the Expenditure of the Ł 5000, from the 5th. of November 1781 to the 21st. of January 1782. which I Trust will be Approved of the Vouchers which were Produced in Council, I dare not Venture to Send, but by a Ship of War.

I also Inclose your Lordship a Copy of the Accounts for Supporting the Troops of Horse, the Refugees, Militia & ca. which I likewise Trust will be Approved of. I have the Honor to be with Perfect Esteem my Lord.

Your Lordships most Obliged and

Obedt. Serv

Ja : Wright.

The Right Honorable Lord George Germain His Majesty's Principal Secretary of State For America &.ca &:ca &:ca

[Endorsed]

Savannah, Georgia

27th. March 1782.

Sir James Wright Bar^t

[No. 64.]

Rx 29th May

Dr. The Right Honble. The Lords Commissioners of the Treasury in pursuance of the address of both Houses of Assembly on the 7th Day of July 1781 for defraying the Expence of Embodying, Paying & Subsisting the Militia & for buying provisions &c. for the Support of the Loyal Refugees & other matters contain'd in the said Address, and an accot: of the Expediture of the Monies recd: for the Bills drawn on their Lordships.

1781.				
June 12th	To James Mossman Esqr: for 100 Barrs. of Rice at 4 1/2 Guins: p barrl:	₤ 489	7	6
	To John Channing Esqr: for 272 Barrs. of Ditto. . . Ditto	1320	4	6
	To Sir Jas: Wright Bart: for 50 Barrs. Ditto. . . 244.13.9			
	300d. Ditto for the Negroes employed on the Fortifications. 2.18.6	247	12	3
July 5	To James Hamilton for 2 puncheons of Rum for the Militia 215 Gas. 4/10	51	19	2
	To Cash pd. advance pay to Six Companies of Militia doing Duty at Ebenezer from the 1st. of July to the 1st of Augt.	188	9	1
	To Ditto paid Colo. Thomas a much destress'd Loyal Refugee & a very Usefull Man doing duty at Ebenezer	15	10	-
10	To Ditto paid Colo. Rogers in part pay as Lieut. Colo. Commands. of the Militia doing Duty at Ebenezer	25	-	-
	To Ditto pd. Lieut. Oneil 1 Mos. Pay on Duty at Ebenezer	6	15	-
12	To Ditto pd. Josh. Maddock Comy. for providing for the Refugees in part purchase of Beef for their Daily Rations p Accot.	40	-	-
	To Ditto pd. Doctr. Folliatt 1 Mos. Pay as Surgeon of Militia	8	10	6
13	To Ditto pd. Jonn. Sell a much distressed Refugee to enable him to purchase Necessaries	5	13	-
	To Ditto paid Joseph Maddock Commy for Providing For the Refugees	21	9	6
	To Ditto paid Wm. Harris Commy for Refugees	21	9	6
	To Ditto paid Robt. Willm. Harris a Loyal & Distressd Refugee driven from his Settlement & enable him to purchase Necessaries	20	10	2
	To Ditto paid Richd. Davis for Negro hire Storing Rice	3	9	8

```
1781
July 10th.   By His Excellency Sir James Wrights sett
             Bills of Excha: No. 1 at 40 Days Sight in
             Favr. of Josa: Tatnall Esqr.                    Ⱡ 300    -   -

             By Ditto No. 2 in favr. of John
             Channing Esqr.                                   1320    4   6

             By Ditto. 3 in favr. of Peter Mill                 50    -   -

             By Ditto. 4 in favr. of James Mossman Esqr         150    -   -

             By Ditto. 5 in favr. of Ditto.    Ditto.          100    -   -

             By Ditto  6 in favr. of John Murray Esqr.         300    -   -

             By Ditto. 7 in favr. of James Herriott Esqr.      100    -   -

     18th    By Ditto. 8 in favr. of John Henderson Esqr.      300    -   -

             By Ditto. 9 in favr. of Willm. Clarke              75    -   -

     19      By Ditto. 10 in favr. of Cecil & Wood             163   12   8

     27      By Ditto  11 in favr. of Lewis Johnston
             Junr. Esqr.                                       120    -   -

Augt  8      By Ditto 12 in favr. of James Belcher             300    -   -
```

1781
July 16   To Ditto pd: Wm. Johnston Adjt. of Militia
          a Loyal & Distress'd Subject taken in Colo.
          Brown's Fort at Augusta a very Usefull Man &
          who came almost naked to Savannah   Ł   9   11   3

          To Ditto paid Capt Crawford for Subsistence
          & to purchase Necessaries   6   -   -

          To Cash paid Colo. Waters a Distressd Loyal
          Subject   39   2   6

          To Ditto paid John Douglass. . . ditto. .. ditto   39   2   6

          To Ditto paid Capt. Ashton a Captn. in the
          Augusta Militia, and a Loyal Subject taken
          in the Fort with Col. Brown at Augusta   6   -   -

          To Ditto paid Major Williams a Major in the
          Militia in the Ceded Lands a very good & Usefull
          Man, a very great Sufferer & who was dangerously
          wounded in the breast & Shoulder & taken with
          Colo. Brown   19   2   6

     17   To Ditto paid Tillet a loyal Subject & a Captain
          in the Militia   1   1   9

     18   To Ditto paid Nathl. Young, a Captn. in the Militia,
          a Loyal Subject taken in the fort with Colo. Brown   5   8   9

     19   To Ditto pd Edwd. Crawford a Capt. in Ditto..Ditto   4   -   -

          To Ditto pd. Jonas Bedford a Loyal & Distress'd
          Refugee.   2   3   6

          To Ditto pd Mm. Johnston a Major of Militia
          taken in the Fort   6   -   -

          To Ditto pd. Doctr. Follia for Medecines &
          attendance to the Militia.   11   3   -

     20   To Ditto pd Expresses at times.   1   11   1

          To Ditto pd Carson Waggon Mastr: Expence of
          Waggons going to Ebenezer   14

          To Ditto pd. Watson & Baldwin two Distree's
          Loyal Refugees   2   3   6

     23   To Ditto pd. Peter Donald Adjutt. of Militia
          his Pay & Expences   9   9   2

1781
July 25   To Ditto pd. Fletchall & Vernon two Loyal
            Refugees to pay the Passage of themselves &
            thirsty Onepersons to Chas. Town having fled
            from the back parts of So. Caroa: on Acco. of
            their Loyalty   Ł 10 14 -

To Messrs. Cecil & Wood for Amot. of 6 hhds
of Rum suppd. the Militia   163 12 8

26   To Cash pd. Buhler Captn. of the Ebenezer
      Militia, pay & Subsistence for himself
      Officers & Men from the 2nd May to the 10th
      July   41 9 1½

To Ditto pd. Ditto for Carting Provisions from
Abercorn to Ebenezer   8 8 -

To Ditto pd Mathias Pittenburgh for Ditto..Ditto   4 13 4

To Ditto pd. Mrs. Strobald for 2 Cows for the
Militia   3 10 -

30   To Ditto pd. David Russell Mayor of the St. George's
      Militia his Pay   10 - -

To Ditto pd. Isaac Lorimer for Amunition Suppd.
the Militia   1 16 9

To Ditto pd. James Weatherford a Capt. in the
Militia & taken in the Fort at Augusta, for his
Subsistence   10 17 6

To Ditto paid Martin Weatherford a Loyal Subject
who made his Escape out of the Fort at Augusta,
while invested by the Rebels, to bring down an
Express from Colo Brown   7 4 8

To Cash paid Alexr. McLean bringing an Express
from Augusta   7 4 8

31   To Ditto paid Captn. Rhan for the Pay & Sus-
      sistence of the Blue Bluff Militia under his
      Command on Actual Service May & June p abstract   37 4 11

To Ditto paid Capt. Rhan for 4 Stears & Sundry
Waggon Utensils   10 5 -

Augt 1   To Ditto paid Capt. Poldwire for 13 head of
       Cattle suppd. the Militia   28 5 -

By amot. brot. forward   Ł 3278 17 2

Aug. 10   By His Excelly Sir Jas Wrights Sett Bills of
        Excha: No. 13 in favr. of James Herriott Esqr.   180 - -

Aug. 2	To Ditto paid Thomas Sims for the Purchase of Beef & Salt	30	15	10
3	To Ditto paid James Herriott for 1568 lbs. Lead at 2d.	13	1	10
	To Ditto paid David Douglass a Loyal Refugee who was taken in the Fort with Colo. Brown	10	17	6
	To Ditto paid James Ingram under the like Circumstances	10	17	6
	To Ditto paid James Stewart under the like Circumstances	10	17	6
	To Ditto paid David Mc Credie for Oznabings & Check for the distree's Refugees	34	7	5
	To Ditto paid Geo. Limebecker & Saml. Lyons two Distressd Subjects	4	7	
	To Ditto paid the Honble Lewis Johnston Esqr. for Monies disburs'd by him to pay the Militia while on Actual Duty, Doctrs. bills attending Two Wounded Men & for 900 yards of Oznabrigs for the Distressd Loyal Refugees	92	17	
11	To Ditto paid John Hopkins for a Stear supplied the Militia	3		
	To Ditto paid Joshua Pearce Comy of Militia in part his Acco.	5		
	To Ditto paid Capt. Tillet 1 Mos Pay for himself 11..12..6 his Lieutenant 6..19..6 his Ensign 5.. 8..6 2 Serjeants 4.. 2..8	28	3	2
14	To Ditto paid Colo Kirkland repairing the redoubt at Ebenezer	5	14	7
	To Ditto paid John Cook for 22 head of Cattle suppd: the Militia	50		
15	To Ditto paid Capt. Perkins a Distress'd Loyal Refugee	4	7	
16	To Ditto paid Jno. Carsan Waggon Mast hire of his Waggon	12	16	-
	To Ditto paid Thos. Sims Cimmissary for his Salary & for Beef Issued to the Distressd Loyal Refugees	41	15	3
22	To Ditto pd. Capt: Philips his Pay as Captain of Militia on Actual service	4		

1781

Augt. 22 To Amount brought forwards   Ŀ 3336 7 6½

          To Cash pd. Josa. Pearce Commy at Ebenezer
          Amot. of his Salary   18 - -

          To Ditto pd. Jno. Briant in full for 9. head
          of Cattle suppd. the Militia   18 - -

       27 To Ditto pd. Richd. Davis for Negro hire   11 13 2

       28 To Ditto pd. Thos. Mills for 11 head of Fat
          Cattle   20 18 2

          To Ditto pd. Jas. McConkey Serjeant 1 Mos. Pay   1 1 4

       29 To Ditto pd. Joseph Maddock for the relief of
          himself Jno Williams & Joshua Ryal distress'd
          Refugees   8 5 4

       30 To Ditto paid William Harris a Distress'd
          Refugee   3 - -

Sep.   4 To Ditto paid Richd. Davies for making Shirts
          &c for Refugees   3 12 -

          To Ditto paid William Powell for 19 head of
          Cattle for Ditto   /15 2 6

          To Ditto paid John Robertson a Distress'd
          Loyal Subject   5 8 9

        7 To Ditto paid Capt. Corker 1 Mos. Pay as
          Capt. of Militia   11 12 6

          To Ditto paid Thos. Simms Comy. of Refugees for
          Beef & Salt Issued to the Loyal Refugees   41 4 5

          To Ditto paid Ditto his Salary 20 Days 5/.   5 - -

          To Capt. Joseph Hunter for 33 Barrs. flour
          purchased for the Militia   155 18 6

       13 To Cash paid Thos Gibbons Junr. for a Waggon   15 4 6

          To Ditto paid John McIvor for Oznabrigs & Check
          for the distressd Refugees & Militia, unable
          to cloath themselves   18 8 6

       14 To Ditto pd. Andrew McLean Esqr. in Considera-
          tion of his great Sufferings & inability to
          Support himself having Lost his all   50 - -

          To Ditto pd. Jesse Webb a distressd Refugee   1 12 8

       17 To Ditto pd. Robt. Ronaldson 2 Mos. Pay as Serjt.
          of Militia.   4 2 4

          To Ditto pd. John Carsan Waggon Mastr.   12 16 -

          To Ditto pd Richd. Davis to pay Negro hire &
          Storage of Provisions   27 4 8

          To Ditto pd. John Bonnell for 4 head fat Cattle   8 14 -

       19 To Ditto pd. Abraham Lyons for Six Swords for
          the Horse Militia   11 4 -

1781			
Sept. 3	By Amount brot forward	₺ 3458	17	2

1781
Sept. 3 By Amount brot forward   ₺ 3458 17 2

By His Excelly Sir James Wrights Sett
Bills of Exha No. 14 in favr. of Wm. Clarke   500 - -

11 By Ditto No. 15 in favr. of John Doran   100 - -

19 To Cash pd. Abraham Brackstone wounded by
the Rebels   1 1 9

To Ditto pd. Peter Gardiner for freight of
Sund. to Ebenezer at times   14 13 7

To Ditto pd. John Oxford a Aged Man wounded by
the Rebels   1 1 9

To Ditto pd. Josa. & Wm. Pearce Comy & Assistant
Comy their Pay   15 12 6

24 To Ditto pd. Lieut. Hausborough 1 Mos. pay   5 9 -

To Ditto pd. Thos Sims Commissary of Issues to
the Distressd Refugees for Beef &c Issued by
him & his Pay 20 Days   48 3 6

28 To Ditto pd. C. Creaner for Cattle for the Militia   8 11 -

29 To Cash pd. Anty. Montell Inspector of Boats his
Salary the 15 Int.   30 16 -

Octr. 1 To Ditto paid David Paines for a heifer for the
Militia   1 17 4

2 To Ditto paid Major Rogers as Colo Commandant of
the Militia at Ebenezer, for Beef purchased by him,
Waggons &c &c for the Militia, also his Contingent
Accot.   229 12 2

To Ditto pd Andrew Robertson a Gentleman with a
large Family obliged to quit his property on
Accot. of the Rebels   21 15 -

4 To Ditto paid Franklin Taylor for making 32
Waistcoats for the Militia   6 8 -

5 To Ditto paid Alexr. Allison freight of Sundry
Stores to Ebenezer   3 5 3

9 To Ditto paid Benjn. Ansley for Boarding Sundry
Loyal Refugees   2 3 6

9 To Ditto paid Richd. Davis his Salry a Comy. of
Stores & for Oznabrigs &c. purchased by him for
the distressd Refugees   21 7 5

1781
Sept. 14 By Amount brot forward   ₺4058 17 2

20 By His Excelly Sir James Wrights set Bills
of Excha No. 16 in favr. of Cecil & Wood   200 - -

1781

Oct. 9   To Cash paid Thomas Netherclift 3 Mos. hire his
Store for Storage of Public Rice   15 - -

13   To Ditto paid The Revd. Mr. Seymour for the
Schooling Washing & board of the Orphan Sons of
Colo. Grierson Kill'd at Augusta   41 7 6

16   To Ditto paid John Carson to purchase Cattle at
Ebenezer   20 - -

   To Ditto paid Thos. Rutherford a Loyal Refugee   4 7 -

17   To Ditto paid Wm. Mangum for 2 head of Cattle
for the Militia   4 - -

19   To Ditto paid Thos. Sims Comy. of Refugees to pay
for Beef Salt &a.   51 19 4

22   To Ditto paid Joseph Hutchinson for 12 Dragoon
Swords   12 2 6

   To Ditto paid Saml. Harrison for 21 Ditto   26 5 -

   To Ditto paid Capt. Corker to purchase Beef
for the Militia   41 4 -

23   To Ditto paid Major Russell to purchase Cattle
for the Refugees   6 - -

24   To Ditto paid Willm. Mangum for Ditto   2 3 6

   To Ditto paid Philip Dill for Ditto   1 15 -

25   To Ditto paid Abraham Lyons for 3 Swords   6 15 4

   To Ditto paid Capt. Ingram for Pay due himself
Officers & Men of the Augusta Volunteer Troop
of Horse   250 14 10

26   To Ditto paid Capt. Philips & Lieut Clarke thr.
Pay   18 12 -

31   To Ditto paid Wm. Ross for Check & Scarlet Cloth
for the Militia   26 17 10

   To Ditto paid Jas. Bulloch for 2 Stears   3 8 6

   To Ditto paid Capt. Jackson 1 Mos. Pay   11 8 -

   To Ditto paid Serjeant Peel 1 Mos. Do.   3 - -

   To Ditto paid Serj: Conner 1 Mos. Do.   3 - -

   To Ditto paid Geo McCauley for Sunds: for the
distress'd Loyalists   30 4 8

1781	To Amount brought forwards	₺ 4845	16	5½

Novr. 1   To Cash pd. John McIver for Sundries for the
Distress'd refugees   30 16 -

To Ditto pd. Colo. Kirkland for Salt &c for Ditto   15 3 8

  5   To Ditto paid Peter Gardiner freight of Sundries
to Ebenezer   9 15 9

To Ditto paid John Smith for 7 Dragoon Swords   7 12 3

To Ditto paid Israel Keiffer for Pasturage   4 - -

To Ditto paid Capt. Crawford 1 Mos. Pay   11 12 6

10   To Ditto paid James Belcher for Sunds. for the
Distress'd Refugees   38 10 -

To Ditto paid Captn. Philips to relieve him from
his Distresses   2 3 6

To Ditto paid Captn. Polhill pay due his Company
while on Actual Service as a horse Patrole   33 6 -

                                                    4998 16 1½

To Sundry Sums due by the Merchants for
Bills Sold on Credit.

James Herriott. . . . . ₺ 95 5 4

Willm Clarke   100 - -

Cecil & Wood   200 - -

Ballance of Cash on hand   113 15 8½

                                           510 1 0½

1781
Novr. 10   To Cash paid Wm. Clarke Ballce. Accot. for
           working on the Fortifications   Ł 10 5 6

           To Ditto paid John Graham Esqr. for Lumber
           &c for the Barracks   77 18 2

      16   To Ditto paid Josiah Adams going for
           Intelligence   5 19 7

           To Ditto paid Negro hire bringing up a Raft
           of Timber for the Barracks   2 1 -

           To Ditto paid Abililech Hawkins for a Horse
           as p Order in Council   9 15 9

           To Ditto paid Ditto as p Do. going Express
           to Augusta in Apl. last   5 8 9

           To Ditto paid my Own Accot. for Timber &c
           for the Barracks as p Accot. passed in Council 35 17 6

      22   To Ditto paid Matthew Baillie a poor Mans
           Passage to Chs. Town   10 10

           To Ditto paid Mrs. Gresham for Intelligence   2 3 6

      23   To Ditto paid Thomas Simpson for Timber for
           the Barracks   2 7 -

Octr. 6   To Ditto paid Lewis Johnston Esqr. for Timber
           & boards for the Barracks as p Accot. passed
           in Council   60 16 3

      11   To Ditto paid F. Fahm for Ironwork &c. about
           a PublicWell   3 11 -

           To Ditto paid Martin Weatherford a p Order in
           Council for a Boat Lost in the Public Service   40 - -

1781
Novr.   By Ballance depending p Accot. rendered up
           to the 5th of November last   Ł 258 5 9

      10   By a Bill of Exhca in favr. of John Graham Esq 100 - -

Decr. 6   By Ditto in favr. of Lewis Johnston Esqr.   60 16 3

Jany, 21   By Ditto in favr. of James Jackson for the
           use of Col Griersons Children   105 - -

           By Ballance due Sir Jas. Wright Bart. this
           21st Jany.   17 7 3

1781	To Cash paid Green going for Intelligence	4	7	-
Octr. 19	To Ditto pd. Wm. Wylly for Timber &c for the Barracks	34	6	-
20	To Ditto pd. Willm. Lejoe Carpenter for Work on the Barracks as p Accot. pass'd in Council	18	13	4
	To Ditto paid Ditto an Accot. for Labourers getting up Timber	3	9	3
26	To Ditto paid Jno. Hopkins going Express by Sea to Chs. Town	27	3	9
27	To Ditto paid Lieut. Pace going into Carolina for Intelligence	18	13	4
	To Ditto pd. Negro Carpenters Accot. Building Barracks from 6th Novr. to the 24th Decr. as p particulars pass'd in Council	65	6	-
1782 Jan. 1	To Ditto pd Josiah Adams Express	2	3	-
8	To Ditto pd. Abra. Gable pulling down a house in the way of the Fort	1	1	9
17	To Ditto pd. Christopher Triebner repairing Bridges by Order Council	5	-	-
21	To Ditto pd. by Bill to Jas Jackson for the Use of the Children of Colo. Grierson as p Resolution in Council 7th Inst.	105	-	-

The Right Honble. The Lords Commissioners of His Majesty's Treasury for raising, Paying & Subsisting two Troops of Horse in the Province of Georgia, and for the purchase of Horses, Arms, Cloathing & Appointments for the said Troops, with an Accot. of the Expenditure of the Monies recd: for the Bills drawn on their Lordships.

1781				
June 14th	To Amount of 55 Horses purchased by B. Cowper Esqr: for the use of The Troops p Receipts	Ł 408	-	-
	To Cash pd. for 2 Waggons for Ditto	30	-	-
21	To Ditto pd. Alexander McLean for recruiting Services	20	13	3
July 4	To Ditto pd. Jacob Russell for altering 100 muskets into Carbines	25	14	8
11	To Ditto pd. Capt. Wm: Johnston to pay for 5 Horses	50	-	-
	To Lewis Johnston Junr: for his Draft on Chs. Town to purchase Swords &c: for the Dragoons	232	6	8
18	To Sawyer Morel & Keal for 25 Saddles & Bridles for Ditto	56	5	-
	To Cecil & Wood for Amount of Sundries Supplied the Troops and for Monies advanced Captains Johnston & Lightenstone for Recruiting Service	119	17	1
	To Cash paid Kerr & Begbie for 9 Mens Saddles at 47/	21	3	-
	To Ditto paid Houstoun & Storr for 8 Ditto 45/	18	-	-
20	To Cash paid Capt. Johnston to pay for Horses	17	1	2
	To Ditto paid Capt. Wm. Johnston his & Capt. Lightenstones Pay Bills for themselves, Officers & Men 2 Mos: Pay up to the 24th of August next p abstract	529	9	10

```
1781
June 6th   By His Excelly. Sir James Wrights Sett Bills
           of Excha. No. 1 at 40 Days Sight in favr. of
           Alexr: Wright Esqr.                              Ŀ 700   -   -

     14    By Ditto No. 2 in favr: of Daniel Silsby        1000   -   -

     22    By Ditto 3 in favr: of Wm. Clarke                 99   -   -

     22    By Ditto 4 in favr: of Geo: Barnes                54   -   -

           By Ditto 5 in favr. of Ceo. Nowland              54   -   -

     25    By Ditto 6 in favr. of Cecil & Wood              600   -   -

           By Ditto 7 in favr: of Ditto                     400   -   -

     26    By Ditto 8 in favr: of James Herriott            250   -   -

July 7     By Ditto 9 in favr: of Lewis Johnston Junr:       50   -   -

     16    By Ditto 10 in favr: of Ditto                     50   -   -

     18    By Ditto 11 in favr. of Ditto                     50   -   -

           By Ditto 12 in favr. of Sawyer Morel & Keal       56   5   -

     19    By Ditto 13 in favr. of Cecil & Wood             119  17   1

Augt. 22   By Ditto 14 in favr. of John Wallace            500   -   -

Sepr.  5   By Ditto 15 in favr. of Houstoun & Storr         300   -   -

Octr. 11   By Ditto 16 in favr. of Wm. Knox Esqr.           100   -   -
```

1781

Date	Description	£	s	d
July 20	To Cash pd. Lieut. McLean for Recruiting Service	1	17	4
	To Ditto pd. Jacob Russell for fixing Rings to 100 Carbines	7	10	-
30	To Ditto pd. Alexr. Scott for attendance on the Horses at Pasture	7	10	-
Augt. 3	To Ditto pd. Mattw. Stewart for making Holsters, Cartouch Boxes, Bridles &c. &c. for the Light Dragoons	108	5	-
11	To Ditto pd. Geo. Hardwick Com. to the Geoa. L. Dragoons for Rations bot: & Issued by him from the 26th June to the 31st of July, Also for 4 Stears purchased for the Use of the Dragoons & dld Capt. Johnston	52	4	7½
14	To Ditto pd: Capt: Patterson for freight of Sundry Packages from Chs: Town for the Use of the Geo. L. Dragoons	28	7	6
15	To Ditto pd. Capt. Johnston for the purchase of 5 Horses	53	-	-
Sepr. 3	To Ditto pd. Capt. Lightenstone for the purchase of 3 Ditto	44	2	9
4	To Cash pd. the Honble Mr. Graham for a Waggon & Horses	34	16	-
5	To Ditto pd: F. Fahm Blacksmith for a Brand	-	14	-
7	To Ditto pd: Capt: Wm: Johnston his & Capt: Lightenstone Pay Bills for themselves Officers & Men 2 Mos. Pay up to the 24th of Octr:	592	9	-

1781

			L		
Sepr. 7	To Ditto pd Ditto his Contingent Accot.		40	16	3

12	To Ditto pd. Capt. Johnston for a horse for the Geo. Dragoons		14	-	-
	To Ditto pd. Capt. Lightenstone for 2 Horses		22	16	9
	To Ditto pd. Capt. Johnston for a Horse		14	-	-
25	To Ditto pd. Capt. Lightenstone for a Horse		14	2	9
Oct 1	To Ditto pd. Martin Weatherford Qr. Mastr. for Cattle		10	-	-
6	To Ditto pd. Ditto for Camp Kettles		1	17	4
9	To Ditto pd. Capt. Lightenstone for a Horse		8	14	-
12	To Ditto pd. Capt. Johnston for 2 Horses		28	6	3
19	To Ditto pd. Ditto for three Horses		49	15	-
29	To Ditto pd. Rachael Hand for a Bay Mare		20	13	3
31	To Ditto pd. Geo. Barnes for a Horse		12	-	-
	To Major Prevost for a Bill in part payment of Sundries purchas'd by him for Equiping the Two Troops of Geo: L: Dragoons p Acc.		700	-	-
Nov. 6th	To Cash pd. James Herriott for his Draft on Chs. Town remitted Majr. Prevost, Ballce. of his Acco. & a Discount of 5 p 6t. on the abo.		83	14	8
		L	3481	3	1½

To Sundry Sums due on Bills Sold Vizt.

John & Wm. Wallace   291..5..-

Lewis Johnston Junr   100..-..-

John Henderson   300..-..-

Ballance of Cash on hand this Day.   510..14.-

	1201	19	-
L	4683	2	1

Savannah in GEORGIA Nov.r

Errors

Nath Hall.

1781

			L		
Octr. 11	By Amount brot. forward		4383	2	1
Novr. 5	By His Excelly Sir Jas. Wrights sett Bills of Excha: No. 17 - in favr. of John Henderson Esqr.		300	-	-

The rolls of Major James Wright, Jr.'s Georgia Loyalists reproduced in this section are from the Ward Chipman Papers, Public Archives
of Canada and are abstracted here with the kind permission of the
Director of the Public Archives of Canada.

Although Georgians served in other Loyalist provincial units,
notably Thomas Brown's King's Carolina Rangers, only the Georgia
Loyalists, formed in 1779, was predominately Georgians.

Muster Roll of Major Wright's Company of the Georgia Loyalists Savannah
Abercorne 6th Dec. 1779.

No.	Rank	Names	Time of Inlistment	Casualties
1.	Major	James Wright, com.	1 May 1779	
1.	Ensign	Thomas Clark, com	13 Aug. 1779	
1.	Chaplin	Revd Edwd. Jenkins	1 Sept 1779	absent wt. Leave
1.	Adjuctant	William Johnston	4 Octr.	
1.	Surgeon	Samuel Beecroft	1 Sept.	absent with Leave
1.	Quarter Mr.	Lauft. Waldron	6 June	
3.	Sergeants	Richard Dunbar	14 June	
		Evan Thomas	16 June	
		John Hutcheson	7 July	discharged 21 December 1779
2.	Corporals	Robert Qarker	10 June 79	absent with leave
		Francis Gambold	8 Sept.	
1.	Drummer	John Wilcox	17 Novr.	
	Privates	John Slater	1 June	
		Thomas Davis	28 June	
		John Lawrence	27 July	
		John Strength	22 Augst.	
5.		Peter Gadby	28 June	
		Joseph Terry	27 June	
		James O'Brien	19 June	
		Henry Lindon	7 June	
		John Thompson	28 June	
10.		John Steel	24 Octr.	
		Daniel Fraser	24 Octr.	
		Thomas Eggleton	26 June	
		William Rudd	11 Septr.	

No.	Rank	Names	Time of Enlistment	Casualties
		Patrick McGraw	7 June	died 4th October
15.		John Smith	28 June	deserted 4th October
		Jesse Parker	28 June	deserted 4th October
		Whitney Shipard	27 June	died 13 October
		William Harris	26 June	died 10 August
		Joseph Brooks	28 June	died 13 October
20.		John Wilson	4 July	died 6 September
		Joseph Smith	18 June	
		William Smith	26 June	discharged 23 July
		Rolly Griffith	27 June	deserted 22 Sept
		John McDonald	2 July	
25.		William Postin	28 June	
		Thomas Dodd	16 Augst.	
		Thomas Serjeant	19 July	died
		James Wilson	26 July	died
		Joseph Hatfield	18 June	discharged 27 July
30.		Peter Turno	28 June	
31		John Robertson	19 June	

Muster Roll of Captain William Patersons Company of the Georgia
Loyalists Abercorn   6 Decr. 1779

No.	Rank	Name	Time of Enlistment	Casualties
1.	Captain	William Paterson Comm.	19 June 79	
1.	Ensign	William Chs. Moore		
3.	Serjeants	Thomas Childers	20 June	deserted 6 August 1779
		George Kennedy	20 June	killed 5 October
		James Ienes[?]	20 June	deserted 19 Octr.
1.	Drummer	Jesse Mall	20 June	
	Privates	Price[?] Innis	20 June	
		James McDull	20 June	deserted 26 July
		James Babesck	20 June	deserted 26 July
		Erasmus Cakley	20 June	deserted 6 Aug.
5.		William Alpkin	20 June	died 5 July
		Peter Meran	20 June	died 11 July
		John Pettello	20 June	died 19 July
		George Hightower	20 June	died 13 Septr.
		William Slater	20 June	died 19 Septr.
10.		Andrew Wineburg	20 June	died 1 October
		John Smart	20 June	died 19 Septr.
		John Spencer	20 June	
		William Neuman	20 June	
		Jonathan Hunt	20 June	
15.		Peter Brumback	20 June	
		Thomas Hooks	20 June	died 24 October
17.		George Stokes	20 June	died 24 October

Muster Roll of Capt. John Bond Randells Coy of the Georgia Loyalists
Abercorn   6 Decr. 1779.

No.	Rank	Name	Time of Enlistment	Casualties
1.	Captain	John B. Randells comm.	27 May 79	
1.	Lieut.	Jacob D. Obman comm.	27 July	
3.	Serjeants	James Quales	10 June	
		Jonah Meoferd	15 June	
		Jonathan Backer	28 June	
3.	Corporals	Abrose Lee	14 June	
		Grove Doran	14 June	Sick in Hospital
		Elijah Wilson	14 June	Sick in Hospital
1.	Drummer	David Hanster	25 June	
	Privates	Michael Locks	11 June	
		Timothy Haly	14 June	
		David Backer	14 June	
		Joseph Barrack	14 June	
5.		Miles Busby	22 June	
		Jacob Fisher	22 June	
		Michael Flanagan	26 June	
		Samuel Sanders	28 June	
		Bond Vail	28 June	
10.		Luke Paul	28 June	
		John Bartrap	28 June	
		William Holloway	28 June	
		Edward Roxberry	28 June	
		Thomas Johnston	28 June	
15.		Elias Johnston	28 June	died 20 October
		Charles Smith	28 June	
		David Evans	28 June	
		Thomas Arnold	28 June	
		James Arnet	28 June	
20.		William Mums	28 Sept.	Died 7 Septr.
		John Powers	28 Sept.	Died 5 October
		William Bolton	28 Sept.	Deserted 11 Octr.

198

No.	Rank	Name	Time of Enlistment	Casualties
		George Patterson	28 Sept.	
		Benjamin Williams	28 Sept.	Killed 5 October
25.		John Mitchell	28 Sept.	Deserted 12 July
		Joseph Cannon	28 Sept.	Died 31 July
		Francis Gerden	5 Sept.	Discharged 17 Septr.
		John Morrison	14 June	Discharged 13 Septr.
		Sherrd Wilkinson	28 June	Deserted 6 August
30.		John Nolly	28 June	Deserted 1 October

Muster Roll of Capt. David Tate's Compy. of the Georgia Loyalists
Abercorn   6 Decr. 1779

No.	Rank	Name	Time of Enlistment	Casualties
2	Captains	John Simpson Comm.	28 May 79	killed 8 October 1779
		David Tate "	25 Octr.	Recruiting
1	Lieut.	David Egan "	1 July	Do
3	Sergeants	Joseph Hughs Enlisted	2 June	Do
		John Marshall "	21 Augst.	Sick
		Paul Mathews	28 June	Died 30 Novr.
2	Corporals	Charles Mencham "	1 June	
		John Evans	5 June	
1	Drummer	Joseph Hughs Jr."	20 July	
	Privates	Samuel Moore "	12 July	
		Alexr. Chisolm "	26 July	
		Simon Price "	10 July	
		Peter Seandlin "	26 July	
5		John Hume "	27 July	
		George Demerin "	28 July	
		Simon Lavine "	28 July	
		Hugh Moore "	4 Sept.	
		Arthur Ashworth "	14 Sept.	
10		Robert Key "	28 Sept.	
		Lewis Pugh "	28 Sept.	Killed 5 July
		David Crosen [?]"	28 Sept.	Died 13 August
		Philip Damford "	28 Sept.	
		David Childers "	27 Sept.	Deserted 6 August
15		John Saunders "	28 Sept.	Died 13 Septr.
		Richard Stevens "	28 Sept.	Died
		Peter Carrier "	28 Sept.	
		Adam Corsee "	28 Sept.	Deserted 22 Septr.
		Peter Japo "	28 Sept.	Deserted 12 July

Muster Roll of Capt. Andrew Hewetts Compy. of the Georgia Loyalists
Abercorn   10 Decr. 1779

No.	Rank	Name	Time of Enlistment	Casualties
1	Captain	Andrew Hewatt comm.	11 June 1779	
1	Lieut.	Edward Cooper		
2	Serjeants	Stephen Curtis	20 June	died 12 October
		Thomas Stockwell	30 Octr	
	Privates	George Barclay	28 June	
		William Christian	28 June	discharged 20 August
		Benjamin Wetherford	28 June	deserted 30 Octr.
		James Cherry	28 June	deserted 1 Octr.
		John Windsor	28 June	deserted 1 Octr.
5		John Windsor Jr.	28 June	deserted 12 Octr.
		John Flcmming	28 June	died 3 Octr.
		John Franks	28 June	died 30 Septr.
		Charles Allenet	28 June	deserted 9 July
10		Thomas Thompson	28 June	died 25 July
		James Wilson	28 June	died 10 July
		Dempsey Perry	28 June	died 11 Septr.
		George Mills	28 June	deserted 23 Septr
		Charles Taylor	28 June	died 4 Septr.
15		James Stery	28 June	
16		Benjamin Windsor	19 Augt.	
20		Gollep Schuphin	28 June	
		Christian Schuphin	28 June	
		Samuel Jeppers	28 June	
		Jonathan Cole	10 July	died 30 July
		David Melvestin	20 July	deserted 23 Septr.
25		Jacob Williams	10 July	
26		Christopher Snider	8 Augst.	

Muster Roll of Capt. Thomas Goldsmiths Compy. of the Georgia Loyalists
Abercorn   6 Decr. 1779

No.	Rank	Name	Time of Enlistment	Casualties
1	Captain	Thomas Goldsmith	Comm. 3 June 1779.	
1	Ensign	Lach. [?] Walden	" 6 June	
1	Sergeant	John Tennay [?]	Enlisted 28 June	
1	Corporal	Allen Carruthers	" 28 June	Died 24 October
1	Drummer	Thomas Dorset[?]	" 28 June	
	Privates	William Corker	" 28 June	
		Thomas Williams	" 28 June	Died 2 August
		James Gibson	" 8 July	
		James Clear [?]	" 18 July	
5		Chapman Hawkins	" 18 July	
		Elias West	" 11 Septr.	
		Patrick Levy	" 25 Septr.	
		James Edwards	" 30 Septr.	
		Jacob Rexbury	" 30 Septr.	Deserted 11 October
10		Nicholas Lazarus	" 30 Septr.	Deserted 11 October
		William Barker	" 30 Septr.	Died 9 October
12		Dennis Carroll	" 30 Septr.	

[Rosters of the Georgia Loyalists from 24 February to 24 December
1781 and for 1782-1783 as part of Lieutenant Colonel Thomas Brown's
King's Rangers are also available from the Public Archives of Canada.
June Clark Hartel is currently working on an index to all Loyalist
units that served in the South during the American Revolution.]

E. JAIL LISTS

1. Jail List, Augusta, 1779.

The following list of prisoners held at the jail in Augusta is reproduced from the original in the Thomas Addis Emmet Collection, New York Public Library and is used here courtesy of the New York Public Library. Similiar Loyalist jail lists for Wilkes and Richmond Counties in 1779 are included in Grace G. Davidson, Early Records of Georgia Wilkes County 2 vols. (1932; reprinted edition, Vidalia, Ga.: Rev. Silas E. Lucas, Jr., 1968), II, 2ff, and in Robert S. Davis, Jr., The Wilkes County Papers, 1773-1833, to be published by the Southern Historical Press in 1980.

A Return of the Prisoners in the Main Guard Augusta Augst. 1779

Names	By Whom Confined	Crimes
Thomas Moore	Colo. Wm. Few	Theft
John Jarvis	Do	An Enemy
John Brock	Colo. George Wells	Do & a Deserter from
John Davis	Col. Wm. Few	An Enemy
Isham Philips	Josa Inman	Prisoner of War
Mark Philips	"	"
John Bonell	"	"
Richd Hackard	"	"
Jacob Thompson	"	"
John Sibby	"	"
Benjn Lamar	"	"
William Hobbs	"	"

[s] Geo. Handley

Actg Major 1st Geor Con.

2. Jail List, Ninety Six, South Carolina, 1779.

Georgians and North and South Carolinians appear on the following list of men held at the Ninety Six, South Carolina jail in 1779. Many of these men were held for having fought on the side of the King at the Battle of Kettle Creek and other skirmishes in Georgia. Others were criminals or deserters from the South Carolina continental regiments.

Sheriff William Moore of Ninety Six District compiled this list as part of his claim for money owed to him by the South Carolina State government. The following is abstracted from the original in William Moore (5335), Accounts Audited growing out of the Revolution in South Carolina, South Carolina Department of Archives and History. Numbers in brackets do not appear on the original manuscript but were included here to make the list easier to understand.

[1]   Wm Moore Esqr. Shff of 96 District for Subsistence of Desserters from the Contl. Regts. of this State at 30s p day and for a fee of 50s for turnkey to each.

    John Moor, deserter from the 3rd Regiment, held for 62 days (Ł95=10:0)

    Jas. McClure, deserter from the 3rd Regiment, held for 13 days (Ł22:0:0)

    Charles Steel, deserter from the 3rd Regiment, held for 10 days (Ł17:10:0)

    Joseph Beasley, deserter from the 5th Regiment, held for 30 days (Ł47:10:0)

[2]   1779
12th April To the following persons prisoners of war from 10 March to 12 April 1779 Inclusive. (Each was held for 34 days at Ł53:10:0 per man.)

John Overstreet	Jacob Singley	Isaac Smith
Hugh Stevenson	Jacob Counts	Nicholas Welch
John Morgan	Peter Dricker	Fredrick Wise
John Ulrick	Daniel Quarder (Luarder?)	John Stnm (Steem?)
Danl. Johnson	Henry Wicker	John Blake
Semion Sanders	goodlip shouldstreet	Sampson Williams
Wm. Robertson	Nicholas Brook	Wm. Young
Elisha Chavis	William Love	Wm. Welch
John Bowder	allen Sharp	Richd. Whitfield
William Chavis	augustus Underwood	James Martin
Fredrick Hartley	Parker Perce (Peree?)	Ben Busby
Joseph Pyatt	absolam Palmore	Jacob Williams
John Finley	Philip Waffington	
John Smith	William Thomas	
John Ryall	Mathias Fisher	
Thomas Webster	Anderson Reynalds	
Jamie Neeley	Thomas Welch	
William almon	Henry Williams	

[3] The following were Committed for Sedition & Removd. to oringburg
[sic Orangeburg] by Habeus Corpus. [Each was held for 34 days
at Ь78:14:0 per man.]

George Mock (Mack?)	James Case	Jesse Brown
Stephen Rijall	James Wallace	William Templeton
John killing	Moses Quals	Edward Caswell
Martin kinner	John Harris	Arthur Ashworth
Jas. Justin (Justice?)	Daniel McRevick	Jeremiah Brantley
John Farmer	Chrisly Whitman	Moses Eason
Joel Farmer	James Chitwood	James Noland
Michal Sties	Shadrick Chitwood	James mann
David Ahart	Philip Whitman	Absolam Palmer
Michal Trudezelle(?)	Moses Chitwood	James Thomas

[4] The following were held for 30 days at Ь72:14:0 each before
being removed to Orangeburg by habeas corpus.

Archad. McDougle	Elexander Smith	Murdock McCloud
Duncan McFarson	Neal Ramsey	Archabab McNeal

[5] To Wm Hallum for 20 days a 30s Turnkey 50s Habeus &c 57:14:0

To Joseph Noble his fees on Habeus &c. Ь32:14:0.

[6] The following were held for an unspecified period of time at
Ь38:14:0 per man before being removed by habeas corpus.

John (the name "Peter" is crossed out here) Buffinton

Sam Buffinton	Joel Sanders	John Nichols
Thomas Sanders	Conrad Golman(?)	John Mills (Wells?)
Abraham Sanders	Jonathan Crow	
Mordicia Sanders	Simon Nichols	

[7] The following were held for unspecified periods of time and for
varying amounts of fees before being removed by habeas corpus.

David Thornton, Ь60:4:0	Colo. John Moore, Ь40:0:0
Wm. Rhodes, Ь38:10:0	abraham Clements, Ь40:0:0
Fredrick Bagwell, Ь12:0:0	Eli Fort, Ь23:10:0
Saml. Morrow, Ь12:0:0	Walter Long, Ь65:10:0
John Thompson, Ь56:10:0	Wm. Glover, Ь17:10:0
Lark Thomas, Ь56:10:0	James Emberson, Ь8:10:0

[8]   The following were held for an unspecified period at £50:0:0
        before being placed in the Continental service by order of a
        court martial.

        Moses Coe   John Harn   Anthony Argo   John Roe

[9]   To James Jones(?) his fees on Comitmt. 29 days &c 46:0:0

        To James killey his fees 50 days &c. 77:10:0

        Richd. Scrugs his fees 26 days &c. 41:10:0

        To Wm. Hooker his fees as a deserter 36 days &c £56:10:0

        To Phillip Hickenbotom his fees 24 days &c. 38:10:0

        To Newt Burfoot his fees 24 days &c. 19:0:0

        To Whealer Herterley [Werterley?] his fees for 10 days &c 17:10:0

        To Wm. Powell his fees 4 days &c. 8:10:0.

[10]   To the goal fees on Commitment of Jas Linley John anderson aquilla
        Hall Saml. Clegg and Charles Draper who were hanged &c. £86:4:0
        Each.

[11]   To the fees on Thomas Green. Imprisonmt. Swore off Nor. Court.
        1779 £50:10:0

        To the fees on Wm Flemings Imprisonmt. Swore off as above
        £30:10:0.

[12]   The State vs. Phillip Coleman John Willard William Pain Edward
        Johnson aquila Hall John Wells [Mills?] & others Six Writs of
        Subpena at £5:0:0.

[13]   The State vs. Henry Seleman one Writ of Subpena Excutd.
        £5:0:0. . .

        To the fees on Henry Millen Imprisonmt. as a deserter from
        3d. Regmt. 100 days &c. £152:10:0.

[14]   The following were Convicted at the Special Court held 22d.
        March 1779 & dischard [sic, discharged] by his Exelency the
        govr. after being Removd by Habeus.

Jesse Purkins	Benjamin Mehaneys	Regan Barber
Rhode Edsors	Sherod Hudson	Beasly Presoit
Benja. Mettons	Henry Senterfit	Edwd. Johnson
James Hart	George Hollingsworth	Wm. Parker
Jesse Jonakin	Wm. Hesterly	Mathew Parker
Moses Clark	Wm. Bryant	Jesse Collins
James Mosley	Walter Holm	William Lindley
Robt. Poole	Thomas Swofford	Thomas Cargill

James Waldroup   Wm. Goodwin

William Pain   Wm. Cunningham

[15]   To Fitus Paulk is fees as above omiting 10 days 63:14:0

       To William Adington his fees as the Last 63:14:0

       To Richard Gray his fees 13 days & Removg. &c. 47:4:0

       To John Donoho his fees as the Last 47:4:0

       Abell. Bowling his fees as the Last 47:4:0

       To John Strum his goal fees 13 days & Turnkey 50s Sworn 3d
       april 1779 40:0:0.

[16]   The following is a seperate list of prisoners in the Audited
       Account of William Moore (5335), identified only as "No. 49."
       It is undated and for varying periods to time and amounts of
       fees.

	Ł.	S.	D.
James Wilson, 35 days	1	15	6
for execution of the same		14	6
Jacob Hawick, days	4	9	3
Robert Gill, days	4	9	3
James McDonald, 89 days	4	4	7
John Watson, 117 days	5	10	3
John Cunningham, 44 days	2	3	4
Andrew McWilliams, 44 days	2	3	4
John Hinniard, 39 days	1	10	7(?)
John Salters, 59 days	2	17	1
Barton Harris, 22 days	1	3	2
Simon Salters, 18 days		19	6
Loderick Hartley, 28 days	1	8	8
ambrose Sanders, 59 days	2	17	1
Saml. Gillbody, 60 days	2	18	
Phillip Hickenbottom, 45 days	2	4	3
Newit Baffort, 30 days	1	10	6
James McMayhan, 20 days	1	1	4
Walter Long, 35 days	1	15	1
William Hooker, 15 days		16	9

	Ł.	S.	D.
William Glover, 70 days	3	7	2
Thomas Kelly, 50 days	2	8	10
Wheler Hesterly, 90 days	4	5	6
Eli Fort, 25 days	1	5	11
Colo. John Moore, 40 days	1	19	8
abram Climmond, 54 days	?	12	6
Saml. Morrow, 32 days	1	12	4
Bairwell, 29 days	1	9	7
Walter Long, 73 days	3	9	11
Daniel McDonal, 46 days	2	5	2
John Palmer moore, 33 days	1	13	3
Guy Williams, 90 days	4	5	6
Thomas Green, 76 days	3	12	8
Samuel Tully, 17 days		18	7
Edward Fort, 26 days	1	7	10
James Emberson, 37 days	1	16	11
Joseph Busby, 65 days	3	2	7
Silas Mc Daniel, 24 days	1	5	

APPENDICES:

POST-REVOLUTIONARY WAR DOCUMENTS THAT RELATE TO REVOLUTIONARY WAR SERVICE

A. Georgia Military Records Book,
Georgia Department of Archives and History.

Since 1777, attempts have been made to draw up as complete a
list of the officers or officers and soldiers who served in Georgia
during the Revolution as possible, using surviving state documents.
None of these attempts have been successful. Some of these lists
were published in George White, Historical Collections of Georgia. . .
(New York: Pudney and Russell, 1855). Other include the "Georgia
Military Affairs," the militia commissions in the State Commission
Book B, and other records reproduced elsewhere in this work.

The following are taken from the "Georgia Military Records Book,"
Georgia Department of Archives and History, an attempt by B. B. de
Graffenried in 1857-1858 to compile a book of state military records
for the period 1779 to 1839. Revolutionary War period documents that
were included in the "Georgia Military Records Book," are reproduced
elsewhere in this work from the original documents.

Among the documents included here is an incomplete list of men
who received Georgia state Revolutionary War pensions and the dates
that they were wounded in the war.

Rank	Name	Reg.	Commencement of Pay	Expiration of Pay
Prvt	James White	2 Reg	Decr. 29, 1778	29th June 1786
Lt	John Greer	Militi	Augt. 15, 1779	29 Sept. 1786
Prvt	Benj Greer	"	Augt. 9, 1780	Sep. 29, 1786
"	Austin Dabney	"	May 25, 1782	Sep. 29, 1786
"	John Newnan	"	Decr. 29, 1778	Decr. 29, 1786
"	Chas Damson [Dawson?]	2nd	Mch. 3d, 1779	Mch. 3d, 1779
"	James White	"	June 29, 1786	Feby 1st 1787
"	John Sceve	"	Apl 1st 1782	Apl 1st, 1787
"	Samuel Whatley	"	Decr 10, 1781	Decr 13, 1786
"	Austen Dabney	Mil.	Sept. 29, 1786	1st Feby 1788
"	James White	2nd	Feby 1, 1787	1 Apl
"	Thomas Hanshaw	2nd	Oct. 1st, 1778	Oct. 1st, 1788
"	Thomas Hanshaw	"	Oct. 1st, 1782	Mch. 1st, 1789

Office of Secatary of Council, Augusta
  28th August 1789
                              This may certify that the
            foregoing statement of monies advanced to
          the Invalids of the Late army and Millitia,
       Amounting to four thousand three hundred and seventy
     six Dollars and 25/56 of a dollar is taken from the Original
  Certificates of the Inspection of Invalids filed in this Office.

                    J Merriwether
                      S.Y.E.C.

An account of Certificates issued to the officers of the Georgia line under and by Virtue of a Resolve of the Honorable the House of Assembly passed at Augusta the 1st day of May 1782

No.	Rank	Names		
1	Capt.	George Handley	L 50	
2	"	" Do "	25	
3	"	" Do "	25	
4	"	" Do "	15	L 115
5	"	John Milton	50	
6	"	" Do "	25	
7	"	" Do "	25	L 115
8	"	" Do "	15	
9	Lt.	Christopher Hillary	50	
10	"	" Do "	65	L 115
11	"	John Morrison	115	L 115
12	"	Henry Allison	115	L 115
13	"	Mayor Philip Son	70	
14	"	" Do "	45. . .	L 115
15	Capt.	Alexander D Cuthbert	50	
16	"	" Do "	50	
17	"	" Do "	15. . .	L 115
18	Lt.	John DuCoins	75	
19	"	Do	28	
20	"	Do	12. . .	L 115
27	"	Thomas Glassock	50	
28	"	Do	25	
29	"	Do	25	
30	"	Do	15. . .	L 115
31	"	Nathnl Pearse	50	
32	"	Do	25	
33	"	Do	25	
34	"	Do	15. . .	115
35	"	Fredrick Shick	50	
36	"	Do	25	
37	"	Do	25	
38	"	Do	15. . .	115
39	"	Josiah Maxwell	60	
40	"	Do	40	
41	"	Do	15. . .	115
42	"	John Mitchell	60	
43	"	Do	40	
44	"	Do	15. . .	115
45	Capt.	Joseph Day	60	
46	"	Do	40	
47	"	Do	15. . .	115
48	"	John Lucas	60	
49	"	Do	40	
50	"	Do	15. . .	115
51	"	Lackland McIntosh	60	
52	"	Do	40	
53	"	Do	15. . .	115
54	"	Richd Willy Dy Qr Mr Gnl	115. .	115
55	Lt.	Edwd Cowen	115. . .	115
57	Capt.	Lackland McIntosh	115. . .	115
60	"	George Melvin	115. . .	115
61	Lt.	Francis Tennil	50	
62	"	Do	40	
63	"	Do	25. . .	115
66	"	John P Wagnon	50	
67	"	Do	40	
68	"	Do	25. . .	115
69	"	Thomas Payne	50	
70	"	Do	40	
71	"	Do	25. . .	115

No.	Rank	Names			
73	Lt.	John Meanly	47		
74	"	Do	40.	. .	115
81		Cornelius Collins	115.	. .	115
82	Capt.	Gideon Booker	115.	. .	115
83	Lieut.	John McIntosh	115.	. .	115
84	Capt.	William McIntosh	115.	. .	115
95		David Reese Dy Judge Advo	115	.	115
97	Lieut	William Jordan	115.	. .	115
98	"	Arthur Hays	115.	. .	115
100	" Col	Joseph Parnill	50		
101	" "	Do	25		
102	" "	Do	25		
103	" "	Do	15.	. .	115
104	Capt.	E. P. Delaplaigr	50		
105	"	Do	25		
106	"	Do	25		
107	"	Do	15.	. .	115
108	Lieut	William Scott	115.	. .	115
109	Capt	Rains Cook	115.	. .	115
110	"	Isaac Hicks	115.	. .	115
111	"	Edward Woods	115.	. .	115
112	Maj	Joseph Law	115.	. .	115
113	Lieut	Thomas Davenport	115.	. .	115
114	Maj	John Habersham	115.	. .	115
115	Capt.	Littlebery Mosby	115.	. .	115
117	Doct	William Read	115.	. .	115
118	Doct	Nathan Brownson	115.	. .	115
119	Capt	Elisha Miller	115.	. .	115
120	Brig Gen	Samuel Elbert	115.	. .	115
121	Capt	Colrein Brossard	115.	. .	115
122	Lieut	Fraser	115.	. .	115
123	Doct	John Waudin	115.	. .	115
124	Col	Leonard Marburry	115.	. .	115
127	Lt	Mosby (Robt)	115.	. .	115
128	Capt.	Job Pray	115.	. .	115
129	"	Igatius Few	115.	. .	115

L 6090

The above sum has been issued by the respective Governors of this State from the year 1782 to 1785, as per check Book lodged in my office.

J. Milton
Secratary State of Georg

State of Georgia
Sectry Office
21 July 1786

MILLEDGEVILLE GEO
JANUARY 27, 1858

This is to certify that the foregoing pages of this book contain true and full copies of sundry pay rolls, muster rolls and other servicable documents, as far as could be collected in the executive department of this state, as evidence of the performance of military service by various companied and persons under the authority of the United States and of various military expeditions called out by and acting under the authority of this state from the time of the Revolutionary to the Mexican War, --that this book was compiled from original documents in the department and as such entitled to full faith and credit as a record of military service.

Given under my hand the day and year aforesaid, B. B. de Graffenried.

B. List of Federal Pensions
for Service in Georgia During the Revolution.

[Paul G. Moss compiled the following list of surviving federal
pensions for service in Georgia during the American Revolution for
Georgia Genealogical Society Quarterly. It is used here with the kind
permission of Leoda Sherry, editor.]

PREFACE:

This Georgia list to U. S. Revolutionary War Pensions was compiled from
the Index to U. S. Revolutionary War Pensions as published by the
National Genealogical Society, in 1966 (Special Publication No. 32).
The index includes the full name of the veteran, the name of the state(s)
from which the service was rendered, and the file number of applications;
and includes those applications which show a reference to Georgia. The
Georgia reference indicates that service was in the Georgia militia, or
that either the pension applicant, the veteran, or a survivor were
residents of Georgia.

An "S", "W", or "R" preceding the file numerals means, respectively,
Survivor of the Revolution, Widow or Rejected claim, as "S4963,"
"W451," "R7304." The abbreviation, "Dis.," means Disability for
which the veteran was pensioned. "BLWt." means Bounty Land Warrant.
("BLWt. 145-100" means that 100 acres of bounty land was granted on
Warrant No. 145 prior to March 3, 1855, and "BLWt. 145-160-55" means
that 160 acres of Bounty Land was granted on Warrant No. 145 under the
act of Congress approved March 3, 1855; and "B.L. Reg. 55" means Bounty
Land Register and that the claim for bounty land under said act was
rejected.) When two applications (a veteran and his widow both applied),
were filed, the letter preceding the file number indicates the decision
of the application las adjudicated. When the words "No papers" appears,
it means that the application papers were burned in the year 1801 or
1814. An asterisk (*) preceding the name shows that an abstract of the
application was published in the National Genealogical Society Quarterly.

The original project for examining the applications for pension and
bounty land was initiated by Mr. Max E. Hoyt and abstracts of the
applications began appearing in the National Genealogical Society
Quarterly in March, 1920, Vol. XVII.

List:

Alexander, Ala., Ga., S32092
Algood, William, Contl., Ga., S41408
Allen, Daniel, Ga., N.C., S32093
Anderson, Bailey, Ga., S. C., Va., S30826
Anderson, William, Ga., BLWt. 6448-160-'55
Andrew, John, Ga., S.C., Mary O. W5623
Andrews, William, ___, Dis. No papers Va., Ga., residence
Anglin, Henry, Ga., S31521

Bailey, Robert, Ga., N.C., S32108
Baker, John, Ga., Va., S39179
Baker, Thomas, Ga., Sea Service, S15299
Banckston (or Bankston), Elijah, Ga., R4780
Bankston, Andrew, Ga., Mary Sorrell or Sorrels or Sorrells, former
  widow, BLWt. 267-160-55; W8746
Bankston, Elijah (See Banckston), Ga., R478
Bankston, Thomas, Ga., N.C., R477
Bard, John, Ga., BLWt. 311-300-Capt., issued July 27, 1795, no papers
Barnett, Joel, Ga., S.C., R534
Barry, John (or Berry), Ga., S39163
Bell, John, Ga., N.C., S.C., S21068
Bentley, Jesse, Ga., Mary Scott R785

Bickham, Abner, Ga., S30274
Bishop, Golden, Ga., S37763
Black, William, Ga. Elizabeth W9730
Bledsoe, Lewis, Ga., N.C., Fanney W17315
Booker, Gideon, Ga., BLWt. 310-300-Capt. Issued 8/8/1797 to
  Abraham Baldwin, Assignee. No papers
Bowen, Joel, Ga., R1065
Bradie, David, Ga., R1128
Brady, William, Ga., S.C., S34671
Briggs, John, Ga., Susannah, R1202
Brooks, Micajah, Ga., S.C., Margaret T., W27694; BLWt. 51752-160-55
Brooks, William, Ga. R1263
Broughton, Job, Ga., N.C., Mary, W8395
Brown, Frederick, Ga., S31576
Brown, James, Ga., R1308
Brownson, Nathan, Cont., Ga., resident of heirs in 1836, BLWt. 2154-400
Brumback, Peter, Cont., Ga., Elizabeth, W8400
Burke, Isham, Ga., S3093
Burks, Edward, Ga., Elizabeth R1457
Burnett, John, Ga., N.C., Moley, R1473
Burnett, Joshua, Ga., S32154
Burney, David, Ga., R1475 1/2
Burton, Richard, Ga., S40761
Butler, Daniel, Ga., Dis. No papers
Butler, William, Ga., R1556; BLWt. 40509-160-55
Bynum, John, Ga., S3111

Calder, John, Ga., Winewood F., (See Caulder)
Camp, Joseph, Ga., (See War of 1812 under BLWt. 40059-80-55 for his
  service in 1796 and 1797)
Campbell, John, Ga., S42640
Carlton, Ambrose, Ga., N.C., S32160
Carsey, John, Ga., S.C., R1736
Carter, Daniel, Cont., Ga., N.C., S.C., S3126
Carter, Giles Landon, Ga., Sela, R1756
Cartledge, James, Ga., S8167
Cartledge, Samuel, Ga., R1790
Cary, Alexander, Ga., R1679
Cash, John, Va., born 2/1/1760 in Amherst Co., Va.; there at enlistment
  in 18__ he was living in Jackson Co., Ga., where he had resided 32
  years; R__
Cash, John, Va., Lucy, W5894, born 4/5/1757 in Amherst Co., Va.; there
  at enlistment. After war lived in Amherst Co., Va., then 13 years
  in Bedford Co., Va. then Elbert Co., Ga., and in Henry Co., Ga., in
  1832.
Cassady, Thomas, Ga. R1788
Castlebury, Paul, Ga., Nancy, W27664; BLWt. 67529-160-55
Caulder, John, Ga., S.C., Winewood F., W8578
Chamberlin, John, Ga., Va., Milly, W6655
Chandler, Mordecai, Ga., S.C., Elizabeth, R1848
Childers, David, Ga., S39298
Childress, Thomas, Ga., (Va. res.), S3147
Claitt, Isaac, Ga. res. in 1828, R20341, (See Cliatt)
Cliatt, Isaac, R20341, Ga., res. in 1828
Cloud, Ezekiel, Ga., Elizabeth, W6920; BLWt. 26643-160-55
Cloud, John, Ga., S.C., Unity, W9389
Cochran, Thomas, Ga., Va., S16350
Coleman, John, Ga., S39339
Coleman, William, Cont., Ga., S39337, enlisted in Va.
Collins, Joseph, Ga., R2179
Connel, Daniel, Ga., S31631
Conner, Daniel, Ga., Martha, R2228
Conyers, John, Ga., S31617
Cook, Benjamin, Ga., Va., Catharine, W8628
* Cook, Benjamin, Ga., SS31622 (See National Genealogical Society
    Quarterly, March, 1944, p. 32)
Cook, Rains, Ga., BLWt. 2161-300
Crabb, Asa, Ga., R2416
Crane, Lewis, Ga., Sophia, R2450

Crawford, John, Ga., N.C., S.C., born in England, S39369
Crawford, John, Ga., N.C., Rebecca, R2470
Crawley, Thomas, Ga., N.C., Va., Margaret, R2476
Culbreath, James, Ga., S8271
Culpepper, Malachi, Ga., R2566
Cunningham, John, Ga., Ann, W6752
Cuthbert, Daniel Alexander (or Alexander or Daniel), Ga., BLWt. 2142-300

Dameron, (or Damaron or Damron), Charles, Ga., Polly, W4173; BLWT.
    2030-160-55
Dameron, George, Ga., S41501
Danielly, Daniel, ___, Ga., res. in 1782, Dis. No papers
Dannelly (or Dannelley), James, Ga., or S.C., R2657
Darden, George, Ga., S.C., S16757
Davenport, Thomas, Ga., BLWt. 1904-300
Davis, Snead, Ga., N.C., S.C. S32205
Dawson, William, Ga., N.C., S.C., S17920
Day, Francis, Ga., N.C., Jane, W6956
Day, Joseph, Ga., BLWt. 2175-300
Deen (or Dean), Julius, Ga., S39436
Deshasure (or Deshazer or Deshasure), Henry, Ga., S.C., born in Va.,
    S16362
Deveaux, Peter, Ga., S37886
*Dickenson, Griffeth, Ga., Va., S20896 (See Quarterly, Sept. '38,
    p. 35 (75)
Dickey, David, Ga., N.C., S.C., S6798
Donathan, Elijah, Ga., Rachel, R3004
Downman, Rawleigh, Ga., BLWt. 1917-300
Dover, Joshua, Ga., R3053
Ducoin, John, Ga., BLWt. 2260-300
Dupuy, William, Ga., S12821

Ealy, John, Ga., S2191
Eastes, Brazile (or Brizele), Ga., N.C., S.C., R3201, (See Estes)
Eastwood, Israel, Ga., born in N.C., S31660
Elbert, Samuel, Ga., BLWt. 1230-500
Elton, Anthony, Penn., born in Ireland, moved to Pa., S.C., Ga., R3335
Emett, William, Ga., born in N.C., S32237
Estes (or Estis or Eastes), Brazel (or Brizele) Ga., N.C., S.C., R3201
Evans, William, Ga., born in Va., S31670

Fain, Ebenezer, Ga., N.C., Va., born in Penn., Mary, R3421
Fariss, (or Farris), William, Ga., res. in 1833, R3456
Fleming, Samuel, Ga., S32248
Fluker, John, Ga., S16382
Ford, Joshua, Ga., S3368
Fraser, John, Ga., R3766
Frazer, John, Ga., Lenah Middaugh, former wid., W3284; BLWt. 19803-
    160-55 (See Rev. War pension claim S7234 of Henry C. T. Middaugh of
    Pike Co., Penn., who died 8/4/1836).
Fry, Benjamin, ___, Ga. agency, Dis. No papers
Fry, Nathan, Ga., S39545
Fuller, Stephen, Ga., S37949

Gage, Aaron, Ga., S2229
Gent, Charles, Ga., S1903
Gibson, Samuel, Ga., R3999
Gilliland, William, Ga., S.C., Susan, W7533; BLWt. 28640-160-55
Girardeau, John, Ga., S17979. He also entered service in S.C., N.C.,
    and Va., but troops not designated and cannot be identified as given
    names of most of his officers are lacking.
Gordon, Jesse, Ga., N.C., Nancy, W13280
Gordon, Richard, N.C., Ga., S3404
Gore, Notley, Ga., N.C., S31070
Gray, John, Ga., Elizabeth, W429; BLWt. 56568-160-55
Green, William, Ga., R4279
Greene (or Green), McKeen, Ga., N.C., S.C., Frances, W7561; BLWt.
    11275-160-55

Gresham, George, Ga., Elizabeth, W2933
Grier (or Greer), Moses, Ga., N.C. He was born in Penn., S32281
Griffin, Edward, ___, Ga., Agency, S13224
Griffin, Samuel, Ga., Elizabeth, R4309
Griver (or Griner), John M., Ga. R4349
Gugel, David, Ga., R4378
Gwin, Jesse, Ga., Va., S8645

Habersham, John, Ga., BLWt. 1226-400
Hadden, William, Ga., Mary, W7697; BLWt. 43503-160-55
Haines, Evan, Ga., Charity, W8897
Hall, James, Ga., S.C., born in Va., Elizabeth, W25471; BLWt. 87048-
  160-55
Hammet, William, Ga., R4528
Hammond, Abner, Ga., S.C., Sarah, W25753; BLWt. 3533-160-55
Hancock, Samuel, Ga., N.C., S.C. S8687
Handley, George, Ga., BLWt. 1255-300
Harris, Matthew, Ga., S31730
Harrison, John, Ga., Rosanna, W3988
*Harrison, Richard, Ga., N.C., Va., Mary W3807; BLWt. 2359-160-55
  (See Quarterly, Drpy. '49, p. 90)
Hatton, Basil, Ga., Md., S8665
Haymon, Henry, Ga., %4798
Heard, John G., Ga., R4822
Heard, Richard, Ga., Elizabeth, W4229
Henderson, Archibald, ___, Ga., res., R4866
Hendrick, Obediah, Ga., S38017
Hicks, Isaac, Ga., BLWt. 1113-300-Capt. Issued 3/12/1794
Highbaugh, George, Ga., R20512
Highnote (or Hignote or Hignot), Philip, Ga., Agness, W10108
Hill, David, Ga., Polly Worldley, former wid., R11867
Hillary, Christopher, Ga., BLWt. 1243-200
Hobbs, Jonathan, Ga., Margaree, R5075
Hodgin, Joseph, Ga., R5091
Holliday, William, Ga., R5149
Hooper, Absalom, S.C., Ga., Sarah, W7813; BLWt. 19510-160-55
Hooper, Jesse, Ga., S1913
Houston, (or Houston) James, Ga., BLWt. 1231-450
Howard, John, Ga., Margaret, R5281
Hunt, Littleton, Va., Ga., ?, N.C., Sarah W3820
Hunter, John W., S.C., Ga., res. at enl. Lincoln Co., N.C., S10899

Jackson, Samuel, Ga., Elizabeth, W945, See N.S. Acc. No. 874; No. 050091
  Not Half Pay.
Johnson, Caleb, Ga., S7081
Johnson, John H., Ga., S.C., Sarah, W4464
Johnston, James, Ga., S36633
Jones, Abraham P., Ga., S38087. In 1819 aged 66 yrs. and res. Wilkes
  Co., Ga., d. 1/28/1831. Wife's name was Ann.
Jones, David, Ga., R5697. Born 3/2/1749 in Chester Co., Pa. Res. at
  enl. Richmond Co., Ga. Res. in 1832, Meriwether Co., Ga.
Jones, Henry, Ga., Va., R5704. Born in Dinwiddie Co., Va. Res. at enl.
  Brunswick Co., Va. Res. in 1839, Barbour Co., Ala.
Jones, Isaac, N.C., Va., S31777. Born 3/30/1761 in N.J. Res. during
  Rev., Frederick Co., Va., and Guilford Co., N.C. Res. in 1836,
  Telfair Co., Ga. Had resided also in Jefferson and Wilkinson Cos., Ga.
Jones, John, S.C., R5717. Died 6/4/1842 in Columbia Co., Ga.
Jones, Jonathan, N.C., S31778. Res. at enl., Onslow Co., N.C. in 1834
  aged 77 yrs. and res. Laurens Co., Ga.
Jones, Matthew, N.C., R5729. Born 8/29/1760 in Isle of Wight Co., Va.
  Res. at enl. Franklin Co., N.C. Res. in 1832, Putnam Co., Ga.
Jones, Franklin, Va., S4441; B. Amelia Co., Va., 5/5/1763. Res. at enl.
  Charlotte Co., Va., (after Rev. in Ga.) res. in 1832, Giles Co., Tenn.
Jones, Solomon, Cont., Ga., N.C., S38083. Enl. in 1776 in Va., in 1927
  aged 66 yrs. Res. McIntosh Co., Ga.; wife, Nancy.
Jones, Thomas C., Ga., S.C., Margaret, W26160; BLWt. 41291-160-55,
  BLWt. 26365-160-55 cancelled, B. 6/19/1765 in S.C. Res. at enl.
  Edgefield Dist., S.C. and Ga. in 1783. Res. in 1834, Blount Co.,
  Ala., and d. there 2/5/1856.

Jones, Thomas, Md., S38093. In 1820, aged 63 yrs. and res. of Hancock
   Co., Ga.
Jones, William, Ga., Va., Milly or Emilia, W11950; BLWt. 9197-160-55;
   enl. in Va. In 1829 aged 70 years and res. of Jasper Co., Ga.
   Died 2/20/1841.
Jordan, Charles, Ga., Frances, R5761
Jordan (or Jourden), Dempsy (or Dempsey), Ga., Sarah, W4462
Jordan, John, Ga., or Va.?, Winnifred, W29726. (Mary Newton, daughter)
Jordan, Samuel, Ga., Margaret, W8224; BLWt. 29335-160-55
Joyner, Benjamin, Ga., N.C., R5779

Karr (or Kerr), Henry, ___, Ga. res Dis. No papers
Kelly, Jacob, Ga., Jane, R5843
Kemp, William, Ga., S.C., R5856
Kendrick, John, ___, Invalid pensioner, No papers, Savannah, Ga.,
   Agency
Killough, Samuel, Ga., S.C., S4475
*Kindrick, John, Ga., b. in Md., Mary, W4255; BLWt. 38509-160-55
   (See National Genealogical Society Quarterly, Sept., '51, p. 103)
Kirkham, Joseph, Ga., R20392

Laffoon, James, Ga., Va., S13694
Lane, Joseph, Ga., BLWt. 1325-400-Maj. Issued 9/5/1790 (or 1791).
   No papers.
Lashley, Edmun (or Edmund), Ga., Delilah, W8014
Lawson, Hugh, Ga., Dis. No papers here, but see Am. State Papers,
   Class 9___ Claims, p. 169.
Layfield, Josiah, ___, Georgia res., BLRej. 95875-55
Lee, Andrew, Ga., S.C., born in Ga., R6241
Lee, Joshua, Ga., born in N.C., S31209
Leverett, Thomas, Ga., Mary G., W4264
Levins, James, Ga., R7607
Lewis, Frances, former wid. of William Palmer, Ga., W8083, which see
Lewis, George, Ga., R6314
Liles, John, Ga., S47930
Lindsay, John, Ga., Dis. No papers
Linn (or Lin), John, Ga., Rachel, R6362
Love, John, Ga., Louisa, R21476
Low (or Lowe), Phillip, Ga., BLWt. 1797-400
Lowrey, Levi, S.C., Ga., Martha, W8091
Lucas, John, Ga., BLWt. 2215-300

Mabry, Reps, Ga., S41809

McConnell, Manual, Ga., S.C., S2773
McCormack, Benjamin, Ga., S31844
McCormack (or McCormak or McCormick), Thomas, Ga., S31857
McCormick, Joseph, Ga., (N.C.?), S32405
McDowell, Robert, Ga., N.C., S.C., S16471
McEntire, John, Ga., S38189
McGee, Thomas, Ga., N.C., S4194. Resident of Va. at enlistment but
   first enlisted in Balto., Md., under Capt. Templeton and Col. Brown.
McHaney, Terry, Ga., S38185
McIntosh, John, Ga., BLWt. 1550-500-Lt. Col Commandant. Issued
   4/14/1799, to John Wright, assignee. No papers.
McIntosh, Lacklin, Ga., BLWt. 1549-850-Brig. Gen. Issued 3/13/1800.
   No papers
McIntosh, Lacklen, Ga., BLWT. 1344-200-Lt. Issued 6/6/1796. Also
   recorded as above under BLWt. 1657. No papers.
McIntosh, William, Ga., BLWt. 1552-300-Capt. Issued 4/14/1799 to John
   Wright, assignee, No papers
McKenney, John, Ga., S31848
McKinney, William, Ga., Va. S16470
McMillon (or McMullen), Rowley (or Rawley), Ga., S16945

Madden, David, Ga., born in Md., S31835
Mallory, John, Va., R6845. Born 3/1/1759 in Orange Co., Va. Res. at
   enl. Louisa Co., Va. After Rev. War, moved to Ga. Res. of Benton
   Co., Ala., in 1835.

Mann, Thomas, Ga., S.C., Sarah, R6876, BLWt. 77545-160-55
Marbury, Leonard, Ga., Ann, W27446
Marbury, Leonard, Ga., N.C., (b. in Md.), R6892
Martin, John, Ga., S.C., S16459, born in S.C.
Martin, William, Ga., R6975
Mason, John, Ga., S9390. Enlisted in Mecklenburg Co., Va.
Mason, Peter, Ga., S38172
Mathers, William H., Ga., S45846
Maxwell, Josiah, Ga., BLWt. 2448-200
May, Beckham (or Beckom or Beckman), Ga., R7049
Meadows, John, Ga., N.C., (b. in N.C.), S7221
Melvin (or Melven), George, Ga., Martha Mathews (or Martha M.), W14491
   BLWt. 175-300
Mercer, Jacob, Ga., S31862
Metcalf, Warner, Ga., N.C., Elizabeth, W4281
Middaugh (or Middough), Henry C.T., Pa., S7234. (See Rev. War Pension
   claim of Lenah Middough (or Middaugh), former wid. of John Frazer,
   Ga., W3284, and wid. of Henry C. Middaugh of Pike Co., Pa., who died
   8/4/1836
Millican, Thomas, Ga., N.C., Mary, R7236
Milton, John, Ga., BLWt. 323-300
Mitchel, John, Ga., BLWt. 2464-200
Mitchell, Reuben, Ga., Ann, W5373
Moler, Joseph, Ga., Md., S9033
Mooney, Driant (or Bryant), Ga., (or Va.), Margaret, R7310
Moore, James, Ga., Res. R7330
Morgan, Asa, Ga., S31870
Morgan, Philip, Ga., Patsey, R7386
Morris, Thomas, Ga., R16555. Ga. Half Pay
*Morrison, Ezra, Ga., S13956 (See Quarterly, Sept. '53, p. 102)
Morrison, John, Ga., BLWt. 2256-200
Mosby, Littleburry, Ga., Va., BLWt. 64-300
Murray, Jack, Ga., Sea Service, R7520

Nail, Reuben, Ga. S31877
Nealy, John, Ga., S.C. S31880
Netherland, Benjamin, Ga., Va., Theodocia, W8487
Newman, John, Ga., S1299
Newton, Joseph, Ga., N.C., Ann, R7635
Nix, George, Ga., S7269
Nolen, Shadrack, Ga., S.C., B. in Va., S4622
Norlyke, Benjah, Ga., S21401
Northcut, Francis, Ga., S21401

Oakley, Erasmus, Ga., Rhoda, W5437; res. at enl. and after Rev.,
   Cumberland Co., Va.
O'Bannon, Benjamin, Ga., S31886
Odum, Seybert, Ga., Agcy., Dis. No papers

Palmer, John, Ga., Susanna, W309
Palmer, (or Palmore), William, Ga., Va., Frances Lewis, former wid.,
   W8083
Pardue, William, Ga., R7923
Parrish, Robert, Ga., S3657
Patterson, Alexander, S.C., Ga., B. in Irel, S7288
Patterson, John, Ga., N.C., S.C., S17626
Payne, Thomas, Ga., BLWt. 1764-200-Lt. Issued 1/28/1797 to Thomas F.
   Scott No papers
Pearre, Nathaniel, Ga., BLWt. 1768-200-Lt. Issued 8/8/1797 to Abraham
   Baldwin, assignee. No papers. (Heitman Historical Register give this
   name as Nathaniel Perry)
Peck, See Peek
Peek (or Peck), Henry, Ga., S16504
Perkins, John, Ga., R8111
Perkins, Moses, Ga., S3677
Peters, Jesse, Ga., S16506
Phipps, John, Ga., Va., S14132

Pittman, James, Ga., Va. #7317
Pride, Burton, Ga., N.C., Elizabeth, W10930; BLWt. 43521-160-55
Pumphrey, Henry, N.C., or Ga., (res. at enl. Natchez), Lucy, W8535
Purcell, George, Va., Margaret Chandler, former widow, W6661
Pyatt, Joseph, Ga., Va. S8986

Queen, Samuel, Ga., Dis., R8541
Queen, William L., Ga., S9462

Rahn, Jonathan, Ga., S32465
Ramsay, John, Ga., Dis. ___ No Papers. See American State Papers,
   Class 9, p. 169. Wounded in his left thigh and left arm by a broad-
   sword, July 6, 1781 near Long Pane Mills
Ray, John, Ga., Mary R8613
Reagan, Darby, Ga., S7359
Reed, Zachariah, Ga., S35615; BLWt. 182-100
Rester, Frederick, Ga., Louisa, R8707
Reynolds, Hamilton, Ga., b. in N.C., R8711
Rooksberry (or Rooksbury), Jacob, Ga., N.C., S.C., Eleanor, W3043
Ryall, Wright, Ga., res. in 1835, Ann, R9119

Sack, John, Ga., S39062
Sapp, William, Ga., R9201
Sarzedas, David, Ga., S39061
Savage, William, Ga., ?, S.C., R9224
Scott, Samuel, Ga., Va., Ann, W5998
Scott, William, Ga., Ann, W19329
Scroggins, Thomas, Ga., res. of widow in 1814, R9326
Seva, John, Ga., Agcy., Dis. No papers
Sharp, John, Ga., b. in Va., S31962
Shelton, Stephen, Ga., Va., Sinah, W6044
Sheppard, William, Ga., R9478

Smith, Alexander, Ga., S.C., b. in York Co., Pa. 1759, res. at enl.
   Columbia Co., Ga., res. in 1833 Merriwether Co., S16530
Smith, Benjamin, Ga., or S.C., R___
Smith, Benjamin, Ga., Va., enl. in Chesterfield Co., Va., there in 1820
   at age 66, S38387
Smith (or Smyth), Ezekiel, N.C., res. at enl. Wayne Co., N.C., res. in
   1833 at age 69 Lawrence Co., Ga., d. June 1839 in Montgomery Co., Ga.,
   Margaret or Peggy, W26480; BLWt. 35690-160-55
Smith, Enoch, N.C., S.C., b. in 1759, Orange Co., N.C., res. during
   Rev., Surry Co., N.C., and NewBerry District, S.C., res. in 1833 Hall
   Co., Ga., S31975
Smith, Hardy, N.C., b. in 1760 in Warren Co., N.C., there at encl. d.
   10/5/1819 in Troup Co., Ga., Elizabeth G., W6096
Smith, Henry, Ga., S.C., b. in Brunswick Co., Va., and there at enl.
   res. in 1834 at age 74 or 75 Harlan Co., Ky. d. there 8/15/1836,
   Elizabeth, W9300
Smith, Henry, S.C., b. 8/18/1759 in Rockingham Co., Va., res. at enl.
   York District, S.C., d. 1/8/1840 in Franklin Co., Ga., Margaret,
   W2183; BLWt. 33764-160-55
Smith, Henry, S.C. b. Sept. 1757 in S.C., res. at enl. Fairfield Dis-
   trict, S.C., d. 6/17/1818 in Jaspar Co., Ga., Sally, W27305
Smith, Hill (or Smith Hill), Va., b. 1761 Chesterfield Co., Va. and
   there at enl., res. in 1833 Oglethorpe Co., Ga., d. 12/1/1838, Eliza-
   beth, W26491
Smith, Isaac, Va., b. in New Kent Co., Va., and there at enl. res. in
   1818 Camden, S.C. at age 61, res. in 1832 Monroe Co., Ga., d. there
   7/20/1834, Ann R., W4338.
Smith, Ivey, N.C., b. about 1759, in Nansemond Co., Va., res. at enl.
   Euplin Co., N.C., res. in 1833 Tattnall Co., Ga. R9746
Smith, James, Ga., Elizabeth, BLWt. 205331-1835
Smith, Jesse, S.C., b. 4/16/1765 in Montgomery Co., N.C., res. at enl.
   Chester Dist., S.C., res. in 1832 Franklin Co., G. and there d.
   4/11/1842, Anna, W2450; BLWt. 34910-160-55

218

Smith, Job, Ga., S.C., b. 12/25/1748 in York Co., Pa., res. during
    Rev., St. Paul's Parish, Ga., and in S.C., d. 11/10/1837 in Pickens
    Dist., S.C., S21983.
Smith, John, Ga., b. in York Co., Pa., 6/23/1761, res. at enl. Ga.,
    res. in 1833 Henry Co., Ga., S31967
Smith, John, Ga., S.C., also served in 1785 and 1786 against Indians,
    b. 1761 in York Co., Pa., res. at enl. Richmond Ga., res. in 1836,
    Henry Co., Ga., R9769.
Smith, John, S.C., native of N.C., enl. in Abbeville Dist., S.C., and
    res. there after Rev. d. 5/1/1802, former widow Barbara Glover, lived
    in Habersham Co., Ga., R4070.
Smith, John, N.C., also served 1789, b. 6/1/1759 in Cumberland Co., Va.,
    res. at enl. Surray Co., N.C., d. 7/18/1838 in Clarke Co., Ga.,
    Polly, R9831.
Smith, John Carraway, S.C., d. 3/15/1800 in Savannah, Ga., Ann Belcher,
    former widow, W4890; BLWt. 2265-300.
Smith, Larkin, Va., b. in Cumberland Co., Va., there at enl., res. in
    1832 Oglethorpe Co., Ga., d. there 10/20/1834, S31974.
Smith, Lawrence, N.C., b. 7/18/1763 in Edgecomb Co., N.C. there at enl.,
    res. in 1836 Harne Co., Ga., res. in 1839 Muscogee Co., Ga., R9784.
Smith, Leonard, or Leonard B., Md., res. at enl. near Bryantown, Md.,
    res. in 1820, Columbia Co., Ga. at age 60, d. in Columbia Co., Ga.
    1/15/1838, Mary W6098; BLWt. 57752-160-55.
Smith, Robert, Va., b. Feb. 1749, res. at enl. Cumberland Co., Va.,
    res. in 1832 Oglethorpe Co., Ga.,R9842.
Smith, Robert, S.C., b. in Ireland, son of Hughy Smith an Irishman who
lives in Charleston, S.C. during the Rev. Enl in Fiarfield Co., S.C.
    d. in Butts Co., Ga. 6/19/53 age about 100 years., Ferguson, R9731;
    BLWt. 8446-160-55
Smith, Samuel, Conn., Conn. Sea Service, b. 3/21/1758 in Southington,
    Hartford Co., Conn. there at enl. res. in 1832 Savannah, Chatham Co.,
    Ga. S31971
Smith, Shadrack, N.C., b. 12/26/1752 in Johnson Co. (Wake), N.C.,
    res. at enl. Wake Co., N.C., res. in 1832 Oglethorpe Co., Ga. S31970
Smith, William, Ga., N.C., S.C., B. 1762 in Derry Co., Ireland res. at
    enl. Mecklenburg Co., N.C., after Rev. in Ga., Ala., and Giles Co.,
    Tenn. R9878.
Smith, William, Va., b. 4/22/1754 in Sussex Co., Va., res. at enl.
    Henry Co., Va., res. in 1833 Clarke Co., Ga. S31976.
Smith, William, S.C., b. 2/26/1763 Moore Co., N.C., res. at enl. Ninety-
    Six Dist., S.C., res. in 1832 Franklin Co., Ga., S31973.
Smith, William C., N.C., Ga., b. in Mecklenburg Co., Va., March 4, 1762,
    res. during Rev., Wake Co., N.C., and Wilkes Co., Ga., res. in 1833
    Lincoln Co., Tenn. S3924.

Snelson, Thomas, Ga., S.C. S17111
Snider, Christian, Ga. R9900
Snider (or Snyder), Jonathan, Ga., Elizabeth, W2185
Sorrel, Mary, former widow of Andrew Bankston, Ga., W8746. Which see.
Southern, Gipson, Ga., S39084
Springer, Benjamin, Ga., N.C., S1592
Stallings, James, Ga., R10041
Stewart, James, N.C., lived in Ga. in 1831, S32534
Stewart, John, Gen. Widow's res. Ga., Manning or Mourning, d. 4/23/1830,
    Parmelia S. Perkins Daughter, R10164
Stewart, Robert, Ga., R10167
Stiles, John, Ga., Lucy, W4820; BLWt. 28622-160-55
Stregel, (or Stregles, Stregels), Nicholas, Ga., Sarah, W1329, BLWt.
    28645-160-55
Strozier, Peter, Ga., Margaret, R10279
Swords, James, Ga., S32202

Tankersly, Joseph, Cont., (Ga. res. in 1828) R20201
Tarvin, George, Ga., S32003
Taylor, Charles, Ga., S.C., b. in Va., S3760
Taylor, John, Ga., res. Richmond Co., N.C. in 1819, S42034

Taylor, Jonathan, Cont. (Va.), lived in Edgefield Dist., S.C., there
in April 1820; m. Joannah Morris; there were many children. Among
them were Pleasant of Dollas Co., Ala.; Wyatt A., of Cahmbers Co.,
Ala.; Cread of Tennessee; Onan of Walton Co., Ga.; Elizabeth, widow
of Phillip Johnson of Carroll Co., Ga.; and Jacky, res. unknown.
W4351
Taylor, Richard C., Va., res. in 1819, Wilkes Co., Ga. at age 74. Lived
with son-in-law John Todd in Morgan Co., Ga., in 1820, S42039.
Taylor, Theophilus, N.C., b. in Va., 1759, moved to Chesterfield Co.,
S.C., then to Franklin Co., Ga., in 1837 (now Habersham Co.), d.
10/4/1845. Children: William, Salley, Holcomb, Jeremiah, Hetty
Holcomb and Delpha Johnson. R10433.
Tearney, Gilbert, Ga., Elizabeth, W9850
Tetard, Benjamin, Ga., BLWt. 2230-400 Surgeon. Issued 8/20/1799.
Tharp, Robert, Ga., N.C., R104789
Thompson, Benjamin, Ga., S32016
Thompson, George, Ga., N.C., Jane, R10535
Thompson, William, Ga., N.C., S.C., R10560
Thrasher, George, Ga., Saluda, W2373, BLWt. 924-160-55
Threadgill, Thomas, Ga., Va., S46345, BLWt. 2054-300
Thurman, John, Ga., Deborah, W6267, BLWt. 27565-160-55
Thurmond, David H., Ga., S32010
Timmons, George, Ga., Va., S6242 (b. S.C.)
Toles, James, Died in Ga., abt. 1813, R10630. Only surviving son,
Sudduth Toles (Appld. 1853, Rankin Co., Miss.)
Toney, Abraham, S.C., Elizabeth, R10642, b. N.D. Sold. Res. Spartanburg
Dist., S.C. 1833, d. 3/8/1837; wid. d. Cherokee Co., Ga. 12/22/1844.
Townsend, Thomas, S.C., Susannah W3889 (b. Augusta Co., Va., d. 1836
Lumpkin Co., Ga.).
Trammel (or Tramell), Dennis, Ga., S.C., Martha R10672
Trammel (or Tramel), Peter, Ga., N.C., R10674
Trout, Anthony Daniel, Ga., S.C., Mary Catherine, W9863; BLWt. 26294-
160-55
Tucker, George, Ga., Martha W6319
Turner, George, Ga., S39110

Wade, Richard, Ga., Entered serv. in Va., b. in Md. R10985
Wagnon, John Peter, Ga., Rebecca, W1109; BLWt. 2456-200-Lieut. Issued
4/7/1796
Walker, Daniel, Ga., Hannah, W4613, b. in Ga.
Walker, John, Ga., S.C., b. in Ireland, W9875
Walker, Littleberry, Ga., R11045
Wall, John, Ga., S38455
Wamack, Johnson, Ga., N.C., S32577, b. in Va.
Ward, William, Ga., S42053, Enl. from Brunswick Co., Va., never resided
in Ga. Lived in N.C. and Va.
Wash, John, Ga., N.C., Va., S17183
Wash, William, Ga., and Va., S32046
Watson, Levin, Ga., S7797
Weatherford, Benjamin, Ga., (Va.), Nancey, W1520
Webb, Austin, Ga., Ailsey, W3902
Webb, John, Ga., S32055
Webb, John, Ga., Elizabeth, R11249
Weeks, Francis, Ga., Nancy, W25934, BLWt. 44287-160-55
Welch, Benjamin, Ga., R20446
Welshel, (or Whelchel), Francis, Judah, R11300 son's res. Ga. in 1854
Wells, Richard, Ga., Va., Susanna, W6473; BLWts. 26162-160-55;
52748-160-55
Whaley, Samuel, Ga., Catharine, W6492; BLWt. 40901-160-55
White, Joseph, Mass., Mass. Sea Service, S32060 Ga. res.
White, Stephen, Not Rev. War, Indian War 1795-1798, BLWts, 85871-40-50;
73589-120-55. Enl. in Va. (later lived in Ala. & Ga.)
Whiteker, William, Ga., S31473
Wigington, George, Ga., S.C., S32600
Wilkinson (or Wilkerson), John, Ga., S11818
Williams, Peter, Ga., Nancy, W6507
Williamson, Littleton, Ga., S3594
Willis, Meshach, Ga., S39124

Willoughby, William, Ga., S36396
Wilshire, John, Ga., Va., S6425
Wilson, Augustin, N.C., S7920 (b. 8/4/1755 in Lunenberg Co., Va., res.
   at enl. Dobbs Co., N.C., res. in 1833 Washington Co., Ga.
Wilson, George, Md., S32076 (b. 7/1/1750 res. at enl. Talbot Co., Md.,
   res. in 1832 Walton Co., Ga.
Wilson, James, Ga., R11664 (b. 4/11/1761 in Raferts Fort, near Broad
   River, S.C., res. at enl. Richmond Co., Ga., res. in 1835, Sumter
   Co., Ala.
Wilson, James, N.C., S.C., R11663 (b. 7/12/1758 in Pa. res. at enl.
   Orange Co., N.C., res. in 1832 Franklin Co., Ga.
Wilson, Peter, Ga., Va., Dis. R11662.

Young, Isham, Ga., N.C., S1889
Young, Levi, Ga., N.C., S.C., Nancy, W9040 (b. in N.J.)

ADDITIONS

Augustine, Bailey, Ga., S.C., and Va., S30826

Bankston, Elijah, Ga., BLRej. 63944
Beckham/Beckcom, Solomon, Ga., Susannah Stacy, R697
Black, John, Ga., Margaret, R890

Castleberry, William M., Ga., S16337
Cloud, John, Ga., S.C., S30935
Cloud, Noah, Ga., S.C., Unity, W9389
Cowan, Edward, Lt. Ga., BLWt. 491 200 Lt. Iss. 8/20/1799
Cuksey/Cucksey, William, Ga., R20354

Darby, Richard, Ga., S32203
Day, Joseph, Ga., R2788
Dickinson, Elijah, Ga., S39443
Duick, Timothy, Pvt., Ga., Mil. Reg. 273482-1855

Findley, Paul, Ga., S.C., W9440
Frazier, John, Ga., Mary W24241 BLWt. 2015-200
Freeman, John, Ga., Res., Catherine, R3777
Fuller, Meshack/Meshac, Ga., Bethany, W4958
Fussell, William, Ga., N.C., S31046

Grant, Thomas, ? Ga., res. of wid. in 1857, Martha H., BLWt. 58691-
   160-55

Howell, Hopkin/Hopkins, Ga., S31749
Howle, William, Ga., S.C., S21303
Howlitt, William, Ga., Elizabeth R5304

Laffoon, Jas., Ga., Va., S13694
Lane, Davis, ___ Rejected book gives res. at Ga., Elizabeth, R6119
Lassiter, James, Ga., Elizabeth, W4259
Linvill, William, Ga., Mary, W5321

McCuller, Alexander, Ga., S4196
Martin, Matt, Ga., S.C., Va., S2726
Maxwell, Beckam/Beckom/Beckman, Ga., R7049
Metcalf, Danza, Ga., N.C., Mary, W4280
Mitchell, Cheney/Chaney, Ga., S38228
Mote, Levi, Ga., S.C., S7245

Northcutt, Francis, Ga., S21401
Nordyke, Benjamin, Ga., R7691

Phelps, Thomas/Tekel, Ga., W5531
Pulliam, William, Ga., R20425

Ramsey, Samuel, Ga., S21437

Sheftall, Sheftall, Ga., S31959
Shehee, John, Cont., Ga., Agcy., and res., S36302
Shick, Frederick, Ga., BLWt. 2109-200 Lt. No date of issue. No papers
Smith, Austin, Va., res. of Lincoln Co., Ga., in 1818, S36318
Stuart, James, Ga., S39088

Taylor, Benjamin, res. Ga., in 1830, sons John, Willis, and William
    lived in Scrivner Co., R10407
Tiner, Joshua, Ga., S32561
Taylor, Robert, Pa., b. Baltimore Co., Md. in 1744 moved to Rockbridge
    Co., Va., during the Rev., res. Jackson Co., Ga., in 1833, S32005

Upton, George, Ga., Charity, W9869

Waddill, John, Ga., N.C., served also 1788-1791, R10977
Williams, John, Va., R11594 res. Forsyth Co., Ga.
Williams, Thomas, Ga., S.C., S7933
Wood, James, Ga., Elizabeth, W4405, b. Va., res. at enl. in Va.
Wooten, Thomas, Ga., Susanna, S11892 and R11861
Wylly, Thomas, Cont., Ga., Sarah, R11535

C. List of Georgia Loyalist Claims

        The following list of Georgia Loyalist claims in the Audit Office
Papers, British Public Record Office was copied by the Microfilm Library,
Georgia Department of Archives and History, for use with their microfilm copies of representative documents from each of the following
claims. To research all of the papers of a particular Loyalist claim,
interested persons should borrow complete microfilm edition of the
Loyalist claims at the Public Archives of Canada, through interlibrary
loan.

Georgia Loyalist Claims

British Public Records Office - London, England

Extract A.O. 13	Bundle #
Barry, George	34, 35
Brailsford, Samuel	34
Brown, Rev. James	34
Brown, Lt. Col. Thomas	34
Casper, Richard	35
Channing, Joanne (wife of John)	34
Channing, John	34
Collis, Robert (2)	34
Combe, Thomas	34
Corry, Lydia (widow of Robert)	34
Crawford, John	35
Davis, Richard	34
Dean, George	34
Dean, Peter	34
D'erbage, George (2)	34
Douglas, Col. John (2)	34
Douglas, Samuel (3)	34
Edgar, James (2)	34
Edwards, Peter (2)	34
Elliott, Grey	34

Farley, Grace (2) (widow of Samuel)	34, 35
Farlie, James	34
Ferguson, Capt. Henry	34, 35
Finlayson, Ann (widow of Henry)	34, 35
Fleming, Mary (widow of Thomas)	35
Flemming, Maj. Thomas	35
Ford, James, esq.	34, 35
Fox, John	34, 35
Fraser, Donald	35
Goodbread, Phillip	35
Goodgion, William	35
Graham, Lt. Col. John	35
Green, George, esq.	35
Hanen, Stephen	35
Henderson, Jean (widow of Arthur)	35
Henderson, John	35
Henry, William	35
Heriot, James	35
Irvine, Dr. John	35
Jackson, James (2)	35
Jenkins, Samuel Hunt, esq.	35
Johnston, George	35
Jollie, Martin	35
Knox, William	35
Lissatt, Patrick	35
Long, George	35
McGorven, David	35
Neil, Margaret (daughter of John)	35
Payne, William	35
PenteCost, Hartwell	35
Plummer, Col. Daniel	35
Rannols, Thomas	35
Simpson, Elizabeth (widow of William)	35
Sloan, James	35
Smith, John	35
Todd, John	35
White, Alexander	35
Wiles, Henry	35
Young, John (3)	35
Young, Capt. Samuel (2)	35
Hayes, John	36
Herriot, James	36
Inglis, John	36
Jackson, James	36
Jackson, James, heirs of	36
Jamison, James	36
Jamison, John	36

Jamison, Neil	36
Jenkins, Samuel Hunt	36
Johnston, Dr. Andrew	36
Johnston, George	36
Johnston, James	36
Johnston, Lewis, esq.	36
Johnston, Lewis, Jr.	36
Johnston, Rachel (widow of Joseph)	36
Johnston, William	36
Jollie, Martin	36
Jones, William	36
Kelsall, John	36
Kelsall, Roger (2)	36
Kincaid, George	36
Kirkland, Moses	36
Knox, William, esq.	36
Lightenstone, John	36
Love, William	36
Lucena, John Charles	36
Lyford, Capt. William	36
Lyle, Col. Matthew	36
Mackenzie, George	36
Manby, Jane (widow of Aaron)	36
Manson, William	36
Martin, James	36
Martindale, John	36
McDonald, Archibald	36
McDonald, Capt. John	36
McDonald, Murdock	36
McGillivray, Lt. Col. John	36
McGillivray, Capt. William	36
Mills, Capt. John	36
Montgomery, Samuel	36
Moore, Eliza (widow of Phillip)	36
Moore, Phillip (2)	36
Moss, William	36
Munro, Simon, esq.	36
Murray, John, esq.	36

Penton, William   36
(included in the claim of Phillip Moore)

Spalding, James   36
(included in the claim of Roger Kelsall)

Bowen, Jane (widow of Samuel)	37
Clark, John	36A
Clark, Capt. William (2)	36A
Corry, Lydia (widow of Robert)	36A
Corry, Robert	36A

Milligan, David   36A
(included in the claim of John Clark)

Patterson, Simon	36A
Polson, Hugh	36A
Polson, Maj. John (2)	36A
Powell, James Edward, esq.	36A
Pryce, Charles, Jr. (2)	36A

Rattan, John	36A
Reid, Robert (2)	36A
Reid, Thomas (3)	36A
Rennie, Rev. John	36A
Ring, William	36A
Robertson, James	36A
Russell, Maj. David	36A
Russell, Emmett	36A
Russell, Jennet (widow of David)	36A
Russell, William	36A
Scales, Ann	37
Seymour, Rev. James	36A
Seymour, James, widow and children	37
Seymour, Jane	37
Shivers, Judith (widow of James)	36A
Simpson, Ama Jean (widow of John) (2)	36A, 37
Simpson, John (2)	36A, 37
Smith, Haddon (2)	36A, 37
Steel, Hugh	36A
Stokes, Anthony, esq. (2)	36A, 37
Storr, John	36A
Strachan, Patrick	37
Stringer, Thomas (2)	36A, 37
Tait, David (2)	37
Tallamach, Thomas	37
Tattnall, John Mulrynee	37
Tattnall, Josiah (4)	37
Telfair, William	37
Thomas, John	37
Thompson, Alexander	37
Thompson, Benjamin	37
Thompson, William	37
Thompson, William A.	37
Triebner, Rev. Christopher Frederick	37
Waldo, Francis	36A
Wallace, James	37
Waters, Thomas	37
Watts, Charles	37
William, Prince	37
Wright, Alexander	37
Wright, James	37
Wright, Jermyn	37
Yonge, Henry, widow and children	37
Baillie, Alex	90
Baillie, George	38, 83
Baillie, John	38
Baillie, Robert	38
Baillou, Isaac	38, 90
Balchenwest, John	38
Barry, George	38, 87
Behler, Jacob	90
Brown, Rev. James	38
Brown, John	90
Brown, Lt. Col. Thomas	38
Bunyie, James (2)	90
Dean, Peter	79
Grasham, John	106

	Bundle #	
Gullan, Thomas	129	
Hall, Nathaniel	100	
Haven, Stephen	83	
Hayes, John C.	80	
Hewatt, Andrew	138	
Knox, William	87	
Leslie, Martha	91	
Lightenstone, John	83	
Manson, William	87	
McGillivray, William	87	
McGown, Alexander	91	
McIntosh, William	91	
Moore, Eliza	91	
Read, William, esq.	138	
Rennie, Rev. J.	83	
Rogers, James	137	
Russell, Janet (widow of David)	79	
Seymour, Rev. James	83	
Sharp, Henry	83	
Smith, Rev. Hadden	83	
Smith, Joseph	83	
Stokes, Anthony, esq.	83,	137
Stractham, Patrick	83	
Taylor, Thomas	87	
Todd, John	138	
Waters, Col. Thomas	38	
Watts, Charles (2)	38,	137
Weatherford, Martin	82	
West, John Belcher	38	
Wood, George	38	
Wood, John (2)	38	
Wright, Alexander	85	
Wright, James	38,	85
Wright, Maj. James	38	
Wright, Jeremyn	37	
Wylly, Alexander	37	
Wylly, Campbell	37	
(included in claim of William Wylly)		
Wylly, Susannah (widow of Alexander) (2)	37	
Wylly, Susannah (daughter of Alexander)	82	
Wylly, William (2)	37	
Yonge, Henry	37	
Yonge, Maj. Henry	38,	83
Yonge, Phillip, widow and children	38	
Yonge, William John (3)	38,	83
Young, Thomas	38	